A Guide To Critical Reviews

Part III

British and Continental Drama
from Ibsen to Pinter

by

James M. Salem

The Scarecrow Press, Inc.
Metuchen, N.J.   1968

To Jennifer

A Guide to Critical Reviews

Part I   American Drama from O'Neill to Albee

Part II   The Musical from Rodgers-and-Hart to Lerner-and-Loewe

Part III   British and Continental Drama from Ibsen to Pinter

Foreword

The purpose of Part III of <u>A Guide to Critical Reviews</u> is to provide a bibliography of critical reviews of modern British and Continental plays produced on the New York stage from the 1909-1910 season to the season of 1965-1966. The productions listed are, for the most part, Broadway productions, though Off Broadway presentations have been included when accurate statistical data could be obtained. Beginning with the 1959-1960 season, selected Off Broadway productions have been included, and beginning with the 1961-1962 season, complete Off Broadway information.

Playwrights included in this bibliography are presented alphabetically, with plays listed alphabetically under each dramatist. No dates are provided because of the complexity of the problem of which date to use--year of composition, original production, translation, or American production. Dates of American productions from 1909 to 1966 are provided, however, with numbers of performances. No conscious effort has been made to include foreign language productions of modern British and Continental plays.

The reviews cited in this volume are those which appeared in American or Canadian periodicals and in the New York <u>Times</u>. With the exception of some now defunct dramatic periodicals like the <u>Dramatic Mirror</u> and the New York <u>Clipper</u>, most of the reviews should be available in college and public libraries. Reviews in other New York newspapers have not been indexed, but <u>New York Theatre Critics' Reviews</u>, which has reprinted reviews from the <u>New York Journal-American</u>, <u>Daily News</u>, <u>Post</u>, <u>Mirror</u>, <u>World Telegram and Sun</u>, <u>Herald Tribune</u>, and <u>Times</u> since 1940, has been cited for plays produced after that date.

As no attempt has been made to include critical articles from the scholarly journals, the student of modern drama should supplement this bibliography with the annual bibliographies in <u>Modern Drama</u>, <u>PMLA</u>, and <u>Educational</u>

v

Theatre Journal. In addition, the "Continuing Checklist" published by The Shaw Review is valuable for items involving George Bernard Shaw, and Bulletin of Bibliography is important for bibliographies on many modern dramatists: Galsworthy, Jones, Pinero, Brieux, Schnitzler, Yeats, Chekhov, and Strindberg. Especially helpful is "A Selected Bibliography of Bibliographies" compiled by Marvin Carlson in Modern Drama, VII (May 1965), 112-118.

I should like to acknowledge a debt of gratitude to Mr. Charles Beard, Head of the Reference Division, and Mrs. Carolyn Thomas, Head of the Circulation Division of the University of Alabama Library; to Professor James B. McMillan, Head of the Department of English; and to Mr. Joseph Ryan. I am also indebted to my wife, Donna, for her assistance in preparing the final manuscript.

University, Alabama   James M. Salem
March 1968

Table of Contents

Alvarez Quintero, Serafin and Joaquin (see Quintero, Serafin and Joaquin Alvarez)

Andreyev, Leonid Nikolayevitch
Anathema
    Productions:
        Opened November 1910.
        Translated by Herman Bernstein. Opened April 10, 1923 for 15 performances
    Reviews:
        Dramatic Mirror 64:7, Nov 30, 1910
        Independent 69:1327-8, Dec 15, 1910
        Nation 91:397-8, Oct 27, 1910
                116:500-1, Apr 25, 1923
        New York Clipper 71:14, Apr 18, 1923
        New York Times p. 16, Apr 11, 1923
                VII, p.1, Apr 15, 1923
Beautiful Sabine Women (see The Sabine Women)

Devil in the Mind
    Productions:
        Adapted by William L. Laurence. Opened May 1, 1931 for 11 performances.
    Reviews:
        Commonweal 14:48-9, May 13, 1931
        New York Times p. 23, May 2, 1931
He Who Gets Slapped
    Productions:
        Adapted by George Zilboorg. Opened January 9, 1922 for 182 performances.
        English version by Judith Guthrie. Opened March 20, 1946 for 46 performances
        (Off Broadway) Season of 1955-1956.
    Reviews:
        Bookman 55:61-2, Mar 1922
        Catholic World 163:168, May 1946
        Current Opinion 72:484-94, Apr 1922
        Dial 72:337-8, Mar 1922
        Dramatic Mirror 95:62, Mar 1922
        Everybody's Magazine 47:112-18, Dec 1922

11

He Who Gets Slapped (cont.)
  Hearst 41:85-7+, Jun 1922
  Independent 108:90-2, Jan 28, 1922
  Life (NY) 79:18, Jan 26, 1922
  Nation 114:103, Jan 25, 1922
      162:409, Apr 6, 1946
  New Republic 29:283-4, Feb 1, 1922
      114:479, Apr 8, 1946
  New York Clipper 69:20, Jan 18, 1922
  New York Theatre Critics' Reviews 1946:426
  New York Times p. 15, Jan 10, 1922
      II, p. 1, Mar 31, 1946
      p. 18, Feb 2, 1956
      VI, p. 28, Feb 12, 1956
  New Yorker 22:42, Mar 30, 1946
  Newsweek 27:84, Apr 1, 1946
  Saturday Review 29:34+, Apr 13, 1946
      39:30, Mar 24, 1956
  Theatre Arts 30:252+, May 1946
  Theatre Magazine 35:141+, Mar 1922
  Time 47:76, Apr 1, 1946
Katerina (Yekaterina Ivanovna)
  Productions:
    Translated by Herman Bernstein. Opened February
      25, 1929 for 19 performances.
  Reviews:
    Commonweal 9:571, Mar 20, 1929
    Dial 86:440-2, May 1929
    New York Times p. 30, Feb 26, 1929
    Vogue 73:164+, Apr 13, 1929
The Life of Man
  Productions:
    Translated by Clarence L. Meader and Fred Newton
      Scott. Opened January 14, 1917 for one perform-
      ance.
  Reviews:
    New Republic 33:176-7, Jan 10, 1923
    New York Times p. 7, Jan 15, 1917
    Theatre Magazine 25:137+, Mar 1917
Love of One's Neighbor
  Productions:
    Translated by Thomas Seltzer. Opened February 19,
      1915 in repertory (Washington Square Players).
  Reviews:
    Green Book 13:1151-2, Jun 1915
The Sabine Women (Beautiful Sabine Women)
  Productions:

Opened March 1920.
Reviews:
    Independent 101:382, Mar 13, 1920
    Weekly Review 2:441-2, Apr 24, 1920
The Waltz of the Dogs
    Productions:
        Translated by Herman Bernstein. Opened April 25,
        1928 for 35 performances.
    Reviews:
        Dramatist 14:1170-71, Jul 1923
        Nation 126:546, May 9, 1928
        New York Times p. 31, Apr 26, 1928
        Theatre Magazine 48:38-9, Jul 1928
        Vogue 71:98, Jun 15, 1928

Anouilh, Jean
Antigone
    Productions:
        English adaptation by Lewis Galantiere, Opened
        February 18, 1946 for 64 performances.
        (Off Broadway) Season of 1959-1960.
    Reviews:
        Catholic World 163:71-2, Apr 1946
        Commonweal 43:525-6, Mar 8, 1946
        Forum 105:752-3, Apr 1946
        Independent Woman 25:100, Apr 1946
        Life 20:73-5, Mar 18, 1946
        Nation 162:269, Mar 2, 1946
                182:347 Apr 21, 1956
        New Republic 114:317, Mar 4, 1946
        New York Theatre Critics' Reviews 1946:450
        New York Times p. 28, Jan 10, 1946
                    II, p. 1, Feb 24, 1946
                    p. 46, Sep 16, 1959
                    p. 52, Dec 14, 1960
        New York Times Magazine pp. 28-9, Jan 27, 1946
        New Yorker 22:40-1, Mar 4, 1946
                35:964, Sep 26, 1959
        Newsweek 27:80, Mar 4, 1946
        Player's Magazine 24:32-4, Nov 1947
                    24:70, Dec 1947
        Saturday Review 29:24-6, Mar 9, 1946
        Time 47:54, Mar 4, 1946
Becket
    Productions:
        Translated by Lucienne Hill. Opened October 5, 1960
        for 193 performances.

Becket (cont.)
  Reviews:
    America 104:275-6, Nov 19, 1960
    Catholic World 192:191-2, Dec 1960
    Christian Century 77:1284-6, Nov 2, 1960
    Coronet 49:14, Jan 1961
    Nation 191:336, Oct 29, 1960
          192:467-8, May 27, 1961
    New Republic 143:22, Oct 17, 1960
    New York Theatre Critics' Reviews 1960:222
    New York Times p. 50, Oct 6, 1960
                  II, p. 1, Oct 16, 1960
    New Yorker 36:73-4, Oct 15, 1960
    Newsweek 56:102, Oct 17, 1960
    Reporter 23:45, Nov 24, 1960
    Saturday Review 43:22, Oct 22, 1960
                    44:26, May 27, 1961
    Theatre Arts 44:9-11, Dec 1960
    Time 76:54, Oct 17, 1960
         77:78, Apr 7, 1961
Colombe (see Mademoiselle Colombe)

Cry of the Peacock
  Productions:
    Adapted by Cecil Robson. Opened April 11, 1950 for
      two performances.
  Reviews:
    New York Theatre Critics' Reviews 1950:316
    New York Times p. 33, Apr 12, 1950
    New Yorker 26:60, Apr 22, 1950
    Newsweek 35:95, Apr 24, 1950
    Theatre Arts 34:16, Jun 1950
Dinner with the Family (see Le Rendevous de Senlis)

Eurydice (see Legend of Lovers)

The Fighting Cock
  Productions:
    Adapted by Lucienne Hill. Opened December 8, 1959
      for 87 performances.
  Reviews:
    America 102:538, Jan 30, 1960
    Nation 189:495-6, Dec 26, 1959
    New Republic 142:20-1, Jan 4, 1960
    New York Theatre Critics' Reviews 1959:192
    New York Times p. 57, Dec 9, 1959
                  II, p. 3, Dec 20, 1959

14

New Yorker 35:111-13, Feb 21, 1959
             35:79-81, Dec 19, 1959
Newsweek 54:83, Dec 21, 1959
Saturday Review 42:29-30, Jun 20, 1959
                42:24, Dec 26, 1959
Time 74:34, Dec 21, 1959
L'Invitation au Chateau (see Ring Round the Moon)

Jeannette (see Romeo and Jeannette)

The Lark (L'alouette)
  Productions:
    Adapted by Lillian Hellman.   Opened Nov 17, 1955 for
      229 performances.
  Reviews:
    America 90:420-1, Jan 23, 1954
            94:363, Dec 24, 1955
            95:109-10, Apr 28, 1956
    Catholic World 182:308-9, Jan 1952
    Commonweal 63:304 Dec 23, 1955
    Holiday 19:77+, Mar 1956
    Life 39:113-14+, Dec 12, 1955
    Nation 181:485-6, Dec 3, 1955
    New Republic 133:21, Dec 5, 1955
    New York Theatre Critics' Reviews 1955:206
    New York Times II, p. 1, Nov 13, 1955
                    II, p. 1, Nov 27, 1955
    New Yorker 31:112+, Dec 3, 1955
    Newsweek 46:110, Nov 28, 1955
    Reporter 13:31, Dec 29, 1955
    Saturday Review 38:24, Feb 19, 1955
    Theatre Arts 39:23, Apr 1955
                 40:63-4+, Mar 1956
                 40:8-10, May 1956
    Time 66:76+, Nov 28, 1955
Legend of Lovers
  Productions:
    Adapted by Kitty Black from Anouilh's play Eurydice.
      Opened December 26, 1951 for 22 performances.
  Reviews:
    Commonweal 55:373-4, Jan 18, 1952
    Nation 174:44, Jan 12, 1952
    New York Theatre Critics' Reviews 1951:125
    New York Times p. 17, Dec 27, 1951
    New Yorker 27:46, Jan 5, 1952
               35:88+, Nov 7, 1959
    Newsweek 39:36, Jan 7, 1952

Legend of Lovers (cont. d)
Saturday Review 35:32, Jan 19, 1952
Theatre Arts 36:71, Mar 1952
Time 59:44, Jan 7, 1952
Mademoiselle Colombe (Colombe)
Productions:
Adapted by Louis Kronenberger. Opened January 6,
1954 for 61 performances.
(Off Broadway) Adapted by Denis Cannan. Opened
February 23, 1965 for 13 performances.
Reviews:
America 90:426, Jan 23, 1954
Catholic World 178:467-8, Mar 1954
Commonweal 59:41-2, Feb 12, 1954
Life 36:59-60+, Feb 15, 1954
Nation 178:77-8, Jan 23, 1954
178:98-9, Jan 30, 1954
New Republic 130:20-1, Jan 25, 1954
New York Theatre Critics' Reviews 1954:397
New York Times II, p. 3, Jan 3, 1954
p. 26, Jan 7, 1954
II. p. 1, Jan 17, 1954
p. 33, Feb 24, 1965
New Yorker 29:52+, Jan 16, 1954
Newsweek 43:59, Jan 18, 1954
65:93, Mar 15, 1965
Saturday Review 37:30-1, Jan 16, 1954
37:59-60, Jan 23, 1954
Theatre Arts 38:14, Mar 1954
Time 63:54, Jan 18, 1954
Poor Bitos (Pauvre Bitos)
Productions:
Translated by Lucienne Hill. Opened November 14,
1964 for 17 performances.
Reviews:
Nation 184:554, Jun 22, 1957
199:415-17, Nov 30, 1964
New Republic 151:20-1, Dec 12, 1964
New York Theatre Critics' Reviews 1964:147
New York Times p. 40, Nov 16, 1964
New Yorker 32:84+, Nov 3, 1956
Newsweek 64:92, Nov 30, 1964
Saturday Review 47:43, Dec 5, 1964
49:55, Mar 5, 1966
Time 84:104, Nov 27, 1964
The Rehearsal
Productions:

Opened November 27, 1952 for four performances.
Adapted by Pamela Hansford Johnson and Kitty Black.
Opened September 23, 1963 for 110 performances.
Reviews:
Commonweal 79:194, Nov 8, 1963
Nation 175:562-3, Dec 13, 1952
      197:245, Oct 19, 1963
National Review 15:406-7, Nov 5, 1963
New Republic 127:23, Dec 22, 1952
New York Theatre Critics' Reviews 1963:285
New York Times p.22, Nov 28, 1952
      p.45, Sep 24, 1963
      II,p.1, Oct 20, 1963
New Yorker 39:133-4, Oct 5, 1963
Newsweek 62:96, Oct 7, 1963
Saturday Review 35:26, Dec 13, 1952
      46:30, Oct 12, 1963
Theatre Arts 47:10-11, Dec 1963
Time 82:63, Oct 4, 1963

Le Rendevous de Senlis (Dinner with the Family)
Productions:
(Off Broadway) Season of 1960-1961.
Reviews:
New York Times p.39, Feb 28, 1961
New Yorker 37:114-15, Mar 11, 1961
Theatre Arts 45:56, May 1961
Time 77:45, Mar 17, 1961

La Repetition Ou L'Amour Puni
Productions:
Opened November 27, 1952 for four performances.
Reviews:
Nation 175:652-3, Dec 13, 1952
New York Theatre Critics' Reviews 1952:175
New York Times p.22, Nov 28, 1952
Saturday Review 35:26, Dec 13, 1952

Ring Round the Moon (L'Invitation au Chateau)
Productions:
Translated by Christopher Fry. Opened November 23, 1950 for 68 performances.
Reviews:
Catholic World 172:307, Jan 1951
Christian Science Monitor Magazine p.13, Dec 2, 1950
Commonweal 52:253, Dec 15, 1950
Nation 171:514, Dec 2, 1950
New Republic 122:21, Jun 5, 1950
      123:22, Dec 25, 1950
New York Theatre Critics' Reviews 1950:189

Ring Round the Moon (L'Invitation au Chateau) (cont. d)
    New York Times II, p. 4, Nov 19, 1950
                    p. 30, Nov 24, 1950
    New Yorker 26:78-9, Dec 2, 1950
    Newsweek 36:74, Dec 4, 1950
    Saturday Review 33:25-6, Dec 16, 1950
    Theatre Arts 32:30, Feb 1948
                 34:29+, Dec 1950
    Time 56:64, Dec 4, 1950
Romeo and Jeannette (Jeannette)
Productions:
    (Off Broadway) Translated by Miriam John.   Opened
      March 24, 1960 for four performances.
Reviews:
    New York Times p. 20, Mar 25, 1960
    Theatre Arts 31:44, May 1947
                 33:40-1, Nov 1950
    Vogue 109:251, Mar 1, 1947
Thieves' Carnival
Productions:
    (Off Broadway) Season of 1954-1955.
Reviews:
    Catholic World 181:148-9, May 1955
    Commonweal 62:183, May 20, 1955
    New Republic 132:28-9, Feb 21, 1955
    New York Times p. 21, Feb 2, 1955
                   II, p. 1, Feb 13, 1955
    New Yorker 31:77-8, Feb 19, 1955
    Saturday Review 38:38, Dec 3, 1955
    Theatre Arts 40:18-19, Jan 1956
Time Remembered
Productions:
    English version by Patricia Moyes.   Opened November
      12, 1957 for 248 performances.
Reviews:
    America 98:355, Dec 14, 1957
    Catholic World 186:304, Jan 1958
    Christian Century 74:1448, Dec 4, 1957
    Dance Magazine 32:9, Feb 1958
    Life 43:73-4+, Dec 9, 1957
    Nation 185:415-16, Nov 30, 1957
    New York Theatre Critics' Reviews 1957:183
    New York Times p. 41, Nov 13, 1957
                   II, p. 1, Nov 24, 1957
    New York Times Magazine p. 71, Oct 27, 1957
    New Yorker 33:77, Nov 23, 1957
    Newsweek 50:84, Nov 25, 1957

18

Reporter 17:35, Dec 12, 1957
Saturday Review 40:23, Nov 30, 1957
Theatre Arts 41:71-2+, Oct 1957
                22:19, Jan 1958
Time 70:91, Nov 25, 1957

Traveller Without Luggage
  Productions:
    Translated by Lucienne Hill.   Opened September 17,
    1964 for 44 performances.
  Reviews:
    Commonweal 81:73, Oct 9, 1964
    Nation 199:202, Oct 5, 1964
    New York Theatre Critics' Reviews 1964:226
    New York Times p.26, Sep 18, 1964
    Newsweek 64:90-1, Sep 28, 1964
    Saturday Review 47:28, Oct 3, 1964
    Time 84:96, Sep 25, 1964
    Vogue 144:66, Nov 1, 1964

The Waltz of the Toreadors
  Productions:
    English version by Lucienne Hill.   Opened January 17,
    1957 for 132 performances.
    English version by Lucienne Hill.   Opened March 4,
    1958 for 31 performances.
  Reviews:
    America 96:656, Mar 9, 1957
    Catholic World 184:469, Mar 1957
                   187:146, May 1958
    Christian Century 74:201, Feb 13, 1957
    Life 42:109-10, Feb 25, 1957
    Nation 184:108, Feb 2, 1957
           186:261, Mar 22, 1958
    New Republic 126:21, Feb 11, 1957
    New York Theatre Critics' Reviews 1957:390
                                      1958:334
    New York Times p.17, Jan 18, 1957
                   II,p.1, Jan 27, 1957
                   p.37, Nov 5, 1958
    New York Times Magazine p.58, Jan 6, 1957
    New Yorker 32:68+, Jan 26, 1957
    Newsweek 49:84, Jan 28, 1957
    Review of Reviews 15:38, Nov 1, 1956
    Saturday Review 39:30, Oct 13, 1956
                    40:24, Feb 2, 1957
    Theatre Arts 41:21+, Mar 1957
    Time 69:50, Jan 28, 1957

Ansky, S. (Solomon Rappaport)
The Dybbuk
   Productions:
      English version by Henry G. Alsberg. Opened
      December 15, 1925 for 120 performances.
      Opened December 13, 1926 for 111 performances in
      repertory.
      Opened December 16, 1926 for 41 performances.
      Translated by H. N. Bialik. Opened February 3, 1964
      for 24 performances.
   Reviews:
      Arts and Decoration 24:66, Feb 1926
      Bookman 63:81, Mar 1926
      Catholic World 122:665-7, Feb 1926
      Dial 80:255-9, Mar 1926
      Independent 116:332, Mar 20, 1926
      Life (NY) 87:20, Jan 14, 1926
               89:21, Jan 27, 1927
      Literary Digest 88:29, Jan 23, 1926
      Nation 122:16, Jan 6, 1926
      New Republic 45:187, Jun 6, 1926
                   49:190-1, Jan 5, 1927
                   118:28, May 24, 1948
      New York Theatre Critics' Reviews 1964:332
      New York Times p.22, Dec 16, 1925
                     VII, p.3, Dec 20, 1925
                     p.27, Dec 17, 1926
                     p.18, Feb 24, 1937
                     p.30, Feb 4, 1964
      Newsweek 63:90, Feb 17, 1964
      Saturday Review 143:559, Apr 9, 1927
      Survey 55:572, Feb 1, 1926
      Theatre Arts 10:72, 79, Feb 1926
                   25:581, Aug 1941
                   32:18, Jun 1948
      Theatre Magazine 43:15+, May 1926
      Vogue 67:74, Feb 15, 1926
      Woman Citizen 10:16, Feb 1926

Anthony, C. L. (pseud. of Dodie Smith)

Archer, William
The Green Goddess
   Productions:
      Opened January 18, 1921 for 175 performances.
   Reviews:
      Bookman 53:276, May 1921

Collier's 67:14, Feb 19, 1921
Current Opinion 71:319-31, Sep 1921
Dramatic Mirror 83:188, Jan 22, 1921
Dramatist 12:1067-9, Jul 1921
Everybody's 45:91-8, Sep 1921
Independent 105:129, Feb 5, 1921
Life (NY) 77:172, Feb 3, 1921
Nation 112:250, Feb 9, 1921
New York Clipper 68:19, Jan 26, 1921
New York Times p.14, Jan 19, 1921
　　　　　　　VI,p.1, Jan 23, 1921
　　　　　　　VI,p.1, Jan 30, 1921
Outlook 127:330-1, Mar 2, 1921
Theatre Magazine 33:224, Mar 1921
　　　　　　　34:84+, Aug 1921
Weekly Review 4:112, Feb 2, 1921

Auden, W. H.
 Ascent of F 6 (with Christopher Isherwood)
 　Productions:
　　　(Off Broadway) Opened April 23, 1939 (Dove Players).
 　Reviews:
　　　Forum 97:355, Jun 1937
　　　New Republic 141:16-17, Nov 23, 1959
　　　Saturday Review 16:20, May 8, 1937
　　　Scholastic 31:23 E, Jan 15, 1938
　　　Scribner's Magazine 102:66+, Sep 1937
　　　Theatre Arts 21:355-6, May 1937
 The Dance of Death
 　Productions:
　　　Opened May 19, 1935 (Federal Theatre Project).
 　Reviews:
　　　Theatre Arts 19:906-8, Dec 1935
 Dog Beneath The Skin (with Christopher Isherwood)
 　Productions:
　　　(Off Broadway) Opened July 21, 1947.
 　Reviews:
　　　Commonweal 46:475-6, Aug 29, 1947
　　　Nation 141:626, Nov 27, 1935
　　　New Republic 85:79 Nov 27, 1935
　　　　　　　141:16-17 Nov 23, 1959
　　　Saturday Review 13:16, Nov 30, 1935
　　　Theatre Arts 19:906-8, Dec 1935

Bagnold, Enid
 The Chalk Garden
 　Productions:

The Chalk Garden (cont.)
    Opened October 26, 1955 for 182 performances.
  Reviews:
    America 94:195, Nov 12, 1955
    Catholic World 182:227, Dec 1955
    Commonweal 63:616, Mar 16, 1956
    Holiday 19:85+, May 1956
    Life 39:164-6, Dec 5, 1955
    Nation 181:426, Nov 12, 1955
          182:477-8, Jun 2, 1956
    New Republic 134:21, Mar 26, 1956
    New York Theatre Critics' Reviews 1955:227
    New York Times p.29, Oct 27, 1955
                  II,p.1, Nov 13, 1955
                  II,p.3, Jan 1, 1956
    New Yorker 31:77, Nov 5, 1955
    Reporter 13:31-2, Dec 29, 1955
    Saturday Review 38:24, Nov 12, 1955
    Theatre Arts 40:16, Jan 1956
                40:66-7, Feb 1956
                41:25, May 1957
    Time 66:96, Nov 7, 1955
The Chinese Prime Minister
  Productions:
    Opened January 2, 1964 for 108 performances.
  Reviews:
    America 110:148, Jan 25, 1964
    Nation 198:80, Jan 20, 1964
    New Republic 150:28, Feb 1, 1964
    New York Theatre Critics' Reviews 1964:393
    New York Times p.14, Jan 3, 1964
                  II,p.1, Jan 12, 1964
    New Yorker 39:69, Jan 11, 1964
    Newsweek 63:70, Jan 13, 1964
    Saturday Review 47:22, Jan 18, 1964
    Time 83:52, Jan 10, 1964
Gertie
  Productions:
    Opened January 30, 1952 for five performances.
  Reviews:
    Commonweal 55:470, Feb 15, 1952
    New York Theatre Critics' Reviews 1952:379
    New York Times p.23, Jan 31, 1952
    New Yorker 27:56, Feb 9, 1952
    Newsweek 39:82, Feb 11, 1952
    Theatre Arts 36:71, Apr 1952
    Time 59:79, Feb 11, 1952

Bahr, Hermann
  The Concert
    Productions:
      Adapted by Leo Ditrichstein.   Opened October 4, 1910
        for 264 performances.
    Reviews:
      Blue Book 12:637-7, Jan 1911
      Columbian 3:698+, Jan 1911
      Dramatist 2:150-1, Apr 1911
      Everybody's 24:120+, Jan 1911
      Green Book 4:1221-2, Dec 1910
      Hampton 25:824-6, Dec 1910
      Harper's Weekly 54:18, Nov 12, 1910
      Life (NY) 56:661, Oct 20, 1910
      Metropolitan Magazine 33:524-5, Jan 1911
      Munsey 44:409-11, Dec 1910
      Pearson 24:800-803, Dec 1910
      Theatre Magazine 12:131-3, Nov 1910
  Josephine
    Productions:
      Adapted by Dr. Washburn Freund.   Opened January 28,
        1918 for 24 performances.
    Reviews:
      Bookman 47:76, Mar 1918
      Dramatic Mirror 78:5, Feb 19, 1918
      Green Book 19:590-1+, Apr 1916
      New York Dramatic News 65:7, Feb 2, 1916
      New York Times p.13, Jan 29, 1918
  The Master
    Productions:
      Adapted by Benjamin F. Glazer.   Opened December 5,
        1916 for 47 performances.
      Adapted by Benjamin F. Glazer.   Opened February 19,
        1918 for 15 performances.
    Reviews:
      Dramatic Mirror 76:5+, Dec 16, 1916
      International 11:29, Jan 1917
      Life (NY) 68:1150, Dec 21, 1916
      New York Dramatic News 63:22, Dec 9, 1916
      New York Times p.7, Dec 6, 1916
                      p.10, Feb 20, 1918
      North American Review 205:135-6, Jan 1917
      Theatre Magazine 25:9+, Jan 1917
  The Mongrel
    Productions:
      Adapted by Elmer Rice.   Translated by Francis C.
        Fay.   Opened December 15, 1924 for 32 performances.

The Mongrel (cont.)
  Reviews:
      Independent 114:51, Jan 10, 1925
      Living Age 324:70-6, Jan 3, 1925
      New York Times p.28, Dec 16, 1924
      Theatre Magazine 40:62 +,Feb 1925
The Poor Fool
  Productions:
      Translated by Mrs. F. E. Washburn Freund. Opened
        August 30, 1916 in repertory (Washington Square
        Players).
  Reviews:
      Dramatic Mirror 77:7, Mar 31, 1917
      Theatre Magazine 25:278, May 1917

Barrie, James M.
  The Admirable Crichton
  Productions:
      Opened March 9, 1931 for 56 performances.
  Reviews:
      Catholic World 133:210, May 1931
      Commonweal 13:581, Mar 25, 1931
      Drama 21:10, Apr 1931
      Dramatist 7:623, Oct 1915
      Life (NY) 97:25, Mar 27, 1931
      Literary Digest 108:17, Mar 28, 1931
      Nation 132:336, Mar 25, 1931
      New York Times p.23, Mar 16, 1931
                     VIII,p.1, Mar 29, 1931
      Theatre Arts 15:373-4, May 1931
  The Adored One (see Legend of Lenora)

  Alice-Sit-by-the-Fire
  Productions:
      Opened February 13, 1911 for 32 performances.
      Opened March 7, 1932 for 32 performances.
  Reviews:
      Bookman 33:136-7, Apr 1911
      Catholic World 135:77, Apr 1932
      Collier's 46:13, Mar 11, 1911
      Commonweal 15:579, Mar 23, 1932
      Dramatist 2:147, Apr 1911
      Green Book 5:900, May 1911
      Life (NY) 57:444, Mar 23, 1911
      New Republic 70:153-4, Mar 23, 1932
      New York Times p.19, Mar 8, 1932
      Theatre Guild Magazine 9:25-6, Apr 1932
      Theatre Magazine 13:xi-xiii, Mar 1911

Barbara's Wedding
  Productions:
    Opened October 8, 1931 for 20 performances.
  Reviews:
    New Republic 68:300, Oct 28, 1931
    New York Times p.21, Oct 9, 1931
The Censor and the Dramatists
  Productions:
    Opened October 14, 1913 for 33 performances.
  Reviews:
    Harper's Weekly 58:24-5, Nov 15, 1913
    New York Dramatic Mirror 70:7, Oct 15, 1913
    New York Times p.13, Oct 9, 1913
                    p.11, Oct 15, 1913
Dear Brutus
  Productions:
    Opened December 23, 1918 for 184 performances.
  Reviews:
    Bellman 26:12-15, Jan 4, 1919
    Current Opinion 66:91-4, Feb 1919
    Dramatic Mirror 80:8, Jan 4, 1919
    Hearst 35:46+, Mar 1919
    Forum 61:243-4, Feb 1919
    Life 73:56, Jan 9, 1919
    Nation 105:601, Nov 29, 1917
           108:30 Jan 4, 1919
    New Republic 17:285, Jan 4, 1919
    New York Times p.7, Dec 24, 1918
                   IV, p.2, Dec 29, 1918
                   p.9, Jan 8, 1919
    Theatre Magazine 29:77+, Feb 1919
                     29:156+, Mar 1919
Half an Hour
  Productions:
    Opened September 25, 1913 for 60 performances.
  Reviews:
    Bookman 38:263-4, Nov 1913
    Dramatic Mirror 70:6 Oct 1, 1913
    Dramatist 5:392-4, Oct 1913
    Everybody's Magazine 29:807-8, Dec 1913
    Green Book 11:166-7, Jan 1914
    Harper's Weekly 58:25-6, Oct 18, 1913
A Kiss for Cinderella
  Productions:
    Opened December 25, 1916 for 152 performances.
    Opened March 10, 1942 for 48 performances.
  Reviews:

A Kiss for Cinderella (cont.)
  Bellman 22:44-6, Jan 13, 1917
  Book News 35:244, Feb 1917
  Bookman 53:172-3, Apr 1921
  Catholic World 155:216, May 1942
  Commonweal 35:561, Mar 27, 1942
  Current Opinion 62:178-82, Mar 1917
  Dramatic Mirror 75:7, Apr 15, 1916
                 76:7, Dec 30, 1916
                 76:15, Dec 30, 1916
  Green Book 17:388+, Mar 1917
  Life (NY) 69:22, Jan 14, 1917
  Nation 102:522-3, May 11, 1916
        104:27, Jan 4, 1917
        154:348-9, Mar 21, 1942
  New Republic 9:269, Jan 6, 1917
               106:398, Mar 23, 1942
  New York Dramatic News 63:40, Dec 30, 1916
  New York Theatre Critics' Reviews 1942:332
  New York Times p.6, Mar 18, 1916
               p.9, Dec 26, 1916
               II,p.6, Jan 7, 1917
               II,p.6, Jan 14, 1917
               p.22, Mar 11, 1942
               VIII,p.15, Mar 15, 1942
  New Yorker 18:29, Mar 2, 1942
  Newsweek 19:59, Mar 23, 1942
  North American Review 205:296-7, Feb 1917
  Theatre Arts 25:86-7+, Feb 1917
               26:289-90, May 1942
  Time 39:46, Mar 23, 1942
The Legend of Lenora (The Adored One)
  Productions:
    Opened January 5, 1914 for 136 performances.
    Opened March 24, 1927 for 16 performances.
  Reviews:
    Bookman 38:612-13, Feb 1914
    Current Opinion 56:194-5, Mar 1914
    International 8:68, Feb 1914
    Green Book 11:406-8+, Mar 1914
    Harper's Weekly 58:5, Feb 14, 1914
    Life (NY) 63:110-11, Jan 15,1914
    North American Review 199:192-3, Feb 1914
    New York Times p.6, Jan 6, 1914
                   p.22, Mar 30, 1927
                   VII, p.1, Apr 3, 1927
    Outlook 106:580-1+, Mar 14, 1914
            106:668-9, Mar 28, 1914

The Little Minister
  Productions:
    Opened January 11, 1916 for 79 performances.
    Opened March 23, 1925 for 16 performances.
  Reviews:
    Dramatic Mirror 75:8, Jan 22, 1916
    Literary Digest 119:31, Jan 12, 1935
    Life (NY) 85:20 Apr 9, 1925
    Nation 102:85, Jan 20, 1916
    New York Times p.13, Jan 12, 1916
                   VI, p.1, Jan 16, 1916
                   p.21, Mar 24, 1925
    Stage 14:92, Aug 1937
    Time 25:55, Jan 7, 1935
    Vanity Fair 43:42 Feb 1935
Mary Rose
  Productions:
    Opened December 22, 1920 for 127 performances.
    Opened March 4, 1951 for 17 performances.
  Reviews:
    Bookman 51:541, Jul 1920
            52:568, Feb 1921
    Current Opinion 69:63-5, Jul 1920
    Catholic World 173:148-9, May 1921
    Commonweal 53:589, Mar 23, 1951
    Dramatic Mirror 83:11, Jan 1, 1921
    Fortnightly Review 113:955-9, Jun 1920
    Independent 105:57, Jan 15, 1921
    Living Age 305:492-4, May 22, 1920
    Nation 112:48, Jan 12, 1921
    New York Clipper 68:18, Dec 29, 1920
    New York Theatre Critics' Reviews 1951:328
    New York Times p.9, Dec 23, 1920
                   VI, p.3, Dec 26, 1920
                   VII, p.1, Apr 3, 1921
                   p.25, Mar 5, 1951
                   II, p.1, Mar 11, 1951
    New Yorker 27:54, Mar 17, 1951
    Outlook 127:11-12, Jan 5, 1921
    School and Society 73:185, Mar 24, 1951
    Touchstone 8:335, Feb 1921
    Theatre Arts 35:17, May 1951
    Theatre Magazine 33:155+, Mar 1921
    Weekly Review 4:18-19, Jan 5, 1921
The New Word
  Productions:
    Opened May 14, 1917 for 48 performances.
    Opened May 6, 1918 for 32 performances.

The New Word (cont.)
Reviews:
    Nation 104:640, May 24, 1917
    New Republic 11:221, June 23, 1917
    New York Times p. 11, May 15, 1917
                      VIII, p. 5, May 20, 1917
                      p. 11, May 7, 1918
    Theatre Magazine 15:344+, Jun 1917
Old Friends
Productions:
    Opened May 14, 1917 for 48 performances.
Reviews:
    Theatre Magazine 25:374, Jun 1917
The Old Lady Shows Her Medals
Productions:
    Opened May 14, 1917 for 48 performances.
    Opened March 7, 1932 for 32 performances.
Reviews:
    Commonweal 15:579, Mar 23, 1932
    Current Opinion 63:23-6, Jul 1917
    Dramatic Mirror 77:5+, May 26, 1917
    Life (NY) 69:910 May 24, 1917
    New Republic 11:221, Jun 23, 1917
    New York Dramatic News 64:2, May 26, 1917
    New York Times p. 11, May 15, 1917
                      VIII, p. 5, May 20, 1917
                      p. 19, Mar 8, 1932
    Theatre Magazine 25:374, Jun 1917
Peter Pan
Productions:
    Opened December 23, 1912 for 24 performances.
    Opened December 21, 1915 for 23 performances.
    Opened November 6, 1924 for 96 performances.
    Opened November 26, 1928 for 48 performances.
    Opened April 24, 1950 for 321 performances.
Reviews:
    Catholic World 171:226-7, Jun 1950
    Christian Science Monitor Magazine p. 4, Apr 29, 1950
    Commonweal 52:127-8, May 12, 1950
    Dramatic Mirror 69:4, Jan 1, 1913
                     75:9, Jan 1, 1916
    Harper's Weekly 56:9-10, Dec 28, 1912
    Life 28:89-90+, May 22, 1950
    Life (NY) 84:18, Nov 27, 1924
    Literary Digest 84:26-7, Jan 17, 1925
    Musical America 70:4, May 1950
    National Magazine 53:195, Dec 1924

New Republic 122:20, May 8, 1950
New York Times p.11, Apr 14, 1913
VIII, p.6, Jan 2, 1916
p.16, Nov 7, 1924
p.36, Nov 27, 1928
p.27, Apr 25, 1950
II, p.1, Apr 30, 1950
New Yorker 26:50+, May 6, 1950
Outlook 139:51-2, Jan 14, 1925
Theatre Magazine 40:19, Jan 1925
Time 55:49, May 8, 1950

The Professor's Love Story
Productions:
Opened February 26, 1917 for 48 performances.
Reviews:
Dramatic Mirror 77:7, Mar 3, 1917
Green Book 17:773+, May 1917
Life (NY) 69:401, Mar 8, 1917
Nation 104:275 Mar 8, 1917
New York Dramatic News 64:2, Mar 3, 1917
New York Times p.9, Feb 27, 1917
III, p.2, Mar 4, 1917
Theatre Magazine 25:212+, Apr 1917

Rosalind
Productions:
Opened September 6, 1915 for 48 performances.
Reviews:
Dramatic Mirror 74:8, Sep 8, 1915
Green Book 14:811-13, Nov 1915
Harper's Weekly 61:302, Sep 25, 1915
New Republic 4:185, Sep 18, 1915

Shall We Join The Ladies?
Productions:
Opened January 13, 1925 for 31 performances.
Reviews:
American Mercury 4:373-4, Mar 1925
Bookman 61:75-6, Mar 1925
New York Times p.19, Jan 14, 1925

A Slice of Life
Productions:
Opened January 29, 1912 for 48 performances.
Reviews:
Bookman 35:171-2, Apr 1912
Dramatic Mirror 67:6, Feb 7, 1912
Everybody's Magazine 26:685-6, May 1912
Life (NY) 59:348-9, Feb 15, 1912
Theatre Magazine 15:75, Mar 1912

The Twelve Pound Look
Productions:
Opened February 13, 1911 for 32 performances.
Reviews:
Bookman 33:136-7, Apr 1911
Collier's 46:13, Mar 11, 1911
Dramatist 2:147, Apr 1911
Green Book 5:900, May 1911
Life (NY) 57:444, Mar 2, 1911
Pearson's Magazine 25:502-3, Apr 1911
Theatre Magazine 13:xi-xiii, Mar 1911

What Every Woman Knows
Productions:
Opened April 13, 1926 for 74 performances.
Opened November 8, 1946 for 21 performances.
Opened December 22, 1954 for 15 performances.
Reviews:
Catholic World 164:260, Dec 1946
             180:389, Feb 1955
Commonweal 45:144, Nov 22, 1946
Nation 163:593, Nov 23, 1946
      180:37, Jan 8, 1955
New Republic 115:723+, Dec 2, 1946
New York Theatre Critics' Reviews 1946:268
                               1954:208
New York Times VIII, p. 1, Apr 18, 1926
             p. 13, Nov 9, 1946
             p. 16, Dec 23, 1954
New Yorker 22:59, Nov 16, 1946
        20:44, Jan 1, 1955
Newsweek 28:97, Nov 18, 1946
       45:43, Jan 3, 1955
Saturday Review 29:28, Nov 30, 1946
           38:25, Jan 8, 1955
Theatre Arts 30:692, Dec 1946
         31:23, Jan 1947
Theatre Magazine 44:13, Jul 1926
Time 63:35, Jan 3, 1955

The Will
Productions:
Opened September 29, 1913 for 32 performances.
Reviews:
American Mercury 77:32, Mar 1914
Bookman 39:263-4, Nov 1913
Dramatist 5:395-6, Oct 1913
Everybody's Magazine 29:808-9, Dec 1913
Harper's Weekly 58:25-6, Oct 18, 1913

Theatre Magazine 18:143, Nov 1913

Baum, Vicki
 A Divine Drudge (with John Golden)
  Productions:
   Opened October 26, 1933 for 12 performances.
  Reviews:
   New York Times p. 22, Oct 7, 1933
   Stage 10:28-9, Aug 1933
 Grand Hotel
  Productions:
   Translated by W. A. Drake.   Opened November 13,
    1930 for 459 performances.
  Reviews:
   Bookman 72:515-16, Jan 1931
   Catholic World 132:460-1, Jan 1931
   Collier's 87:19+, Apr 11, 1931
   Commonweal 13:497, Mar 4, 1931
   Drama 21:11-12, Jan 1931
   Life (NY) 96:34-5, Dec 5, 1930
   Literary Digest 107:19-21, Dec 13, 1930
   New Republic 65:72, Dec 3, 1930
   New York Times p. 30, Nov 14, 1930
                 IX, p. 1, Nov 23, 1930
                 IX, p. 2, Nov 23, 1930
   Outlook 156:554, Dec 3, 1930
   Sketch Book 8:25, Jan 1931
   Theatre Arts 15:896-8, Nov 1931
   Theatre Guild Magazine 9:38-40, Oct 1931
   Theatre Magazine 53:24+, Jan 1931
                    53:33-5+, Feb 1931
 Summer Night (with Benjamin Glazer)
  Productions:
   Opened November 2, 1939 for 4 performances.
  Reviews:
   Commonweal 31:96, Nov 17, 1939
   New York Times p. 17, Nov 3, 1939
   Newsweek 14:32, Nov 13, 1939

Beckett, Samuel
 Endgame
  Productions:
   (Off Broadway) 1958
   (Off Broadway) Opened February 11, 1962 in repertory.
  Reviews:
   Christian Century 75:282, Mar 5, 1958
   Nation 186:145-6, Feb 15, 1958

Endgame (cont.)
New York Times p. 32, Jan 29, 1958
II, p. 1, Feb 16, 1958
p. 27, Feb 12, 1962
VI, p. 30, Feb 25, 1962
Newsweek 59:79, Feb 26, 1962
Saturday Review 41:28, Feb 15, 1958
Theatre Arts 42, 26, Apr 1958
Happy Days
Productions:
(Off Broadway) Opened September 17, 1961 for 28 performances.
(Off Broadway) Opened September 28, 1965 for 16 performances.
Reviews:
Christian Century 78:1208-9: Oct 11, 1961
Commonweal 75:69-70, Oct 13, 1961
Nation 193:234-5, Oct 7, 1961
201:258-9, Oct 18, 1965
New Republic 145:45-6, Oct 2, 1961
New York Times II, p. 1, Sep 17, 1961
p. 36, Sep 18, 1961
II, p. 1, Oct 1, 1961
New Yorker 37:119, Sep 30, 1961
Saturday Review 44:38, Oct 7, 1961
Theatre Arts 45:57-8, Nov 1961
Time 78:74, Sep 29, 1961
Krapp's Last Tape
Productions:
(Off Broadway) Opened January 14, 1960 for 582 performances.
(Off Broadway) Opened September 12, 1961 for 32 performances.
(Off Broadway) Opened October 31, 1965 for 168 performances.
Reviews:
Christian Century 77:256, Mar 2, 1960
Nation 190:153, Feb 13, 1960
New Republic 142:21, Feb 22, 1960
New York Times p. 37, Jan 15, 1960
II, p. 1, Jan 31, 1960
New Yorker 35:75, Jan 23, 1960
Saturday Review 43:28, Jan 30, 1960
Play
Productions:
(Off Broadway) Opened January 4, 1964 for 121 performances.

Reviews:
Commonweal 79:484-5, Jan 24, 1964
Nation 198:106, Jan 27, 1964
New Republic 150:30, Feb 1, 1964
New York Times p. 35, Jan 6, 1964
                p. 46, Mar 25, 1964
Saturday Review 47:25, Jan 25, 1964
Time 83:64, Jan 17, 1964
Vogue 143:22, Feb 15, 1964

Waiting for Godot
Productions:
Opened April 19, 1956 for 59 performances.
Opened January 21, 1957 for 6 performances.
Reviews:
America 95:182+, May 12, 1956
        95:265, Jun 9, 1956
Catholic World 183:227-8, Jun 1956
Commonweal 61:365-6, Dec 31, 1954
            64:203, May 25, 1956
            66:188+, May 17, 1957
Life 40:155-6+, May 7, 1956
Nation 182:387+, May 5, 1956
New Republic 134:20-1, May 14, 1956
New York Theatre Critics' Reviews 1957:385
New York Times II, p. 1, Apr 5, 1956
             p. 21, Apr 20, 1956
             II, p. 1, Apr 29, 1956
             p. 25, Jan 22, 1957
New Yorker 32:89, May 5, 1956
         32:25-6, May 19, 1956
Newsweek 47:76, Apr 30, 1956
        48:102, Sep 24, 1956
Reporter 13:43, Oct 20, 1955
Saturday Review 39:32, May 5, 1956
            39:46, May 19, 1956
            40:25, Feb 9, 1957
Theatre Arts 40:18, Jun 1956
         40:33-5+, Aug 1956
         41:16, Apr 1957
Time 67:55, Apr 30, 1956
      69:108, Mar 18, 1957

Becque, Henry
Parisienne
Productions:
Adapted by Ashley Dukes. Opened July 24, 1950 for
16 performances.

Parisienne (cont.)
  Reviews:
    Christian Science Monitor Magazine p. 9, Jul 29, 1950
    New Republic 123:22, Aug 28, 1950
    New York Times p. 24, Jul 25, 1950
    Newsweek 36:74, Aug 7, 1950

Behan, Brendan
  The Hostage
    Productions:
      Opened September 20, 1960 for 127 performances.
      (Off Broadway) Opened December 12, 1961 for 545
        performances.
    Reviews:
      America 104:130, Oct 22, 1960
      Atlantic 203:65-7, Jun 1959
      Catholic World 192:126-7, Nov 1960
      Commonweal 75:389, Jan 5, 1962
      Horizon 3:113-14, Jan 1961
      Nation 191:236, Oct 8, 1960
      New Republic 143:20-1, Oct 3, 1960
      New York Theatre Critics' Reviews 1960:239
      New York Times p. 42, Sep 21, 1960
                    II, p. 1, Oct 2, 1960
                    II, p. 1, Oct 30, 1960
                    p. 55, Dec 13, 1961
      New Yorker 35:156, Apr 18, 1959
                 36:128, Oct 1, 1960
                 37:57-8, Dec 23, 1961
      Newsweek 56:57, Oct 3, 1960
      Reporter 23:45, Nov 24, 1960
      Saturday Review 43:32, Oct 8, 1960
                      45:30, May 19, 1962
      Theatre Arts 44:8-9, Nov 1960
      Time 76:59, Oct 3, 1960
  Quare Fellow
    Productions:
      (Off Broadway) Season of 1958-1959.
    Reviews:
      Catholic World 188:420, Feb 1959
      Commonweal 69:438-9, Jan 23, 1959
      New York Times p. 34, Nov 28, 1958
      New Yorker 34:119-20, Dec 6, 1958
      Newsweek 52:66-7, Dec 8, 1958
      Saturday Review 41:27-8, Dec 13, 1958
      Theatre Arts 43:66, Feb 1959

34

Time 70:82, Jul 29, 1958
        72:78+, Dec 8, 1958
Vogue 133:95+, Jan 1, 1959

Benavente, Jacinto
  The Bonds of Interest
    Productions:
        Translated by John Garrett Underhill.   Opened April 19,
        1919 for 32 performances.
        Translated by John Garrett Underhill.   Opened October
        14, 1929 for 24 performances.
    Reviews:
        Bellman 26:574-7, May 24, 1919
        New Republic 19:25, May 3, 1919
        New York Times p. 9, Apr 15, 1919
                       IV, p. 2, Apr 20, 1919
                       p. 34, Oct 15, 1929
        Poet Lore 32:244-50, Jun 1921
        Theatre Arts 13:878, Dec 1929
        Theatre Magazine 29:341+, May 31, 1919
                         50:66, Dec 1929
        Weekly Review 1:45, May 24, 1919
  Field of Ermine
    Productions:
        Adapted by John Garrett Underhill.   Opened
        February 8, 1935 for 11 performances.
    Reviews:
        Drama 13:101, Dec 1922
        New Republic 82:78, Feb 27, 1935
        New York Times p. 10, Feb 9, 1935
        Theatre Arts 19:248, Apr 1935
  His Widow's Husbands
    Productions:
        Translated by John Garrett Underhill.   Opened
        October 31, 1917 in repertory (Washington Square
        Players).
    Reviews:
        New York Times p. 13, Nov 1, 1917
  The Passion Flower
    Productions:
        Translated by John Garrett Underhill.   Opened
        January 13, 1920 for 144 performances.
    Reviews:
        Arts and Decoration 12:344, Mar 1920
        Dramatic Mirror 82:131, Jan 29, 1920
        Independent 102:157, May 1, 1920
        Nation 110:152-3, Jan 21, 1920

35

The Passion Flower (cont.)
    New York Clipper 67:25, Jan 21, 1920
    New York Times p.12, Jan 14, 1920
    Theatre Magazine 31:183-4, Mar 1920
    Weekly Review 2:161, Feb 14, 1920
Saturday Night
  Productions:
    Opened October 25, 1926 for 13 performances.
  Reviews:
    New Republic 48:323, Now 10, 1926
    New York Times p.25, Oct 26,1926
                        VIII, p.1, Nov 7, 1926
    Theatre Arts 11:11, Jan 1937

Benelli, Sem
  The Jest (La Beffa)
  Productions:
    Adapted by Jean Richepin. Opened December 5, 1910
      in repertory as La Beffa.
    Opened April 9, 1919 for 77 performances.
    Opened September 19, 1919 for 179 performances.
    Opened February 4, 1926 for 77 performances.
  Reviews:
    Arts and Decoration 12:396-7, Apr 1920
    Bellman 26:489-92, May 3, 1919
    Bookman 63:214, Apr 1926
    Current Opinion 66:364-7, Jun 1919
    Dial 66:534-7, May 31, 1919
    Drama 10:140-5, Jan 1920
    Forum 61:28-9, May 1919
    Hearst 36:46-7+, Jul 1919
    Literary Digest 61:28-9, May 10, 1919
    Nation 108:618-19, Apr 19, 1919
    New Republic 19:55, May 10, 1919
                 19:397, Jul 23, 1919
    New York Times p.9, Apr 10, 1919
                    IV,p.2, Apr 20, 1919
                    IV,p.2, May 4, 1919
                    IV,p.2, May 18, 1919
                    IV,p.2, Sep 28, 1919
                    p.22, Feb 5, 1926
                    VIII,p.1, Feb 14, 1926
    Theatre Magazine 29:324, May 1919
                     29:352-4, Jun 1919
                     30:159, Sep 1919
                     43:11, Apr 1926
    Vogue 67:126+, Apr 1, 1926

Weekly Review 1:131, Jun 21, 1919
                    2:626, Jun 16, 1920

Bernard, Jean-Jacques
Invitation to A Voyage
  Productions:
      Translated by Ernest Boyd.   Opened October 4, 1928
      for 19 performances.
  Reviews:
      American Mercury 15:504, Dec 1928
      New York Times p. 17, Oct 5, 1928
      Vogue 72:122+, Nov 24, 1928
Martine
  Productions:
      Translated by Helen Grayson.   Opened April 4, 1928
      for 16 performances.
  Reviews:
      New Republic 54:272-3, Apr 18, 1928
      New York Times p. 19, Apr 15, 1928
      Vogue 71:114, Jun 1, 1928

Besier, Rudolph
The Barretts of Wimpole Street
  Productions:
      Opened February 9, 1931 for 370 performances.
      Opened February 25, 1935 for 24 performances.
      Opened March 26, 1945 for 88 performances.
  Reviews:
      Arts and Decoration 34:46, Apr 1931
      Bookman 73:182-3, Apr 1931
      Canadian Forum 12:316, May 1932
      Catholic World 133:79-80, Apr 1931
                     161:169, May 1945
      Commonweal 13:469, Feb 25, 1931
                 41:648, Apr 13, 1945
      Golden Book 13:64-6, May 1931
      Harper's Bazaar 79:116-17+, Oct 1945
      Life (NY) 97:18, Feb 27, 1931
      Life 18:105-8, Apr 16, 1945
      Literary Digest 108:18-19, Mar 7, 1931
      Nation 132:224-5, Feb 25, 1931
             139:419, Oct 10, 1934
      New Republic 112:447, Apr 9, 1945
      New York Times p. 25, Feb 10, 1931
                     VIII, p. 1, Feb 15, 1931
                     VIII, p. 1, Feb 22, 1931

The Barretts of Wimpole Street (cont.)
                          VIII, p. 3, Feb 7, 1932
                          p. 16, Feb 26, 1935
                          p. 23, Mar 27, 1945
                          II,p. 1, Apr 1, 1945
     Newsweek 25:87, Apr 9, 1945
     Outlook 157:311, Feb 25, 1931
     Saturday Review 7:726, Apr 11, 1931
                          28:20-2, Apr 7, 1945
     Sketch Book 8:21, Jul 1931
     Theatre Arts 15:273-7, Apr 1931
                      19:258, Apr 1935
     Theatre Magazine 53:8+, Mar 1931
                          53:24, Apr 1931
     Time 45:88, Apr 9, 1945
     Vanity Fair 35:38+, Mar 1931
     Vogue 77:77+, Apr 1, 1931
     Woman's Journal ns16:12-13, Mar 1931
     Yale Review 20:817-18, Summer 1931
Don
  Productions:
     Opened December 30, 1909 in repertory.
  Reviews:
     Bookman 31:139-41, Apr 1910
     Current Literature 48:421-7, Apr 1910
     Dramatic Mirror 63:5, Jan 8, 1910
     Dramatist 2:155-6, Apr 1911
     Forum 43:188-9, Feb 1910
     Hampton 24:410, Mar 1910
     Harper's Weekly 54:25, Jan 22, 1910
     Life (NY) 55:92, Jan 3, 1910
     Metropolitan Magazine 32:390-1, Jun 1910
     Theatre Magazine 11:35-6+, Feb 1910
Her Country (with Sybil Spottiswood)
  Productions:
     Opened February 21, 1918 for 76 performances.
  Reviews:
     Dramatic Mirror 78:5, Mar 9, 1918
     Green Book 19:773+, May 1918
     New Republic 14:177, Mar 9, 1918
     New York Dramatic News 65:3, Mar 2, 1918
     New York Times p. 12, Feb 22, 1918
     Theatre Magazine 27:207, Apr 1918
                          27:260-8, Apr 1918
Lady Patricia
  Productions:
     Opened February 26, 1912 for 32 performances.

Reviews:
 American Playwright 1:75-6, Mar 1913
 Bookman 35:172-3, Apr 1912
 Collier's 48:34, Mar 16, 1912
 Dramatic Mirror 67:6, Feb 28, 1912
 Dramatist 3:244-5, Apr 1912
 Everybody's Magazine 26:688, May 1912
 Green Book 7:907-9+, May 1912
             7:975-7, May 1912
 Leslie's Weekly 114:193, Mar 14, 1912
 Life (NY) 59:540, Mar 14, 1912
 Munsey 47:282, May 1912
 Nation 93:321, Oct 5, 1911
 Red Book 19:177-82, May 1912
 Theatre Magazine 15:108+, Apr 1912

A Lesson in Love (with May Edgington)
 Productions:
 Opened September 24, 1923 for 72 performances.
 Reviews:
 Bookman 58:306, Nov 1923
 Nation 117:412, Oct 10, 1923
 New York Times p.10, Sep 25, 1923
             II, p.1, Sep 30, 1923
 Theatre Magazine 38:75, Nov 1923

Olive Latimer's Husband
 Productions:
 Opened January 7, 1910 for one performance.
 No Reviews.

Secrets (with May Edgington)
 Productions:
 Opened December 25, 1922 for 168 performances.
 Reviews:
 Current Opinion 75:61-6+, Jul 1923
 Drama 14:57, Nov 1923
 Nation 116:128, Jan 31, 1923
 New York Clipper 70:20, Jan 10, 1923
 New York Times p.11, Dec 26, 1922
             VII, p.1, Dec 31, 1922
 Theatre Magazine 37:15, Feb 1923
             37:28+, Apr 1923

Betti, Ugo
 Corruption in the Palace of Justice
 Productions:
 (Off Broadway) Translated by Henry Reed. Opened
 October 8, 1963 for 103 performances.
 Reviews:

Corruption in the Palace of Justice (cont.)
    Catholic World 198:199-200, Dec 1963
    Nation 197:306, Nov 9, 1963
    New Republic 149:26+, Dec 21, 1963
    New York Times p. 49, Oct 9, 1963
    New Yorker 39:100+, Oct 19, 1963
    Newsweek 62:72, Nov 18, 1963
    Theatre Arts 48:68, Jan 1964
    Time 82:75, Oct 25, 1963
The Gambler
  Productions:
    Adapted by Alfred Drake and Edward Eager.   Opened
      October 13, 1952 for 24 performances.
  Reviews:
    Commonweal 56:119, Nov 7, 1952
    New Republic 127:23, Oct 27, 1952
    New York Theatre Critics' Reviews 1952:241
    New York Times p. 40, Oct 14, 1952
    New Yorker 28:78-80, Oct 25, 1952
    Saturday Review 35:26, Nov 1, 1952
    Theatre Arts 36:25-6, Dec 1952
    Time 60:76, Oct 27, 1952
Island of the Goats
  Productions:
    English version by Henry Reed.   Opened October 4,
      1955 for 7 performances.
  Reviews:
    New York Theatre Critics' Reviews 1955:260
    New York Times p. 40, Oct 5, 1955
    New Yorker 31:81, Oct 15, 1955
    Theatre Arts 39:23, Dec 1955
The Queen and the Rebels
  Productions:
    (Off Broadway) Opened February 25, 1965 for 22
     performances.
  Reviews:
    New York Times p. 16, Feb 26, 1965
    New Yorker 41:80, Mar 6, 1965
Time of Vengeance
  Productions:
    (Off Broadway) Season of 1959-1960.
  Reviews:
    Nation 190:19, Jan 2, 1960
    New York Times p. 39, Dec 11, 1959
                 II, p. 1, Dec 27, 1959
Troubled Waters
  Productions:

(Off Broadway)   Translated by Gino Rizzo and William
     Meriwether.   Opened June 3, 1965 for 5 performances.
  Reviews:
     Nation 200:681, Jun 21, 1965
     New York Times p. 40, Jun 4, 1965

Birabeau, Andre
  Dame Nature
     Productions:
     Adapted by Patricia Collinge.   Based on Wedekind's
        The Awakening of Spring.   Opened September 26,
        1938 for 48 performances.
     Reviews:
        Commonweal 28:644, Oct 14, 1938
        Nation 147:362, Oct 8, 1938
        New Republic 96:271, Oct 12, 1938
        New York Times p. 24, Sep 27, 1938
        Newsweek 12:28, Oct 10, 1938
        Theatre Arts 22:782-3, Nov 1938
        Time 32:49, Oct 10, 1938
  Little Dark Horse
     Productions:
     Adapted by Theresa Helburn.   Opened November 16,
        1941 for 9 performances.
     Reviews:
        New York Theatre Critics' Reviews 1941:218
        New York Times p. 14, Nov 14, 1941

Bolitho, William
  Overture
     Productions:
     Opened December 5, 1930 for 41 performances.
     Reviews:
        Arts and Decoration 34:48, Feb 1931
        Bookman 73:72, Mar 1931
        Catholic World 132:593-4, Feb 1931
        Commonweal 13:217-18, Dec 24, 1930
        Drama 21:14, Jan 1931
        Nation 131:714+, Dec 24, 1930
        New Republic 65:165-6   Dec 24, 1930
        New York Times p. 31, Nov 25, 1930
                        p. 26, Dec 8, 1930
                        IX, p. 1, Dec 14, 1930
        Outlook 156:629, Dec 17, 1930
        Theatre Arts 15:96+, Feb 1931
        Theatre Magazine 53:24-5, Feb 1931
        Vanity Fair 35:82, Feb 1931
        Vogue 77:39+, Feb 1, 1931

Bolt, Robert
 Flowering Cherry
  Productions:
     Opened October 21, 1959 for 5 performances.
  Reviews:
     New York Theatre Critics' Reviews 1959:247
     New York Times p. 46, Oct 22, 1959
     New Yorker 35:136, Oct 31, 1959
     Theatre Arts 43:88, Dec 1959
     Time 74:30, Nov 2, 1959
 A Man For All Seasons
  Productions:
     Opened November 22, 1961 for 637 performances.
     Opened January 27, 1964 for 17 performances.
  Reviews:
     America 106:452, Jan 6, 1962
             107:184-7, Apr 28, 1962
     Catholic World 194:255-6, Jan 1962
     Christian Century 79:87-9, Jan 17, 1962
     Commonweal 75:317-18, Dec 18, 1961
     Life 52:55-7+, Jan 12, 1962
     Nation 193:480, Dec 9, 1961
     New Republic 145:28-30, Dec 11, 1961
     New York Theatre Critics' Reviews 1961:164
     New York Times II, p. 1, Nov 19, 1961
                     p. 51, Nov 23, 1961
                     II, p. 1, Dec 3, 1961
                     II, p. 1, Sep 23, 1962
                     p. 24, Jan 28, 1964
     New Yorker 37:117, Dec 2, 1961
     Newsweek 58:78, Dec 4, 1961
     Reporter 26:38, Jan 4, 1962
     Saturday Review 44:27, Dec 16, 1961
                     45:27, Sep 15, 1962
     Theatre Arts 46:10-11 Feb 1962
     Time 78:64 Dec 1, 1961

Bolton, Guy
 Adam and Eva (with George Middleton)
  Productions:
     Opened September 13, 1919 for 312 performances.
  Reviews:
     Current Opinion 68:782-8, Jun 1920
     Dramatic Mirror 80:1503, Sep 25, 1919
     Dramatist 10:969-70, Oct 1919
     Hearst 38:41-3+, Jul 1920
     Life (NY) 74:548-9, Sep 25, 1919

New York Times p. 15, Sep 16, 1919
                 IV, p. 2, Sep 21, 1919

Anastasia
Productions:
Adapted from a play by Marcelle Maurette.   Opened
December 29, 1954 for 272 performances.
Reviews:
America 92:461, Jan 29, 1955
Catholic World 180:386, Feb 1955
Commonweal 61:582-3, Mar 4, 1955
Life 38:32-3, Feb 14, 1955
Nation 180:24, Jan 22, 1955
New Republic 132:22, Feb 7, 1955
New York Theatre Critics' Reviews 1954:192
New York Times p. 13, Dec 30, 1954
                 II, p. 1, Jan 16, 1955
New Yorker 30:66, Jan 8, 1955
Newsweek 45:62, Jan 10, 1955
Saturday Review 38:31, Jan 15, 1955
Theatre Arts 39:19+, Mar 1955
              39:28+, Jun 1955
              40:34-61, May 1956
Time 65:35, Jan 10, 1955

The Cave Girl (with George Middleton)
Productions:
Opened August 18, 1920 for 37 performances.
Reviews:
Dramatic Mirror p. 9, Jul 3, 1920
                p. 371, Aug 28, 1920
Independent 103:261, Sep 4, 1920
New York Clipper 68:19, Aug 25, 1920
New York Times p. 12, Aug 19, 1920
Theatre 32:242, Oct 1920

Chicken Feed (Wages for Wives)
Productions:
Opened September 24, 1923 for 144 performances.
Reviews:
New York Times p. 10, Sep 25, 1923
Theatre Magazine 38:56+, Nov 1923

Child of Fortune
Productions:
Adapted from Wings of the Dove by Henry James.
Opened November 13, 1956 for 23 performances.
Reviews:
Commonweal 65:383, Jan 11, 1957
New York Theatre Critics' Reviews 1956:209
New York Times p. 41, Nov 14, 1956

43

Child of Fortune (cont.)
    New Yorker 32:124, Nov 24, 1956
    Saturday Review 39:50, Dec 1, 1956
    Theatre Arts 41:27, Jan 1957
    Time 68:58, Nov 26, 1956
Children (with Tom Carlton)
    Productions:
    Opened October 4, 1915 in repertory (Washington
        Square Players).
    Reviews:
    Dramatic Mirror 75:8, Apr 1, 1916
    New York Times p. 9, Mar 21, 1916
The Fallen Idol
    Productions:
    Opened January 23, 1915 for nine performances.
    Reviews:
    Current Opinion 58:177-8, Mar 1915
    Dramatic Mirror 73:24, Jan 27, 1915
    Green Book 13:765-6, Apr 1915
    Life (NY) 65:196, Feb 4, 1915
    New York Dramatic News 60:17, Jan 30, 1915
    New York Times p. 9, Jan 25, 1915
    Theatre Magazine 21:149, Mar 1915
The Five Million (with Frank Mandel)
    Productions:
    Opened July 8, 1919 for 91 performances.
    Reviews:
    Current Opinion 67:160-4, Sep 1919
    Forum 62:243-4, Aug 1919
    Hearst 36:42-3+, Oct 1919
    New York Times p. 14, Jul 9, 1919
    Theatre Magazine 30:149, Sep 1919
Golden Wings (R. A. F.) (with William Jay)
    Productions:
    Opened December 8, 1941 for six performances.
    Reviews:
    New York Theatre Critics' Reviews 1941:178
    New York Times p. 46, Dec 9, 1941
    Newsweek 18:61, Dec 22, 1941
    Theatre Arts 26:79, Feb 1942
Grounds for Divorce (see entry under Vajda, Ernest)

The Light of the World (with George Middleton)
    Productions:
    Opened January 6, 1920 for 31 performances.
    Reviews:
    Dramatic Mirror 82:51, Jan 15, 1920

Life (NY) 75:148, Jan 22, 1920
New York Clipper 67:25, Jan 14, 1920
New York Times p.17, Jan 7, 1920
Theatre Magazine 31:142, Feb 1920
The Nightcap (with Max Marcin)
Productions:
Opened August 15, 1921 for 96 performances.
Reviews:
Dramatic Mirror 84:285, Aug 20, 1921
New York Clipper 69:24, Aug 14, 1921
New York Times p.18, Aug 16, 1921
Theatre Magazine 34:236, Oct 1921
Weekly Review 5:215, Sep 3, 1921
Nobody Home (with Paul Rubens)
Productions:
Opened April 20, 1915 for 135 performances.
Reviews:
Dramatic Mirror 73:8, Apr 28, 1915
Green Book 14:59-60, Jul 1915
14:191-2, Jul 1915
Life (NY) 65:808, May 16, 1915
Theatre Magazine 21:280+, Jun 1915
Nobody's Business (with Frank Mandel)
Productions:
Opened October 22, 1923 for 40 performances.
Reviews:
New York Times p.17, Oct 23, 1923
VIII, p.1, Oct 28, 1923
Polly Preferred
Productions:
Opened January 11, 1923 for 184 performances.
Reviews:
New York Clipper 70:14, Jan 17, 1923
New York Times p.13, Jan 12, 1923
Polly With A Past (with George Middleton)
Productions:
Opened September 8, 1917 for 315 performances.
Reviews:
Bookman 46:284-5, Nov 1917
Dramatic Mirror 77:5+, Sep 15, 1917
Green Book 18:774-8, Nov 1917
Life (NY) 70:466, Sep 20, 1917
New York Dramatic News 64:6, Sep 15, 1917
New York Times p.7, Sep 7, 1917
II, p.5, Sep 16, 1917
Theatre Magazine 26:197+, Oct 1917
R.A.F. (see Golden Wings)

The Rule of Three
    Productions:
        Opened February 16, 1914 for 80 performances.
    Reviews:
        Bookman 39:145, Apr 1914
        Dramatic Mirror 71:6, Feb 18, 1914
        Green Book 11:776, May 1914
                    11:972-4, Jun 1914
                    11:1058-68, Jun 1914
        Hearst 25:685-700, May 1914
        Life (NY) 63:409, Mar 5, 1914
        Munsey 51:585, Apr 1914
        New York Dramatic News 59:20, Feb 21, 1914
        New York Times p.11, Feb 17, 1914
        Theatre Magazine 19:170+, Apr 1914
    Theatre (see entry under Maugham, W. Somerset)

    Wages for Wives (see Chicken Feed)

Bourdet, Edouard
    Best Sellers (Vient de Paraitre)
    Productions:
        Adapted by Dorothy Cheston Bennett. Opened May 3,
            1933 for 53 performances.
    Reviews:
        Catholic World 137:338-9, Jun 1933
        Nation 136:594, May 24, 1933
        New Outlook 161:49, Jun 1933
        New York Times p.20, May 4, 1933
        Stage 10:11, Jun 1933
        Time 21:52, May 15, 1933
        Vogue 81:60, Jun 15, 1933
The Captive
    Productions:
        Adapted by Arthur Hornblow, Jr. from La Prisonnière.
            Opened September 29, 1926 for 160 performances.
    Reviews:
        American Mercury 9:502-3, Dec 1926
                        10:373-5, Mar 1927
        Bookman 64:479, Dec 1926
        Dramatist 18:1327, Jan 1927
        Independent 44:14+, Dec 1926
        Life (NY) 88:23, Oct 21, 1926
        Nation 123:408, Oct 20, 1926
        New Republic 48:324, Nov 10, 1926
        New York Times p.23, Sep 30, 1926
        Theatre Arts 10:810-11, Dec 1926

Theatre Magazine 45:22+, Feb 1927
Vanity Fair 27:69+, Dec 1926
Vogue 68:82, Dec 1926

The Other Rose

Productions:
Adapted by George Middleton. Opened December 20, 1923 for 84 performances.

Reviews:
American Mercury 1:247, Feb 1924
New York Times p.15, Dec 21, 1923
VII, p.1, Dec 30, 1923
Theatre Magazine 39:15, Feb 1924

La Prisonnière (see The Captive)

The Rubicon

Productions:
Adapted by Henry Baron. Opened February 21, 1922 for 132 performances.

Reviews:
New York Clipper 70:22, May 8, 1922
New York Times p.13, Sep 22, 1922

The Sex Fable (The Weaker Sex) (Le Sexe Faible)

Productions:
English text by Jane Hinton. Opened October 20, 1931 for 33 performances.

Reviews:
Catholic World 134:336-7, Dec 1931
Commonweal 15:18-19, Nov 4, 1931
Nation 133:525, Nov 11, 1931
New York Times p.26, Oct 21, 1931
Outlook 159:312, Nov 4, 1931
Vanity Fair 36:90+, Apr 1931
Vogue 78:57+, Dec 15, 1931

Times Have Changed (Les Temps Difficiles)

Productions:
Adapted by Louis Bromfield. Opened February 15, 1935 for 32 performances.

Reviews:
Catholic World 141:90-1, Apr 1935
Commonweal 21:570, Mar 15, 1935
New York Times p.28, Feb 19, 1935
Stage 12:24-5, Apr 1935
Theatre Arts 19:254-6, Apr 1935
19:471, Jun 1935
Vanity Fair 44:37, May 1935

Viente de Paraitre (see Best Sellers)

The Weaker Sex (see The Sex Fable)

Brecht, Bertolt
Arturo Ui
  Productions:
    Adapted by George Tabori. Opened November 11,
    1963 for eight performances.
  Reviews:
    Catholic World 198:263-4, Jan 1964
    Commonweal 79:314+, Dec 6, 1963
    Nation 197:403-4, Dec 7, 1963
    New Republic 149:26, Dec 21, 1963
              153:34, Aug 7, 1965
    New York Theatre Critics' Reviews 1963:203
    New York Times p. 49, Nov 12, 1963
              II, p. 1, Nov 24, 1963
    New Yorker 36:66-8, Jul 2, 1960
    Newsweek 62:71, Nov 25, 1963
    Saturday Review 46:24, Nov 30, 1963
Baal
  Productions:
    (Off Broadway) Adapted by Eric Bentley. Opened
    May 6, 1965 for 43 performances.
  Reviews:
    Commonweal 82:413-14, Jun 18, 1965
    Nation 196:381, May 4, 1963
          200:625-8, Jun 7, 1965
    New York Times p. 33, May 7, 1965
              II, p. 1, Jun 6, 1965
    New Yorker 41:158+, May 15, 1965
    Newsweek 65:81, Jun 7, 1965
    Time 85:64, May 14, 1965
Brecht On Brecht (see entry under Tabori, George)

Caucasian Chalk Circle
  Productions:
    English version by Eric Bentley. Opened March 24,
    1966 for 77 performances (Repertory Theatre of
    Lincoln Center).
  Reviews:
    America 114:603-4, Apr 23, 1966
    Commentary 41:76-7, Jun 1966
    Commonweal 84:177, Apr 29, 1966
    Life 60:15, Apr 22, 1966
    Nation 183:202, Sep 8, 1956
         202:436-7, Apr 11, 1966
    New Republic 119:27-8, Sep 6, 1948

154:30+, Apr 16, 1966
New York Times II, p. 3, Mar 20, 1966
p. 35, Mar 25, 1966
II, p. 1, Apr 10, 1966
New Yorker 31:62-4, Jul 16, 1955
38:159-60, May 12, 1962
42:122, Apr 2, 1966
Newsweek 67:90-1, Apr 4, 1966
Saturday Review 44:39, Nov 18, 1961
49:53, Apr 1, 1966
Time 87:63, Apr 1, 1966
Vogue 147:54, Jun 1966

The Exception and the Rule
Productions:
(Off Broadway) Opened February 10, 1962 for one
performance.
(Off Broadway) Adapted by Eric Bentley. Opened
May 20, 1965 for 141 performances.
Reviews:
America 113:62, Jul 10, 1965
Commonweal 82:414, Jun 18, 1965
New York Times p. 19, Mar 21, 1965
II, p. 1, Jun 6, 1965
Newsweek 65:81, Jun 7, 1965

Galileo
Productions:
(Off Broadway) Translated by Charles Laughton.
Opened December 7, 1947 for six performances.
Reviews:
Catholic World 166:74, Oct 1947
Commonweal 47:255-6, Dec 19, 1947
New Republic 117:36, Dec 29, 1947
New York Times p. 21, Aug 1, 1947
Newsweek 30:60, Dec 29, 1947
Theatre Arts 31:68-70, Dec 1947
32:12-13, Feb 1948
Vogue 111:192, Apr 1, 1948

The Good Woman of Setzuan
Productions:
Adapted by Eric Bentley. Opened December 18,
1956 for 24 performances.
(Off Broadway) Translated by Eric Bentley. Opened
March 10, 1963 for 12 performances.
Reviews:
Catholic World 184:385-6, Feb 1957
Christian Century 74:138, Jan 30, 1957
Nation 184:27, Jan 5, 1957

The Good Woman of Setzuan (cont.)
New York Theatre Critics' Reviews 1956:161
New York Times p. 41, Dec 19, 1956
II, p. 1, Dec 30, 1956
New Yorker 32:45-6, Dec 29, 1956
Saturday Review 40:24, Jan 5, 1957
49:55, Jun 4, 1966
Theatre Arts 41:26, Feb 1957
In the Jungle of Cities
Productions:
(Off Broadway) Translated by Gerhard Nellhaus.
Opened December 20, 1960 for 66 performances.
(Off Broadway) Translated by Gerhard Nellhaus.
Opened November 2, 1961 for 80 performances.
Reviews:
Nation 192:18-19, Jan 7, 1961
New Republic 142:30-1, Jan 9, 1961
New York Times p. 39, Dec 21, 1960
II, p. 1, Jan 15, 1961
New Yorker 36:42-3, Dec 31, 1960
Theatre Arts 45:10-11+, Mar 1961
Man Is Man
Productions:
(Off Broadway) Translated by Gerhard Nellhaus.
Opened September 18, 1962 for 175 performances.
Reviews:
Commonweal 77:72, Oct 12, 1962
New Republic 147:26+, Oct 1, 1962
New York Times p. 31, Sep 19, 1962
New Yorker 39:98+, Sep 29, 1962
A Man's Man
Productions:
(Off Broadway) Adapted by Eric Bentley. Opened
September 19, 1962 for 175 performances.
Reviews:
America 107:862, Oct 6, 1962
Commonweal 77:72, Oct 12, 1962
Nation 195:207-8, Oct 6, 1962
New Republic 147:26+, Oct 1, 1962
New York Times p. 30, Sep 20, 1962
New Yorker 38:98+, Sep 29, 1962
Theatre Arts 47:67, Feb 1963
Time 80:81, Sep 28, 1962
Mother
Productions:
Based on a novel by Maxim Gorki. Translated by
Paul Peters. Opened November 19, 1935 for 36

performances.
Reviews:
    Catholic World 142:469, Jan 1936
    Commonweal 23:162, Dec 6, 1935
    Nation 141:659-60, Dec 4, 1935
    New Republic 85:175, Dec 18, 1935
    New York Times p. 26, Nov 20, 1935
    Theatre Arts 20:13-15, Jun 1936
    Time 26:68, Dec 2, 1935

Mother Courage and Her Children
Productions:
    Adapted by Eric Bentley.   Opened March 28, 1963
      for 52 performances.
Reviews:
    Catholic World 197:143-4, May 1963
    Commonweal 78:141-2, Apr 26, 1963
    Nation 182:557-8, Jun 30, 1956
           196:314-15, Apr 13, 1963
    New Republic 148:35-6, Apr 13, 1963
           152:29, Jun 26, 1965
    New York Theatre Critics' Reviews 1963:362
    New York Times p. 5, Mar 30, 1963
           p. 51, Apr 1, 1963
    New Yorker 39:71, Apr 6, 1963
    Newsweek 61:85, Apr 8, 1963
    Reporter 28:39-40, May 9, 1963
           28:8, Jun 6, 1963
    Saturday Review 46:20, Apr 13, 1963
    Theatre Arts 26:251-2, Apr 1942
           33:26-7, Jun 1949
           46:19-22, Jun 1962
           47:14-15, May 1963
    Time 81:56, Apr 5, 1963

The Private Life of the Master Race
Productions:
    (Off Broadway) English version by Eric Bentley.
      Opened June 11, 1945.
Reviews:
    Commonweal 42:262-3, Jun 29, 1945
    New Republic 112:871, Jun 25, 1945
           113:48, Jul 9, 1945
    New York Times p. 28, Jun 13, 1945
           II. p. 1, Jun 17, 1945

Bridie, James (Osborne H. Mayor)
The Anatomist
Productions:

The Anatomist (cont.)
    Opened October 24, 1932 for eight performances.
Reviews:
    New York Times p. 24, Oct 25, 1932
    Theatre Arts 17:24, Jan 1933
Daphne Laureola
Productions:
    Opened September 18, 1950 for 56 performances.
Reviews:
    Catholic World 172:148, Nov 1950
    Christian Science Monitor Magazine p. 8, Sep 23, 1950
    Commonweal 52:630, Oct 6, 1950
    Nation 171:295, Sep 30, 1950
    New Republic 123:22, Oct 2, 1950
    New York Theatre Critics' Reviews 1950:272
    New York Times II, p. 1, Sep 17, 1950
                      p. 38, Sep 19, 1950
                      II, p. 1, Sep 24, 1950
                      II, p. 1, Oct 15, 1950
    New Yorker 26:52+, Sep 30, 1950
    Newsweek 36:82, Oct 2, 1950
    Saturday Review 33:30-1, Oct 14, 1950
    Theatre Arts 34:11, Nov 1950
    Time 56:56, Oct 2, 1950
A Sleeping Clergyman
Productions:
    Opened October 8, 1934 for 40 performances.
Reviews:
    Catholic World 140:211, Nov 1934
    Commonweal 20:618, Oct 26, 1934
    Literary Digest 118:24+, Oct 20, 1934
    Nation 139:486-7, Oct 24, 1934
    New Republic 80:314, Oct 24, 1934
    New York Times p. 16, Oct 9, 1934
                      IX, p. 2, Oct 28, 1934
    Stage 12:8, Nov 1934
    Theatre Arts 17:769-70, Oct 1933
                  18:899, Dec 1934
    Time 24:38, Oct 22, 1934
Storm Over Patsy (see entry under Frank, Bruno)

Tobias and the Angel
Productions:
    Opened April 28, 1937 for 22 performances.
Reviews:
    Commonweal 26:78, May 14, 1937
    Nation 144:543-4, May 8, 1937

New York Times p. 16, Apr 29, 1937

Brieux, Eugene
 Accused
　Productions:
　　English version by George Middleton.　Opened
　　　September 29, 1925 for 95 performances.
　Reviews:
　　Life (NY) 86:26, Oct 22, 1925
　　Nation 121:446-7, Oct 14, 1925
　　New York Times p. 20, Sep 30, 1925
　　　　　　　　VIII, p. 1, Oct 11, 1925
　　Theatre Magazine 42:16, Dec 1925
 The Affinity
　Productions:
　　Translated by Laurence Irving.　Opened January 3,
　　　1910 for 24 performances.
　Reviews:
　　Dramatic Mirror 63:5, Jan 15, 1910
　　Forum 43:191, Feb 1910
 The Americans in France
　Productions:
　　Opened August 3, 1920 for 7 performances.
　Reviews:
　　Current Opinion 68:488-94, Apr 1920
　　Dramatic Mirror p. 237, Apr 7, 1920
　　Hearst 38:78, Oct 1920
　　Independent 103:229, Aug 28, 1920
　　New York Clipper 68:78, Aug 11, 1920
　　New York Times p. 14, Aug 4, 1920
　　Theatre 32:185, Dec 1920
　　Weekly Review 3:95-6, Jul 28, 1920
　　　　　　　　3:215-16, Sep 8, 1920
 Damaged Goods
　Productions:
　　Opened March 14, 1913 for 66 performances.
　　Adapted by Henry Herbert.　Translated by John
　　　Pollock.　Opened May 17, 1937 for 8 performances.
　Reviews:
　　Blue Book 17:665-8, Aug 1913
　　Bookman 37:431, Jun 1913
　　Current Opinion 54:296-7, Apr 1913
　　Dial 54:288, Apr 1, 1913
　　Dramatic Mirror 69:6-7, Mar 19, 1913
　　　　　　　　69:5, Mar 26, 1913
　　　　　　　　69:6, Apr 16, 1913
　　Dramatist 6:525-7, Jan 1915

53

Damaged Goods (cont.)
   Everybody's Magazine 29:677-9, Nov 1913
   Harper's Weekly 58:18-19, Oct 25, 1913
   International 7:107, Apr 1913
   Life (NY) 61:628, Mar 27, 1913
   Munsey 50:93-4, Oct 1913
   New York Times p.13, Mar 15, 1913
                  p.27, Mar 18, 1937
   Red Book 21:497-500, Jul 1913
   Theatre Magazine 17:134, May 1913
The Letter of the Law (The Red Robe)
 Productions:
   Opened February 23, 1920 for 89 performances.
 Reviews:
   Dramatic Mirror 82:367, Feb 28, 1920
   Independent 101:382, Mar 13, 1920
   Nation 110:340-1, Mar 13, 1920
   New York Clipper 67:25, Jan 25, 1920
                    68:19, Mar 3, 1920
   New York Times V, p.5, Feb 29, 1920
   Theatre Magazine 31:253 Apr 1920
   Weekly Review 2:264, Mar 13, 1920
Madame Pierre
 Productions:
   Adapted by Arthur Hornblow, Jr. Opened February 15,
    1922 for 37 performances.
 Reviews:
   Bookman 55:179, Apr 1922
   Independent 108:264, Mar 11, 1922
   Nation 114:236, Mar 1, 1922
   New Republic 30:198-9, Apr 12, 1922
   New York Clipper 70:20, Feb 22, 1922
   New York Times p.11, Feb 16, 1922
                  VI, p.1, Feb 19, 1922
   Theatre Magazine 35:236, Apr 1922
Maternity
 Productions:
   Translated by Benjamin F. Blanchard. Adapted by
    Richard Bennett. Opened January 6, 1915 for 21
    performances.
 Reviews:
   Bookman 40:639-40, Feb 1915
   Dramatic Mirror 73:8, Jan 13, 1915
   Dramatist 3:203-5, Oct 1911
   Green Book 13:768, Apr 1915
   New Republic 1:26, Jan 23, 1915
   New York Dramatic News 60:17, Jan 16, 1915

New York Times p.13, Jan 7, 1915
        VII, p. 6, Jan 10, 1915
    North American Review 201:267-9, Feb 1915
    Theatre Magazine 21:56-7+, Feb 1915
The Red Robe (see Letter of the Law)

The Three Daughters of Monsieur Dupont
    Productions:
        Translated by Laurence Irving.   Opened April 13,
        1910 for 21 performances.
    Reviews:
        Bookman 31:419-20, Jun 1910
        Dramatic Mirror 63:7, Apr 23, 1910
        Hampton's Magazine 24:826-8, Jun 1910
        Life (NY) 55:767, Apr 28, 1910
        Pearson's Magazine 23:835-40, Jun 1910
        Theatre Magazine 11:131, May 1910

Bruckner, Ferdinand
 Criminals
    Productions:
        (Off Broadway) Opened December 20, 1941 for 15
        performances.
    Reviews:
        Current History ns1:568, Feb 1942
        New York Times p.24, Dec 22, 1941
        Theatre Arts 26:86, Feb 1942
 Gloriana (Elizabeth von England)
    Productions:
        Opened November 25, 1938 for 5 performances.
    Reviews:
        New York Times p.18, Nov 26, 1938
 Nathan the Wise
    Productions:
        Adapted from a play by Gotthold Ephriam Lessing.
        Opened April 3, 1942 for 28 performances.
    Reviews:
        Catholic World 155:214-15, May 1942
        Commonweal 35:647-8, Apr 17, 1942
        New Yorker 18:31, Apr 11, 1942
        New York Theatre Critics' Reviews 1942:321
        New York Times p.15, Mar 12, 1942
                      p.18, Apr 4, 1942
        Newsweek 19:68, Apr 13, 1942
        Theatre Arts 26:290, May 1942
        Time 39:57, Apr 13, 1942

Camus, Albert
Caligula
  Productions:
    Adapted by Justin O'Brien.   Opened February 16,
      1960 for 38 performances.
  Reviews:
    America 102:775, Mar 26, 1960
    Christian Century 77:352-4, Mar 23, 1960
    Life 48:85-8, Mar 7, 1960
    Nation 190:213-14, Mar 5, 1960
    New Republic 142:21-2, Feb 29, 1960
    New York Theatre Critics' Reviews 1960:365
    New York Times p. 31, Feb 17, 1960
                    II, p. 1, Feb 28, 1960
    New Yorker 36:100+, Feb 27, 1960
                55:90, Feb 29, 1960
    Newsweek 55:90, Feb 29, 1960
    Saturday Review 43:36, Mar 5, 1960
    Theatre Arts 44:59, Apr 1960
    Time 75:51, Feb 29, 1960

Capek, Karel
Makropoulos Secret (Komedie)
  Productions:
    Adapted by Randal C. Burrell.   Opened January 21,
      1926 for 88 performances.
    Adapted by Tyrone Guthrie.   Opened December 3,
      1957 for 33 performances.
  Reviews:
    America 98:404, Jan 4, 1958
    Catholic World 186:386, Feb 1958
    Christian Century 75:17, Jan 1, 1958
    Commonweal 67:336-7, Dec 27, 1957
    Life (NY) 87:18, Feb 18, 1926
    Nation 185:483, Dec 21, 1957
    New York Theatre Critics' Reviews 1957:161
    New York Times p. 12, Jan 22, 1926
                    p. 52, Dec 4, 1957
    New Yorker 33:84-5, Dec 14, 1957
    Saturday Review 40:22, Dec 28, 1957
    Theatre Arts 42:26, Feb 1958
    Theatre Magazine 43:18, Apr 1926
    Time 70:45, Dec 16, 1957
The Mother
  Productions:
    English version by Paul Selver and Miles Mallen.
      Opened April 25, 1939 for 4 performances.

Reviews:
    Commonweal 30:76, May 12, 1939
    Nation 148:539, May 6, 1939
    New York Times p.26, Apr 26, 1939
    Newsweek 13:22, May 8, 1939
    Theatre Arts 23:402, Jan 1939

R.U.R. (Rossom's Universal Robots)
  Productions:
    Opened October 9, 1922 for 184 performances.
    English version by Paul Selver. Opened December 3,
      1942 for 4 performances.
  Reviews:
    Bookman 56:478-80, Dec 1922
    Catholic World 116:504-5, Jan 1923
    Current Opinion 74:61-74, Jan 1923
    Collier's 70:23, Dec 9, 1922
    Drama 13:90-1, Dec 1922
    Forum 68:973-4, Nov 1922
    Independent 109:321-2, Nov 25, 1922
    Life (NY) 80:20, Nov 2, 1922
    Literary Digest 75:30-1, Nov 4, 1922
    Nation 115:478, Nov 1, 1922
    New Republic 32:251-2, Nov 1, 1922
    New York Clipper 70:20, Oct 18, 1922
    New York Theatre Critics' Reviews 1942:152
    New York Times p.16, Oct 10, 1922
               VIII, p.1, Oct 15, 1922
               VIII,p.1, Oct 22, 1922
               p.30, Dec 4, 1942
    Newsweek 20:93, Dec 14, 1942
    Saturday Review 136:79, Jul 21, 1923
    Theatre Magazine 36:375, Dec 1922

The World We Live In (The Insect Comedy) (with Josef Capek)
  Productions:
    Adapted by Owen Davis. Opened October 31, 1922
      for 111 performances.
    Adapted by Owen Davis. Opened June 3, 1948 for
      14 performances.
  Reviews:
    Bookman 56:610-11, Jan 1923
    Catholic World 116:501-3, Jan 1923
    Commonweal 48:235, Jun 18, 1948
    Drama 13:130-1, Jun 1923
    Forum 110:20-2, Jul 1948
    Independent 109:320-1, Nov 25, 1922
    Living Age 313:617-20, Jun 3, 1922
    Nation 115:556, Nov 22, 1922

The World We Live In (The Insect Comedy) (with Josef Capek)
(cont.)
    New Republic 118:28-9, Jun 21, 1948
    New York Clipper 70:20, Nov 8, 1922
    New York Times p. 16, Nov 1, 1922
                  p. 26, Jun 4, 1948
    School and Society 67:478, Jun 26, 1948

Carroll, Paul Vincent
Kindred
    Productions:
    Opened December 26, 1939 for 16 performances.
    Reviews:
        Commonweal 31:266, Jan 12, 1940
        New York Times p. 17, Dec 27, 1939
        Newsweek 13:34, Jun 19, 1939
                 15:38, Jan 8, 1940
        Theatre Arts 24:165-6, Mar 1940
The Old Foolishness
    Productions:
    Opened December 20, 1940 for 3 performances.
    Reviews:
        Commonweal 33:282-3, Jan 3, 1941
        New York Theatre Critics' Reviews 1940:182
        New York Times p. 20, Dec 21, 1940
        New Yorker 16:30, Dec 28, 1940
        Theatre Arts 25:97, Feb 1941
Shadow and Substance
    Productions:
    Opened January 26, 1938 for 274 performances.
    Reviews:
        Catholic World 146:724-5, Mar 1938
        Commonweal 27:440, Feb 11, 1938
                   27:525, Mar 4, 1938
        Independent Woman 17:147, May 1938
        Literary Digest 125:22, Feb 19, 1938
        Nation 146:162, Feb 5, 1938
        New Republic 94:45, Feb 16, 1938
        New York Times p. 16, Jan 27, 1938
                       X, p. 1, Feb 6, 1938
                       X, p. 1, Apr 24, 1938
                       IX, p. 3, Oct 23, 1938
        Newsweek 11:24, Jan 31, 1938
        One Act Play Magazine 1:942-3, Feb 1938
        Stage 15:50, Feb 1938
              15:6+, Mar 1938
        Scribner's Magazine 102:66, Sep 1937

Theatre Arts 22:167-8, Mar 1938
Time 31:38, Feb 7, 1938
Vogue 91:108, Mar 15, 1938

The Strings, My Lord, Are False

Productions:
Opened May 19, 1942 for 15 performances.
Reviews:
Commonweal 36:159, Jun 5, 1942
Nation 154:637, May 30, 1942
New York Theatre Critics' Reviews 1942:287
New Yorker 18:32, May 30, 1942
Newsweek 19:67, Jun 1, 1942
Theatre Arts 26:659, Oct 1942

Things That Are Caesar's

Productions:
Opened October 17, 1932 for four performances.
Reviews:
New York Times p. 23, Oct 18, 1932

The Wayward Saint

Productions:
Opened February 17, 1955 for 21 performances.
Reviews:
America 92:629-30, Mar 12, 1955
Catholic World 181:68, Apr 1955
Commonweal 61:655, Mar 25, 1955
Nation 180:226, Mar 12, 1955
New York Theatre Critics' Reviews 1955:362
New York Times p. 17, Feb 18, 1955
                    II, p. 1, Feb 27, 1955
New Yorker 31:67-70, Mar 5, 1955
Newsweek 45:58-9, Feb 28, 1955
Saturday Review 38:26, Mar 5, 1955
Theatre Magazine 39:20+, May 1955
Time 65:60, Feb 28, 1955

The White Steed

Productions:
Opened January 10, 1939 for 136 performances.
Reviews:
Catholic World 148:727-8, Mar 1939
Commonweal 29:386, Jan 27, 1939
Nation 148:100-2, Jan 21, 1939
New Republic 98:17, Feb 8, 1939
New York Times p. 16, Jan 11, 1939
Newsweek 12:20, Aug 29, 1938
           13:24-5, Jan 23, 1939
North American Review 277, no. 2:371, Jun 1939
One Act Play Magazine 2:673-4, Jan 1939

The White Steed (cont.)
    Stage 16:10+, Feb 1939
    Theatre Arts 23:172-3, Mar 1939
    Time 33:20, Jan 23, 1939
The Wise Have Not Spoken
  Productions:
    (Off Broadway) Opened February 1954.
  Reviews:
    New York Times p. 35, Feb 11, 1954
    New Yorker 30:66, Feb 20, 1954
    Theatre Arts 30:356, Jun 1946

Casella, Alberto
  Death Takes A Holiday
  Productions:
    Adapted by Walter Ferris. Opened December 26,
      1929 for 180 performances.
    Adapted by Walter Ferris. Opened February 16,
      1931 for 32 performances.
  Reviews:
    Catholic World 130:725-6, Mar 1930
    Commonweal 11:369, Jan 29, 1930
    Life (NY) 95:20, Jan 17, 1930
    Literary Digest 104:18, Jan 18, 1930
    Nation 138:342, Mar 21, 1934
    New Republic 61:275-6, Jan 29, 1930
    New York Times VIII, p. 2, Jan 5, 1930
                 p. 22, Jan 29, 1930
                 p. 29, Feb 17, 1931
    Saturday Review 151:832, Jun 27, 1931
              157:391, Apr 7, 1931
    Theatre Arts 14:191-2, Mar 1930
    Vogue 75:122, Feb 15, 1930

Chambers, C. Haddon
  The Great Pursuit (The Idlers)
  Productions:
    Opened May 22, 1916 for 29 performances.
  Reviews:
    Book News 34:403, May 1916
    Dramatic Mirror 75:8, Apr 1, 1916
               75:4, Apr 8, 1916
               75:2, Apr 15, 1916
    Life (NY) 67:644, Apr 6, 1916
    Harper's Weekly 62:376, Apr 8, 1916
    Nation 102:366, Mar 30, 1916
    New York Dramatic News 63:13, Aug 19, 1916
    Theatre Magazine 23:274, May 1916

Passers-by
  Productions:
    Opened September 14, 1911 for 124 performances.
  Reviews:
    Blue Book 14:676-9, Feb 1912
    Bookman 34:239+, Nov 1911
    Dramatic Mirror 66:10, Sep 20, 1911
    Dramatist 3:212-14, Jan 1912
    Everybody's 25:822-4, Dec 1911
    Green Book Album 6:1197, Dec 1911
                      6:1205-6, Dec 1911
    Leslie's Weekly 113:356, Sep 28, 1911
    Life (NY) 67:644, Apr 6, 1916
    Munsey 46:277, Nov 1911
    Pearson 26:652-6, Nov 1911
    Red Book 18:369+, Dec 1911
    Theatre Magazine 13:117, Oct 1911
The Saving Grace
  Productions:
    Opened September 30, 1918 for 96 performances.
  Reviews:
    Bookman 50:163-4, Sep 1919
    Dramatic Mirror 79:543, Oct 12, 1918
    Forum 60:621, Nov 1918
    Green Book 20:954-7, Dec 1918
    Life (NY) 72:524-5, Oct 10, 1918
    Nation 105:602, Nov 29, 1917
    New York Dramatic News 65:6, Oct 12, 1918
    New York Times p.11, Oct 1, 1918
    Theatre Magazine 28:277, Nov 1918
Tante
  Productions:
    Opened October 28, 1913 for 79 performances.
  Reviews:
    Bookman 38:365, Dec 1913
    Book News 32:217, Dec 1913
    Dramatic Mirror 70:10, Nov 5, 1913
    Dramatist 5:441-2, Jan 1914
    Everybody's 30:257-60, Feb 1914
    Green Book 11:72-3, Jan 1914
    Life (NY) 62:838, Nov 13, 1913
    New York Dramatic News 58:21, Nov 8, 1913
    New York Times p.11, Oct 29, 1913
                    VII, p.9, Nov 2, 1913
    Theatre Magazine 18:173-4, Dec 1913
The Thief
    Opened October 16, 1911 for 16 performances.
  No Reviews.

The Tyranny of Tears
    Productions:
        Opened September 29, 1913 for 32 performances.
    Reviews:
        Dramatic Mirror 70:6, Oct 1, 1913
        Dramatist 5:397-8, Oct 1913
        New York Times p.13, Sep 30, 1913
        Theatre Magazine 18:143, Nov 1913

Chekhov, Anton
Anniversary
    Productions:
        (Off Broadway)   Season of 1960-1961.
    Reviews:
        Nation 192:419, May 13, 1961
        New York Times p.26, Apr 21, 1961
A Bear
    Productions:
        Opened February 19, 1915 in repertory (Washington
            Square Players).
        Translated by Roy Temple House. Opened August 30,
            1916 in repertory (Washington Square Players).
        Opened February 5, 1948 for 14 performances.
    Reviews:
        New York Times p.29, Feb 6, 1948
The Cherry Orchard
    Productions:
        Opened January 1923 in repertory (Moscow Art Theatre).
        Opened November 1923 in repertory (Moscow Art
            Theatre).
        Translated by George Calderon. Opened March 5,
            1928 for five performances.
        Translated by Constance Garnett. Opened October 15,
            1928 for 63 performances.
        Translated by Constance Garnett. Opened September 23,
            1929 for 14 performances.
        Translated by Constance Garnett. Opened March 6,
            1933 for 30 performances.
        Translated by Irina Skariatina. Opened January 25,
            1944 for 96 performances.
        Translated by Irina Skariatina. Opened January 1,
            1945 for eight performances.
        (Off Broadway) Opened November 14, 1962 for 61
            performances.
        Opened February 9, 1965 for 11 performances.
    Reviews:
        America 94:167, Nov 5, 1955

108:121-2, Jan 19, 1963
Catholic World 129:78+, Apr 1929
               158:584-5, Mar 1944
Commonweal 17:693, Apr 19, 1933
           39:420, Feb 11, 1944
           63:223, Dec 2, 1955
Dramatist 6:590, Jul 1915
Independent 110:97-8, Feb 3, 1923
Life 16:101-2+, Feb 28, 1944
Literary Digest 99:27, Dec 8, 1928
Nation 127:461, Oct 31, 1928
      158:167, Feb 5, 1944
      186:522, Jun 7, 1958
      201:87-8, Aug 16, 1965
New Republic 110:180-1, Feb 7, 1944
           110:211, Feb 14, 1944
           133:30, Nov 21, 1955
           152:26-8, Feb 27, 1965
New York Clipper 70:14, Jan 31, 1923
New York Theatre Critics' Reviews 1944:276
New York Times p.18, Jan 23, 1923
                  VII,p.1, Feb 4, 1923
                  p.20, Mar 6, 1928
                  VIII,p.1, Mar 11, 1928
                  p.20, Mar 7, 1933
                  p.22, Jan 26, 1944
                  II,p.1, Feb 6, 1944
                  p.16, Jan 2, 1945
                  p.46, Nov 15, 1962
                  p.46, Feb 10, 1965
New Yorker 38:118+, Nov 24, 1962
          41:54+, Feb 20, 1965
Newsweek 65:93-4, Feb 22, 1965
Scholastic 44:20, Apr 10, 1944
Theatre Arts 12:316, May 1928
           18:199-202, Apr 1944
Time 43:94, Feb 7, 1944
Vogue 72:98, Dec 8, 1928

A Country Scandal

Productions:
  (Off Broadway) Translated and adapted by Alex Szogyi.
  Opened May 5, 1960 for 203 performances.

Reviews:
  America 103:362+, Jun 11, 1960
  Nation 190:459-60, May 21, 1960
  New York Times p.21, May 6, 1960
                  II,p.1, May 15, 1960

A Country Scandal (cont.)
New Yorker 36:94+, May 14, 1960
Saturday Review 43:26, May 28, 1960
I Forgot
Productions:
Opened February 16, 1935 for 53 performances
(Moscow Art Players).
Reviews:
New York Times p. 24, Mar 12, 1935
Ivanoff
Productions:
Opened November 1923 in repertory (Moscow Art
Theatre).
(Off Broadway) Season of 1958-1959.
Adapted by John Gielgud. Translated by Ariadne
Nicolaeff. Opened May 3, 1966 for 47 performances.
Reviews:
America 113:812-13, Jun 4, 1966
Commonweal 69:496-7, Feb 6, 1959
84:283, Jun 4, 1966
Life 60:16, May 27, 1966
Nation 202:661-2, May 30, 1966
New Republic 123:21, Jul 3, 1950
New York Times p. 23, Nov 27, 1923
II, p. 3, Oct 5, 1958
p. 42, Oct 8, 1958
II, p. 1, Oct 19, 1958
New Yorker 34:58+, Oct 18, 1958
42:114, May 14, 1966
Newsweek 67:98, May 16, 1966
Saturday Review 41:26, Oct 25, 1958
49:10, May 7, 1966
49:47, May 21, 1966
Time 87:75, May 13, 1966
On the Harmfulness of Tobacco
Productions:
Opened February 5, 1948 for 14 performances.
Reviews:
New York Times p. 29, Feb 6, 1948
On the High Road (On the Highway)
Productions:
(Off Broadway) Season of 1960-1961.
Reviews:
Nation 192:419, May 13, 1961
New York Times p. 26, Apr 21, 1961
The Sea Gull
Productions:

Opened May 20, 1916 in repertory.
Opened April 9, 1929 for 31 performances.
Translated by Constance Garnett. Opened September
  16, 1929 for 63 performances.
Opened February 25, 1930 for five performances.
Translated by Stark Young. Opened March 28, 1938
  for 41 performances.
Adapted by Mina Rostova, Kevin McCarthy, and
  Montgomery Clift. Opened May 11, 1954 for 40
  performances.
(Off Broadway) Translated by Alex Szogyi. Opened
  March 21, 1962 for 11 performances
(APA Repertory).
Translated by Eva Le Gallienne. Opened April 5, 1964
  for 16 performances (National Repertory Theatre).
Reviews:
  America 91:257+, May 29, 1954
          96:310, Dec 8, 1956
  Arts and Decoration 32:67, Nov 1929
  Catholic World 130:1, Dec 1929
          147:214-15, May 1938
          179:307, Jul 1954
          184:227, Dec 1956
  Commonweal 10:21,564, May 8, Oct 2, 1929
          27:692, Apr 15, 1938
          60:269, Jun 18, 1954
          76:87, Apr 1962
  Nation 129:366-7, Oct 2, 1929
          146:422-3, Apr 9, 1938
          178:469-70, May 29, 1954
          183:415, Nov 10, 1956
  New Republic 7:175, Jun 17, 1916
          60:205, Oct 9, 1929
          94:305, Apr 13, 1938
          146:37, May 1962
  New York Theatre Critics' Reviews 1954:327
                                    1964:298
  New York Times p. 9, May 23, 1916
          p. 32, Apr 10, 1929
          p. 34, Sep 17, 1929
          p. 19, Mar 29, 1938
          p. 38, May 12, 1954
          II, p. 1, May 23, 1954
          p. 42, Mar 22, 1962
          II, p. 1, Apr 1, 1962
          p. 36, Apr 6, 1964
  New Yorker 30:70+, May 22, 1954

The Sea Gull (cont.)
      38:115-116, Apr 7, 1962
    Newsweek 11:22, Apr 11, 1938
    Saturday Review 37:22-3, May 29, 1954
    Stage 15:10-11, May 1938
    Theatre Arts 13:401-2, Jun 1929
             22:327-8, May 1938
             38:33, Aug 1954
             41:26, May 1957
    Time 31:36-7, Apr 11, 1938
          63:71, May 24, 1954

The Three Sisters

Productions:
    Opened January 1923 in repertory.
    Opened November 8, 1926 for 39 performances.
    Translated by Bernard Guilbert Guerney. Adapted by
    Samuel Rosen. Opened October 14, 1939 for nine
    performances.
    Opened December 21, 1942 for 123 performances.
    English version by Randall Jerrell. Opened June 22,
    1964 for 119 performances.
    Opened February 11, 1965 for eight performances
    (Moscow Art Theatre).

Reviews:
    America 102:55, Oct 10, 1959
           111:54, Jul 11, 1964
    Catholic World 156:597-8, Feb 1943
    Commonweal 31:14, Oct 27, 1939
              37:326, Jan 15, 1943
              62:127, May 6, 1955
    Current History 3:548, Feb 1943
    Dial 82:79, Jan 1927
    Fortune 107:808-16, May 1920
    Harper's 231:32, Sep 1965
    Life 14:33-5, Jan 4, 1943
    Nation 123:488, Nov 10, 1926
          156:31, Jan 2, 1943
          180:293-4, Apr 2, 1955
          189:218-19, Oct 10, 1959
          199:37-9, Jul 27, 1964
    New Republic 6:256-8, Jul 8, 1916
               100:369, Nov 1, 1939
               107:857, Dec 28, 1942
               132:22, Mar 21, 1955
               133:30, Nov 21, 1955
               152:26-8, Feb 27, 1965
    New York Theatre Critics' Reviews 1942:135

New York Times p. 12, Jan 30, 1923
               p. 24, Oct 27, 1926
               VIII,p. 1, Nov 7, 1926
               p. 23, Oct 16, 1939
               p. 21, Dec 22, 1942
               VIII,p. 1, Dec 27, 1942
               p. 24, Jun 23, 1964
               II,p. 1, Jul 5, 1964
               p. 15, Feb 12, 1965
New Yorker 18:32, Jan 2, 1943
           35:96-8, Oct 3, 1959
           40:56, Jul 4, 1964
           41:96, Feb 27, 1965
Newsweek 21:64, Jan 4, 1943
         64:45, Jul 6, 1964
         65:94, Feb 22, 1965
Saturday Review 46:34, Aug 24, 1963
                47:25, Jul 18, 1964
Theatre Arts 11:9-10, Jan 1927
             22:407-10, Jun 1938
             23:862-3, Dec 1939
             27:73-6, Feb 1943
             28:603-6, Oct 1943
             39:87, May 1955
             47:13, Aug 1963
Theatre Magazine 45:17-18, Jan 1927
Time 40:45-6+, Dec 2, 1942
     84:72, Jul 3, 1964
Vogue 69:80+, Jan 1, 1927
A Tragedian in Spite of Himself
  Productions:
    Opened February 5, 1948 for 14 performances.
  Reviews:
    New York Times p. 29, Feb 6, 1948
Uncle Vanya
  Productions:
    Opened November 1923 in repertory (Moscow Art
    Theatre).
    Opened May 24, 1929 for two performances.
    Adapted by Rose Caylor. Opened April 15, 1930 for
    80 performances.
    Adapted by Rose Caylor. Opened September 22, 1930
    for 16 performances.
    Translated by Constance Garnett. Opened May 13,
    1946 for five performances.
    (Off Broadway) Season of 1955-1956.

Uncle Vanya (cont.)
Reviews:
America 94:646, Mar 10, 1956
Catholic World 131:388-9, Jun 1930
                163:357, Jul 1930
                183:65, Apr 1956
Christian Century 11:742-3, Apr 30, 1930
Commonweal 44:166, May 31, 1946
            67:75-6, Apr 20, 1956
Life (NY) 95:16, May 9, 1930
Nation 130:554+, May 7, 1930
        162:671, Jun 1, 1946
        182:147, Feb 18, 1956
New Republic 62:299-300, Apr 30, 1930
             114:805, Jun 3, 1946
New York Theatre Critics' Reviews 1946:389
New York Times p. 17, May 25, 1929
               p. 26, Apr 16, 1930
               II,p. 1, May 19, 1946
               II,p. 3, Jan 29, 1956
               p. 25, Feb 1, 1956
               II,p. 1, Feb 12, 1956
Newsweek 27:84, May 27, 1946
          62:45, Aug 5, 1963
Saturday Review 29:32-4, Jun 1, 1946
                39:24, Feb 18, 1956
Theatre Arts 14:460-1, Jun 1930
             27:721-2, Dec 1943
Theatre Magazine 51:42-3+, Jun 1930
Time 47:66, May 27, 1946
      67:48, Feb 13, 1956
Vogue 75:68-9, Jun 7, 1930
The Wedding
Productions:
Opened February 5, 1948 for 14 performances.
(Off Broadway) Season of 1960-1961.
Reviews:
New York Times p. 29, Feb 6, 1948
               p. 26, Apr 21, 1961
New Yorker 37:123, May 6, 1961

Chiarelli, Luigi
The Mask and the Face (La Maschera e il Volto)
Productions:
Opened September 10, 1924 for 13 performances.
Adapted by W. Somerset Maugham. Opened May 8,
1933 for 40 performances.

Reviews:
    Catholic World 137:337-8, Jun 1933
    Commonweal 18:107, May 26, 1933
    Nation 136:593-4, May 24, 1933
    New Outlook 161:48, Jun 1933
    New Republic 75:46-7, May 24, 1933
    New York Times p. 27, Sep 11, 1924
                    p. 18, Mar 20, 1933
    Stage 10:32-3, Jun 1933
          10:7-9, Jun 1933
    Time 21:52, May 15, 1933
    Vogue 81:39+, Jun 15, 1933

Christie, Agatha
Hidden Horizon
    Productions:
    Opened September 19, 1946 for 12 performances.
    Reviews:
    New York Theatre Critics' Reviews 1946:340
    New York Times p. 42, Sep 20, 1946
Ten Little Indians
    Productions:
    Opened June 27, 1944 for 426 performances.
    Reviews:
    New York Theatre Critics' Reviews 1944:160
    New York Times p. 21, Jun 28, 1944
    Newsweek 24:94, Jul 10, 1944
    Time 44:72, Jul 10, 1944
Witness for the Prosecution
    Productions:
    Opened December 16, 1954 for 645 performances.
    (Off Broadway) Opened March 4, 1966 for nine matinees
       (ANTA).
    Reviews:
    Catholic World 180:386-7, Feb 1955
    Collier's 135:6+, Apr 1, 1955
    New Republic 132:20, Mar 7, 1955
    New York Theatre Critics' Reviews 1954:216
    New York Times p. 35, Dec 17, 1954
                  II, p. 1, Dec 26, 1954
    Theatre Arts 39:14-15+, Mar 1955

Claudel, Paul
L'Annonce Faite à Marie (see The Tidings Brought to Mary)

Christophe Colomb
    Productions:

Christophe Colomb (cont.)
    Opened January 30, 1957
  Reviews:
    America 90:420-1, Jan 23, 1954
    Catholic World 185:67, Apr 1957
    Nation 184:147, Feb 16, 1957
    New Republic 136:20, Mar 18, 1957
    New York Theatre Critics' Reviews 1957:369
    New York Times p.20, Jan 31, 1957
    New Yorker 29:74+, Oct 24, 1953
    Newsweek 49:67, Feb 11, 1957
    Saturday Review 40:22, Jan 26, 1957
    Theatre Arts 41:21, Apr 1957
    Time 69:70, Feb 11, 1957
Noontide (Partage de Midi)
  Productions:
    (Off Broadway) Adapted by Howard Hart. Opened Jun
    1, 1961 for 70 performances.
  Reviews:
    America 105:471-3, Jun 24, 1961
    Commonweal 74:427-8, Jul 28, 1961
    New York Times p.37, Jun 2, 1961
    New Yorker 37:94+, Jun 10, 1961
    Saturday Review 44:51, Jun 17, 1961
The Tidings Brought to Mary (L'Annonce Faite à Marie)
  Productions:
    (Off Broadway) Translated by L. M. Sill. Opened
    December 25, 1922 for 32 performances.
  Reviews:
    Commonweal 36:158, Jun 5, 1942
    Dial 62:98, Feb 8, 1917
        74:215-16, Feb 1923
    Freeman 6:472-3, Jan 24, 1923
    Nation 105:48, 175-6, Jul 12, 1917
        116:102, Jan 24, 1923
    New York Clipper 70:20, Jan 10, 1923
                    70:14, Jan 17, 1923
    New York Times p.20, Dec 25, 1922
                    VII,p.1, Dec 31, 1922
    Outlook 133:18-20, Jan 17, 1923

Cocteau, Jean
  Antigone
  Productions:
    (Off Broadway) Opened December 27, 1962 for 13
    performances.
  Reviews:

New York Times p.5, Dec 29, 1962
New Yorker 38:77, Jan 12, 1963

The Eagle Has Two Heads
  Productions:
    Adapted by Ronald Duncan. Opened March 19, 1947
      for 29 performances.
  Reviews:
    Commonweal 45:613-14, Apr 4, 1947
    Harper's Bazaar 81:198-9, Feb 1941
    Nation 164:403+, Apr 5, 1947
    New Republic 116:38, Mar 31, 1947
    New York Theatre Critics' Reviews 1947:421
    New York Times p.39, Mar 20, 1947
    New Yorker 23:52+, Mar 29, 1947
    Newsweek 29:84, Mar 31, 1947
    Saturday Review 30:40, Apr 12, 1947
    Theatre Arts 30:705-6, Dec 1946
                 31:45, May 1947
                 31:16+, May 1947
    Time 49:78, Mar 31, 1947

The Infernal Machine
  Productions:
    Adapted by Albert Bermel. Opened February 3, 1958
      for 40 performances.
  Reviews:
    America 98:614, Feb 22, 1958
    Catholic World 187:69, Apr 1958
    Christian Century 75:283, Mar 5, 1958
    New Republic 119:27, Jul 5, 1948
    New York Theatre Critics' Reviews 1958:373
    New Yorker 30:163, Oct 9, 1954
               33:60-1, Feb 15, 1958
    Theatre Arts 42:27, Apr 1958
    Time 71:84+, Feb 17, 1958
         30:32-3, Dec 20, 1937

Intimate Relations (Les Parents Terribles)
  Productions:
    (Off Broadway) Translated by Charles Frank. Opened
      November 1, 1962 for 76 performances.
  Reviews:
    New York Times p.27, Nov 2, 1962
                   II,p.1, Nov 25, 1962
    New Yorker 38:148, Nov 10, 1962

Orphee
  Productions:
    (Off Broadway) Translated by Carl Wildman. Opened
      December 27, 1962 for 13 performances.

Orphee (cont.)
  Reviews:
    New York Times p. 5, Dec 29, 1962
    New Yorker 38:77, Jan 12, 1963
  Les Parents Terribles (see Intimate Relations)

Colton, John
  Drifting (with D. H. Andrews)
  Productions:
    Opened January 2, 1922 for 63 performances.
  Reviews:
    Dramatic Mirror 95:17, Jan 7, 1922
    New York Clipper 69:20, Jan 11, 1922
    New York Times p. 20, Jan 3, 1922
                    VI,p. 1, Jan 22, 1922
    Theatre Magazine 35:155+, Mar 1922
  Nine Pine Street (with Carleton Miles)
  Productions:
    Opened April 27, 1933 for 28 performances.
  Reviews:
    Catholic World 137:336-7, Jun 1933
    New Outlook 161:48, Jun 1933
    New York Times p. 15, Apr 28, 1933
    Newsweek 1:28, May 6, 1933
    Stage 10:6+, Jun 1933
    Time 21:52, May 8, 1933
    Vogue 81:53+, Jun 1, 1933
  Rain (with Clemence Randolph)
  Productions:
    Opened November 7, 1922 for 648 performances.
    Opened September 1, 1924 for 104 performances.
    Opened February 12, 1935 for 47 performances.
  Reviews:
    Bookman 56:611-12, Jan 1923
    Catholic World 141:86-7, Apr 1935
    Commonweal 21:513 Mar 1, 1935
    Current Opinion 74:187-95, Feb 1923
    Dramatist 14:1154, Apr 1923
    Golden Book 22:106-7, Jul 1935
    Hearst 43:93-5, Apr 1923
    Life (NY) 80:18, Nov 30, 1922
    Literary Digest 119:20, Feb 23, 1935
    Nation 115:585-6, Nov 29, 1922
    New Republic 33:349, Feb 21, 1923
    New York Clipper 70:20, Nov 15, 1922
    New York Times p. 18, Nov 8, 1922
                    VIII,p. 2, Feb 10, 1935

p. 24, Feb 13, 1935
VIII, p. 1, Feb 17, 1935
Theatre Arts 19:257, Apr 1935
Theatre Magazine 37:25, Jan 1923
37:28+, Feb 1923
Time 25:56, Feb 25, 1935
Saint Wench
Productions:
Opened January 2, 1933 for 12 performances.
Reviews:
New York Times p. 19, Jan 3, 1933
p. 18, Jan 13, 1933
Shanghai Gesture
Productions:
Opened February 1, 1926 for 206 performances.
Opened February 13, 1928 for 16 performances.
Reviews:
Bookman 63:215, Apr 1926
Life (NY) 87:21, Mar 4, 1926
New York Times p. 20, Feb 2, 1926
p. 26, Feb 14, 1928
Theatre Magazine 43:5+, Apr 1926
Vogue 67:134, Apr 1, 1926

Copeau, Jacques
Brothers Karamazov (with Jean Croue)
Productions:
Translated by Rosalind Ivan. Opened January 3, 1927
for 56 performances.
Reviews:
Bookman 65:71, Mar 1927
Current Opinion 64:178-83, Mar 1918
Independent 118:270, Mar 5, 1927
Nation 124:72, Jan 19, 1927
New Republic 49:247, Jan 19, 1927
New York Times p. 20, Jan 4, 1927
Vogue 67:81+, Mar 1, 1927

Coward, Noel
The Astonished Heart (see Tonight At Eight-Thirty)

Bitter Sweet
Productions:
Opened November 5, 1929 for 159 performances.
Opened May 7, 1934 for 16 performances.
Reviews:
American Mercury 19:117-18, Jan 1930

Bitter Sweet (cont.)
    Life (NY) 94:20, Nov 29, 1929
    New York Times p.23, Nov 19, 1929
    Outlook 154:32, Jan 1, 1930
    Theatre Magazine 51:44-5, Jan 1930
Blithe Spirit
  Productions:
    Opened November 5, 1941 for 657 performances.
    Opened September 6, 1943 for 32 performances.
  Reviews:
    Catholic World 154:335-6, Dec 1941
    Commonweal 35:123-4, Nov 21, 1941
    Life 11:69-71, Sep 29, 1941
    Harper's Bazaar 75:76, Nov 1941
    Nation 153:491, Nov 15, 1941
    New Republic 105:701, Nov 24, 1941
    New York Times p.26, Nov 6, 1941
                    X,p.1, Nov 16, 1941
                    II,p.1, Sep 12, 1943
    New Yorker 17:37, Nov 15, 1941
    Newsweek 18:57, Nov 17, 1941
    Theatre Arts 26:8-9, Jan 1942
    Theatre Magazine 37:28, Jan 1942
    Time 38:67, Nov 17, 1941
Conversation Piece
  Productions:
    Opened October 23, 1934 for 55 performances.
  Reviews:
    Catholic World 140:340-1, Dec 1934
    Literary Digest 118:20, Nov 3, 1934
    Theatre Arts 18:899-90, Dec 1934
    Time 24:30, Nov 5, 1934
Design for Living
  Productions:
    Opened January 24, 1933 for 135 performances.
  Reviews:
    Arts and Decoration 38:41, Mar 1933
    Catholic World 136:715-16, Mar 1933
    Commonweal 17:441, Feb 15, 1933
    Literary Digest 115:16, Feb 11, 1933
    Nation 136:187-8, Feb 15, 1933
    New Outlook 161:48, Mar 1933
    New Republic 73:350-2, Feb 8, 1933
    New York Times p.32, Oct 12, 1933
    Player's Magazine 9:11, Mar-Apr 1933
    Stage 10:12, Feb 1933
    Theatre Arts 17:257-8, Apr 1933

Time 21:21, Jan 20, 1933
Vogue 81:72, Mar 15, 1933

Easy Virtue
  Productions:
    Opened December 7, 1925 for 147 performances.
  Reviews:
    Bookman 62:705, Feb 1926
    Nation 121:739-40, Dec 23, 1925
    New Republic 45:133-4, Dec 23, 1925
    New York Times p. 28, Dec 8, 1925
    Theatre Magazine 43:16+, Feb 1926
    Vogue 67:108, Feb 1, 1926

Fallen Angels
  Productions:
    Opened December 1, 1927 for 36 performances.
    Opened January 17, 1956 for 239 performances.
  Reviews:
    Catholic World 134:590-1, Feb 1932
    Commonweal 63:542, Feb 24, 1956
    Nation 182:125, Feb 11, 1956
    New York Theatre Critics' Reviews 1956:389
    New York Times p. 20, Dec 2, 1927
                   p. 27, Jan 18, 1956
    New Yorker 31:58-60, Jan 28, 1956
    Newsweek 47:43-4, Feb 6, 1956
    Saturday Review 4:452, Dec 17, 1927
    Theatre Arts 40:17, Mar 1956
    Time 67:34, Jan 30, 1956

Family Album (see Tonight At Eight-Thirty)

Fumed Oak (see Tonight At Eight-Thirty)

Hands Across the Sea (see Tonight At Eight-Thirty)

Hay Fever
  Productions:
    Opened October 5, 1925 for 49 performances.
    Opened December 29, 1931 for 95 performances.
  Reviews:
    Bookman 62:478, Dec 1925
    Nation 121:468-9, Oct 21, 1925
    New York Times p. 25, Oct 5, 1925
                   VIII, p. 2, Dec 6, 1931
                   p. 25, Dec 30, 1931
    New Yorker 40:200-1, Nov 21, 1964

Look After Lulu
  Productions:

Look After Lulu (cont.)
>Based on Georges Feydeau's Occupe-toi d'Amelie.
Opened March 3, 1959 for 3 performances.
(Off Broadway) Opened April 2, 1965 for 9 performances.
Reviews:
>America 100:726, Mar 21, 1959
Catholic World 189:157, May 1959
Commonweal 70:24-5, Apr 3, 1959
Nation 188:262, Mar 21, 1959
New York Theatre Critics' Reviews 1959:356
New York Times p. 35, Mar 4, 1959
New Yorker 35:80+, Mar 14, 1959
Newsweek 53:90, Mar 16, 1959
Theatre Arts 43:24+, May 1959
Time 73:59, Mar 16, 1959

The Marquise
Productions:
>Opened November 14, 1927 for 80 performances.
Reviews:
>New York Times p. 26, Nov 15, 1927
Saturday Review 4:452, Dec 17, 1927
Theatre Magazine 47:38-9, Feb 1928
Vogue 71:120, Jan 15, 1928

Nude with Violin
Productions:
>Opened November 14, 1957 for 86 performances.
Reviews:
>America 98:355, Dec 14, 1957
Catholic World 186:308, Jan 1958
Christian Century 74:1449, Dec 4, 1957
Commonweal 67:489: Feb 7, 1958
Dance Magazine 32:9, Feb 1958
Nation 185:416, Nov 30, 1957
New York Theatre Critics' Reviews 1957:180
New York Times p. 36, Nov 15, 1957
New Yorker 33:78-80, Nov 23, 1957
Newsweek 50:84, Nov 25, 1957
Reporter 17:35-6, Dec 12, 1957
Saturday Review 40:23, Nov 30, 1957
Theatre Arts 41:30-1, May 1957
>>42:20, Jan 1958
Time 70:91, Nov 25, 1957

Point Valaine
Productions:
>Opened January 16, 1935 for 55 performances.
Reviews:

New Republic 81:363, Feb 6, 1935
New York Times p. 22, Jan 17, 1935
                VIII,p.1, Feb 3, 1935
Newsweek 5:26, Jan 26, 1935
Player's Magazine 11:11, Mar-Apr 1935
Theatre Arts 19:167+, Mar 1935
Time 25:63, Jan 28, 1935

Present Laughter
  Productions:
    Opened October 29, 1946 for 158 performances.
    Opened January 31, 1958 for 6 performances.
  Reviews:
    Catholic World 164:261, Dec 1946
    Commonweal 45:116, Nov 15, 1946
    Life 21:116, Oct 28, 1946
    Nation 163:565, Nov 16, 1946
    New Republic 115:628, Nov 11, 1946
    New York Theatre Critics' Reviews 1946:283
    New York Times p. 31, Oct 30, 1946
    New Yorker 22:56+, Nov 9, 1946
    Saturday Review 29:24-6+, Nov 23, 1946
    Theatre Arts 31:18, Jan 1947
    Time 41:65, May 10, 1943
         48:55, Nov 11, 1946

Private Lives
  Productions:
    Opened January 27, 1931 for 256 performances.
    Opened October 4, 1948 for 248 performances.
  Reviews:
    Arts and Decoration 35:83, Jul 1931
    Bookman 73:523, Jul 1931
    Catholic World 132:719-20, Mar 1931
                   168:160, Nov 1948
    Life (NY) 97:18, Feb 20, 1931
    Life 25:64-5, Dec 27, 1948
    Nation 132:165, Feb 11, 1931
           167:444, Oct 16, 1948
    New Republic 66:19, Feb 18, 1931
                 119:27, Nov 1, 1948
    New York Theatre Critics' Reviews 1948:209
    New York Times p. 24, Jan 28, 1931
                   p. 30, Oct 5, 1948
                   II,p.1, Nov 7, 1948
    Outlook 157:234, Feb 11, 1931
    New Yorker 24:53, Oct 16, 1948
    Newsweek 32:88, Oct 18, 1948
    Saturday Review 31:30-2, Oct 23, 1948

Private Lives (cont.)
    Theatre Magazine 53:25, Apr 1931
    Time 52:82, Oct 18, 1948
    Vogue 77:87+, Mar 15, 1931
Quadrille
  Productions:
    Opened November 3, 1954 for 150 performances.
  Reviews:
    America 92:283, Dec 4, 1954
    Catholic World 180:307, Jan 1955
    Commonweal 61:288, Dec 10, 1954
    Life 33:166, Oct 13, 1952
    Nation 179:450, Nov 20, 1954
    New York Theatre Critics' Reviews 1954:259
    New York Times p. 39, Nov 4, 1954
                  II,p. 1, Nov 14, 1954
    New Yorker 30:103, Nov 13, 1954
    Newsweek 44:98, Nov 15, 1954
    Saturday Review 37:27, Nov 27, 1954
    Theatre Arts 38:20-5+, Nov 1954
                39:16+, Jan 1955
    Time 64:62, Nov 15, 1954
    Vogue 124:125, Dec 1954
Red Peppers (see Tonight At Eight-Thirty)

Shadow Play (see Tonight At Eight-Thirty)

Still Life (see Tonight At Eight-Thirty)

This Was A Man
  Productions:
    Opened November 23, 1926 for 31 performances.
  Reviews:
    Bookman 64:734, Feb 1927
    New York Times p. 27, Nov 24, 1926
                VIII,p. 1, Nov 28, 1926
    Theatre Magazine 45:15, Feb 1927
    Vogue 69:120, Jan 15, 1927
This Year of Grace
  Productions:
    Opened November 7, 1928 for 157 performances.
  Reviews:
    American Mercury 16:120-1, Jan 1929
    Dial 86:245, Mar 1929
    Life (NY) 92:11, Nov 30, 1928
    New Republic 57:15-17, Nov 21, 1928
    Theatre Magazine 49:60, Jan 1929
    Vogue 72: 55, Dec 22, 1928

Tonight At Eight-Thirty (A Repertory of One-Act Plays)
  Productions:
    Opened November 24, 1936 for 118 performances.
    Plays presented included:
    The Astonished Heart
    Family Album
    Fumed Oak
    Hands Across the Sea
    Red Peppers
    Shadow Play
    Still Life
    Ways and Means
    We Were Dancing
    Opened February 20, 1948 for 26 performances.   Plays
    presented included:
    Family Album
    Fumed Oak
    Hands Across the Sea
    Red Peppers
    Shadow Play
    Ways and Means
  Reviews:
    Catholic World 144:471-2, Jan 1937
                   167:72-3, Apr 1948
    Commonweal 25:193, Dec 11, 1936
                47:521, Mar 5, 1948
    Nation 166:285, Mar 6, 1948
    New Republic 89:217, Dec 16, 1936
    New York Theatre Critics' Reviews 1948:329+
    New York Times p. 17, Nov 25, 1936
                   p. 23, Nov 28, 1936
                   XII, p. 5, Dec 6, 1936
                   p. 16, Mar 2, 1937
                   p. 8, Feb 21, 1948
    New Yorker 24:50, Mar 6, 1948
    Newsweek 8:20-2, Dec 5, 1936
    Saturday Review 15:5, Dec 19, 1936
    Stage 14:56-7, Dec 1936
    Theatre Arts 21:18+, Jan 1937
    Time 28:39, Dec 7, 1936
    Vogue 111:150, Apr 1, 1948
The Vortex
  Productions:
    Opened September 16, 1925 for 157 performances.
  Reviews:
    Bookman 62:319, Nov 1925
    Life (NY) 86:20, Oct 8, 1925

The Vortex (cont.)
      Nation 121:469, Oct 21, 1925
      New Republic 44:177, Oct 7, 1925
      New York Times p. 20, Sep 17, 1925
                      VII,p. 1, Sep 27, 1925
      Theatre Magazine 42:22, Jul 1925
Ways and Means (see Tonight At Eight-Thirty)

We Were Dancing (see Tonight At Eight-Thirty)

The Young Idea
   Productions:
      Opened March 18, 1932 for 3 performances.
   No Reviews.

Dane, Clemence
   A Bill of Divorcement
      Productions:
         Opened October 10, 1921 for 173 performances.
      Reviews:
         Bookman 54:376-7, Dec 1921
         Current Opinion 72:199-209, Feb 1922
         Dramatic Mirror 84:557, Oct 15, 1921
         Everybody's 46:92-8, Feb 1922
         Hearst 41:45-7+, Apr 1922
         Independent 107:110, Oct 29, 1921
         Leslie's Weekly 133:835-6, Dec 17, 1921
         Life (NY) 78:18, Nov 3, 1921
         Nation 113:545, Nov 9, 1921
         New Republic 27:198, Jul 13, 1921
                      29:130, Dec 28, 1921
         New York Clipper 69:20, Oct 19, 1912
         New York Times p. 22, Oct 11, 1921
                         VI,p. 1, Oct 16, 1921
                         VI,p. 1, Oct 23, 1921
         Theatre Magazine 34:385-6, Dec 1921
                          35:84+, Feb 1922
   Come of Age (Music by Richard Addinsell)
      Productions:
         Opened January 12, 1934 for 35 performances.
         Opened January 23, 1952 for 30 performances.
      Reviews:
         Catholic World 138:731, Mar 1934
                        174:463, Mar 1952
         Commonweal 55:445-6, Feb 8, 1952
         Literary Digest 117:23, Feb 24, 1934
         Nation 138:140, Jan 31, 1934

New Outlook 163:49, Feb 1934
New Republic 77:368, Feb 7, 1934
New York Theatre Critics' Reviews 1952:382
New York Times p.16, Jan 13, 1934
                X,p.6, Jan 21, 1934
                p.22, Jan 24, 1952
                II,p.1, Feb 3, 1952
New Yorker 27:48+, Feb 2, 1952
Newsweek 3:34, Jan 20, 1934
Saturday Review 10:476, Feb 10, 1934
                35:23, Feb 9, 1952
Stage 11:9+, Feb 1934
Theatre Arts 18:170, Mar 1934
                36:19+, Apr 1952
Time 59:40, Feb 4, 1952

Granite
Productions:
Opened February 11, 1927 for 70 performances.
Opened January 13, 1936 fpr eight performances.
Reviews:
Independent 118:445+, Apr 23, 1927
Nation 124:250, Mar 30, 1927
        142:138, Jan 29, 1936
New York Times p.13, Feb 12, 1927
                p.24, Jan 14, 1936
Pictorial Review 37:51, Apr 1936

The Mariners
Productions:
Opened March 28, 1927 for 16 performances.
Reviews:
Bookman 65:450, Jun 1927
Life (NY) 89:21, Apr 14, 1927
Nation 124:405, Apr 13, 1927
New Republic 50:223-4, Apr 13, 1927
New York Times p.22, Mar 29, 1927
                VIII,p.1, Apr 3, 1927
Vogue 69:84-5, May 15, 1927

The Way Things Happen
Productions:
Opened January 28, 1924 for 24 performances.
Reviews:
American Mercury 1:370-1, Mar 1924
Canadian Magazine 62:449-50, Apr 1924
Life (NY) 83:18, Feb 14, 1924
New York Times p.17, Jan 29, 1924
                VII,p.1, Feb 3, 1924
Theatre Magazine 39:15, Apr 1924

Will Shakespeare
  Productions:
    Opened January 1, 1923 for 80 performances.
  Reviews:
    Bookman 57:53-4, Mar 1923
    Current Opinion 74:315-23, Mar 1923
    Independent 110:72-4, Jan 20, 1923
    Literary Digest 71:24-5, Dec 24, 1921
    Literary Review 3:497-8, Mar 3, 1923
    Nation 116:102, Jan 24, 1923
    New Republic 33:252-3, Jan 31, 1923
    New York Clipper 70:20, Jan 10, 1923
    New York Times p. 14, Jan 2, 1923
                   VII, p. 1, Jan 21, 1923
    North American Review 215:574-6, Apr 1922
    Outlook 133:164-6, Jan 24, 1923
    Theatre Magazine 35:158-61+, Mar 1922
                     37:20, Mar 1923

Delaney, Shelagh
  A Taste of Honey
  Productions:
    Opened October 4, 1960 for 376 performances.
  Reviews:
    Catholic World 193:127-8, May 1961
    Commonweal 74:496, Sep 8, 1961
    Ebony 16:71-4, Feb 1961
    Horizon 3:102-3, Mar 1961
    Nation 188:461-2, May 16, 1959
           191:334+, Oct 29, 1960
    New Republic 143:22, Oct 17, 1960
    New York Theatre Critics' Reviews 1960:225
    New York Times p. 46, Oct 5, 1960
                   II, p. 1, Nov 6, 1960
                   p. 43, May 17, 1961
    New Yorker 34:97-8, Feb 7, 1959
               36:73, Oct 15, 1960
    Newsweek 56:102, Oct 17, 1960
    Reporter 23:46, Nov 24, 1960
    Saturday Review 43:22, Oct 22, 1960
    Theatre Arts 43:16-17+, May 1959
                 44:10-11, Dec 1960
    Time 76:54, Oct 17, 1960
  The Lion in Love
  Productions:
    (Off Broadway) Opened April 25, 1963 for 6 per-
      formances.

82

Reviews:
    America 108:63-4+, July 13, 1963
    New York Times p. 28, April 26, 1963
    New Yorker 39:90+, May 4, 1963
    Newsweek 61:83, May 6, 1963
    Theatre Arts 47:64-5, Jun 1963
    Time 81:76, May 3, 1963

Deval, Jacques
Another Love
Productions:
    Translated and adapted by George Oppenheimer. Open-
    ed March 19, 1934 for 16 performances.
Reviews:
    New York Times p. 26, Mar 20, 1934
Bathsheba
Productions:
    Opened March 26, 1947 for 29 performances.
Reviews:
    Catholic World 165:168, May 1947
    Commonweal 45:647, Apr 11, 1947
    New Republic 116:42, Apr 7, 1947
    New York Theatre Critics' Reviews 1947:415
    New York Times p. 40, Mar 27, 1947
    New Yorker 23:50, Apr 5, 1947
    Newsweek 29:80, Apr 7, 1947
    Time 49:77, Apr 7, 1947
Boudoir
Productions:
    Opened February 7, 1941 for 11 performances.
Reviews:
    New York Theatre Critics' Reviews 1941:388
    New York Times p. 18, Feb 8, 1941
Her Cardboard Lover
Productions:
    Adapted by Valerie Wyngate and P. G. Wodehouse.
    Opened March 21, 1927 for 100 performances.
Reviews:
    Bookman 65:447, Jun 1927
    Dial 82:535, Jun 1927
    Life (NY) 89:31, Apr 7, 1927
    Nation 124:380, Apr 6, 1927
    New Republic 50:194-5, Apr 6, 1927
    New York Times p. 30, Mar 22, 1927
    Vogue 69:84, May 15, 1927
Lorelei
Productions:

Lorelei (cont.)
Productions:
Opened November 29, 1938 for 7 performances.
Reviews:
Catholic World 148:472, Jan 1939
Nation 147: 637, Dec 10, 1938
Newsweek 12:24, Dec 12, 1938
New York Times p. 21, Nov 30, 1938
Theatre Arts 23:95-6, Feb 1939
Mademoiselle
Productions:
Adapted by Grace George. Opened October 18, 1932
for 103 performances.
Reviews:
Arts and Decoration 38:57, Dec 1932
Catholic World 136:336-7, Dec 1932
Commonweal 17:49, Nov 9, 1932
Nation 135:465, Nov 9, 1932
New Outlook 161:47, Dec 1932
New Republic 73:128-9, Dec 14, 1932
New York Times p. 22, Oct 19, 1932
Stage 10:28-9, Dec 1932
Theatre Arts 17:17-18, Jan 1933
Vanity Fair 39:53, Jan 1933
Oh, Brother!
Productions:
Opened January 19, 1945 for 23 performances.
Reviews:
New York Theatre Critics' Reviews: 1945:195
New York Times p. 26, Jun 20, 1945
New Yorker 21:32, Jun 30, 1945
Tonight in Samarkand (with Lorenzo Semple, Jr.)
Productions:
Opened February 16, 1955 for 29 performances.
Reviews:
America 92:657, Mar 19, 1955
Catholic World 181:66-7, Apr 1955
Nation 180:226, Mar 12, 1955
New York Theatre Critics' Reviews 1955:365
New York Times p. 22, Feb 17, 1955
New Yorker 31:50, Feb 26, 1955
Newsweek 45:58, Feb 28, 1955
Saturday Review 38:26, Mar 5, 1955
Theatre Arts 39:15+, May 1955
Time 65:60, Feb 28, 1955
Tovarich
Productions:

English version by Robert E. Sherwood. Opened
October 15, 1936 for 356 performances.
Adapted by Robert E. Sherwood. Opened May 14,
1952 for 15 performances.
Reviews:
Catholic World 144:335-6, Dec 1936
                175:309, Jul 1952
Commonweal 25:20, Oct 30, 1936
            56:224, Jun 6, 1952
Life 3:22-3 Dec 20, 1937
Literary Digest 122:22, Oct 31, 1936
Nation 143:530, Oct 31, 1936
New Republic 89:21, November 4, 1936
New York Theatre Critics' Reviews 1952:281
New York Times p.19, Apr 25, 1935
                IX,p.1, May 19, 1935
                p.35, Sep 29, 1936
                IX,p.2, Oct 4, 1936
                X,p.1, Oct 15, 1936
                p.31, Oct 16, 1936
                X,p.1, Oct 25, 1936
                X,p.2, Apr 25, 1937
                p.39, May 15, 1952
Newsweek 8:40, Oct 24, 1936
          10:30, Dec 20, 1937
Saturday Review 35:26, May 31, 1952
Theatre Arts 19:481, Jul 1935
              20:919-23, Dec 1936
              36:82, Jul 1952
Time 28:47, Oct 26, 1936
     31:29, Jan 3, 1938
A Weak Woman
Productions:
Adapted by Ernest Boyd. Opened January 26, 1926
for 49 performances.
Reviews:
Bookman 63:216-17, Apr 1926
New York Times p.16, Jan 27, 1926

Drinkwater, John
Abraham Lincoln
Productions:
Opened December 15, 1919 for 193 performances.
Opened October 21, 1929 for eight performances.
Reviews:
Arts and Decoration 12:264, Feb 1920
Bookman 50:551-5, Feb 1920

Abraham Lincoln (cont.)
    Collier's 65:13+, Feb 7, 1920
    Current Opinion 67:93-7, Aug 1919
                68:351-2, Mar 1920
    Dramatist 10:974-5, Oct 1919
    Everybody's 42:66-7, Apr 1920
    Hearst 37:38-9+, Mar 1920
    Independent 101:86, Jan 17, 1920
              101:170-1, Jan 31, 1920
    Life (NY) 74:1070-1, Dec 25, 1919
    Literary Digest 59:29-30, Dec 28, 1918
              61:28-9, Jun 28, 1919
              64:30-2, Jan 3, 1920
              64:33-4, Mar 6, 1920
    Living Age 300:623-6, Mar 8, 1919
              304-790-2, Mar 27, 1920
              310:493-4, Aug 20, 1921
    Nation 109:292-3, Aug 30, 1919
           110:858-9, Jan 3, 1920
    New Republic 20:268-9, Oct 1, 1919
              21:148, Dec 31, 1919
    New York Dramatic Mirror 81:2023, Jan 1, 1920
    New York Times IV,p. 2, Jul 6, 1919
              p. 18, Dec 16, 1919
              VIII,p. 21, Dec 21, 1919
    North American 210:824-36, Dec 1919
    Outlook 123:537-8, Dec 24, 1919
    Review 1:710-11, Dec 27, 1919
    Theatre Magazine 31:89+, Feb 1920
    Touchstone 6:269-75, Feb 1920
Bird in Hand
 Productions:
    Opened April 4, 1929 for 500 performances.
    Opened November 10, 1930 for 65 performances.
    Opened October 19, 1942 for eight performances.
 Reviews:
    American Mercury 17:249, Jun 1929
    Catholic World 129:203-4, May 1929
    Commonweal 10:50, May 15, 1929
    Life (NY) 93:20, Apr 26, 1929
    Nation 128:514, Apr 24, 1929
           155:458, Oct 31, 1942
    New York Theatre Critics' Reviews 1942:200
    New York Times p. 28, Apr 5, 1929
              X,p. 1, Apr 14, 1929
              p. 6, Nov 11, 1930
              p. 24, Oct 20, 1942

Outlook 151:670, Apr 24, 1929
Theatre Magazine 50:43, Aug 1929
Vogue 73:104, Jun 8, 1929
Mary Stuart
  Productions:
    Opened March 21, 1921 for 40 performances
  Reviews:
    Arts and Decoration 15:23, May 1921
    Bookman 53:277-8, May 1921
    Current Opinion 70:631-40, May 1921
    Drama 11:266-7,297, May 1921
            11:265-6, May 1921
    Dramatic Mirror 83:527, Mar 26, 1921
    Independent 105:329, Apr 2, 1921
    Life (NY) 77:500, Apr 7, 1921
    Nation 112:564-6, Apr 13, 1921
    New Republic 26:162, Apr 6, 1921
    New York Clipper 69:23, Mar 30, 1921
    New York Times p.15, Mar 22, 1921
    Outlook 128:12-13, May 4, 1921
    Players Magazine 25:119, Feb 1949
    Review 4:322-4, Apr 6, 1921
    Saturday Review 134:502, Oct 7, 1921
    Theatre Magazine 33:318,320, May 1921
                     33:401,416, Jun 1921
    Weekly Review 4:323-4, Apr 6, 1921
    Yale Review 11:425-6, Jan 1922
Robert E. Lee
  Productions:
    Opened November 20, 1923 for 15 performances.
  Reviews:
    American Mercury 1:118, Jan 1924
    Current Opinion 75:317-31, Sep 1923
    Dial 76:612, Dec 1923
    Life (NY) 82:18, Dec 13, 1923
    Literary Digest 78:30-1, Sep 8, 1923
                    79:30-1, Dec 1, 1923
    New York Times III,p.15, Aug 16, 1923
    Theatre Magazine 38:12, Sep 1923
                     39:5+, Jan 1924

Duerrenmatt, Friedrich
  The Physicists
    Productions:
      Adapted by James Kirkup.   Opened October 14, 1964
        for 55 performances.
    Reviews:

The Physicists (cont.)
    Christian Century 80:301-2, Mar 6, 1963
    Commonweal 81:237-8, Nov 13, 1964
    Life 57:89-90, Nov 20, 1964
    Nation 196:380, May 4, 1963
          199:340, Nov 9, 1964
    New York Theatre Critics' Reviews 1964:193
    New York Times p. 52, Oct 14, 1964
              II,p. 1, Oct 25, 1964
    Newsweek 64:102, Oct 26, 1964
    Saturday Review 47:31, Oct 31, 1964
    Time 84:67, Oct 23, 1964
    Vogue 144:152, Dec 1964
Romulus
 Productions:
    Adapted by Gore Vidal. Opened January 10, 1962 for
    69 performances.
 Reviews:
    America 106:772-3, Mar 10, 1962
    Christian Century 79:233, Feb 21, 1962
    Nation 194:106-7, Feb 3, 1962
    National Review 12:173-4, Mar 13, 1962
    New Republic 146:20+, Jan 29, 1962
    New York Theatre Critics' Reviews 1962:380
    New York Times p. 27, Jan 11, 1962
              p. 25, Mar 2, 1962
    New Yorker 37:63, Jan 20, 1962
    Newsweek 59:50, Jan 22, 1962
    Saturday Review 45:29, Jan 27, 1962
    Theatre Arts 46:62-3, Mar 1962
    Time 79:68+, Jan 19, 1962
The Visit
 Productions:
    Adapted by Maurice Valency.   Opened May 5, 1958
    for 189 performances.
    Adapted by Maurice Valency.   Opened March 8, 1960
    for 16 performances.
 Reviews:
    America 99:299, May 31, 1958
    Catholic World 187:312, Jul 1958
    Christian Century 75:668-9, Jun 4, 1958
    Commonweal 68:377-9, Jul 11, 1958
    Life 44:91-4, Jun 2, 1958
    Nation 186:455-6, May 17, 1958
    New York Theatre Critics' Reviews 1958:294
    New York Times p. 40, May 6, 1958
              II,p. 1, May 18, 1958

II, p. 1, Sep 7, 1958
      p. 38, Mar 9, 1960
New Yorker 34: 87, May 17, 1958
            36: 118+, Mar 19, 1960
Reporter 18: 27, Jun 12, 1958
Saturday Review 41: 30-1, May 24, 1958
Theatre Arts 42: 17+, May 1958
Time 71: 83, May 19, 1958

Dunsany, Lord (E. J. M. D. Plunkett)
  The Gods of the Mountains
    In repertory. November 1916 and January 1919.
    Reviews:
      Bookman 44: 471+, Jan 1917
      Dramatic Mirror 76: 7, Dec 9, 1916
                      80: 231, Feb 15, 1919
      Forum 51: 782-90, May 1914
      New York Times p. 11, Nov 28, 1916
                      II, p. 6, Dec 3, 1916
                      IV, p. 2, Jan 26, 1919
      North American Review 205: 134, Jan 1917
  The Golden Doom
    In repertory. November 1916 and January 1919.
    Reviews:
      Bookman 44: 476, Jan 1917
      Dramatic Mirror 80: 231, Feb 15, 1919
      New York Times p. 9, Dec 5, 1916
  If
    Productions:
      Opened October 25, 1927 for 27 performances.
    Reviews:
      Life (NY) 90: 25, Nov 17, 1925
      New York Times p. 26, Oct 26, 1927
                      IX, p. 1, Oct 30, 1927
      Saturday Review 4: 320, Nov 19, 1927
      Theatre Magazine 47: 40, Jan 1928
  King Argimenes
    In repertory. November 1916 and January 1919.
    Reviews:
      Bookman 44: 473-4, Jan 1917
      Dramatic Mirror 80: 231, Feb 15, 1919
      New York Times p. 9, Dec 19, 1916
  The Laughter of the Gods
    In repertory. January 15, 1919.
    Reviews:
      Dramatic Mirror 80: 160, Feb 1, 1919
      Nation 108: 132, Jan 25, 1919

89

The Laughter of the Gods (cont.)
    New York Dramatic News 65: 8, Jan 25, 1919
    New York Times p. 11, Jan 16, 1919
                    IV, p. 2, Jan 26, 1919
A Night at an Inn
  Productions:
    Opened April 15, 1918 for 16 performances.
    Opened May 9, 1930 for one performance.
  Reviews:
    Bookman 44: 470+, Jan 1917
    Current Opinion 60: 411, Jun 1916
                    63: 91-4, Aug 1917
    Dramatic Mirror 78: 584, Apr 27, 1918
                    83: 1073, Jun 25, 1921
    Independent 106: 17, Jul 23, 1921
    New York Times p. 11, Apr 16, 1913
    Theatre Magazine 24: 18+, Jul 1916
The Queen's Enemies
  Productions:
    Opened December 18, 1916 in repertory.
  Reviews:
    Bookman 44: 471+, Jan 1917
    Dramatic Mirror 76: 7, Nov 25, 1916
    New York Times p. 9, Nov 15, 1916
                    II, p. 6, Nov 19, 1916
The Tents of the Arabs
  In repertory.   January 15, 1919.
  Reviews:
    Dramatic Mirror 80: 374, Mar 15, 1919
    Life (NY) 73: 416, Mar 13, 1919
    New York Times p. 9, Mar 4, 1919
    Theatre Magazine 29: 207-8, Apr 1919

Dyer, Charles
  Rattle of A Simple Man
  Productions:
    Opened April 17, 1963 for 94 performances.
  Reviews:
    New York Theatre Critics' Reviews 1963: 340
    New York Times p. 39, Apr 18, 1963
    New Yorker 39: 82, Apr 27, 1963
    Saturday Review 46: 23, May 4, 1963
    Theatre Arts 47: 10-11, Jun 1963
    Time 81: 58, Apr 26, 1963

Eliot, T. S.
  The Cocktail Party

Productions:
   Opened January 21, 1950 for 409 performances.
Reviews:
   American Mercury 70:557-8, May 1950
   Catholic World 170:466, Mar 1950
                  171:469, Sep 1950
   Commonweal 51:463, Feb 3, 1950
              51:507, Feb 17, 1950
   Life 27:16, 18, Sep 26, 1949
   Nation 170:94-5, Jan 28, 1950
   New Republic 122:30, Feb 13, 1950
   New York Theatre Critics' Reviews 1950:373
   New York Times p. 17, Jan 23, 1950
                  II, p. 1, Jan 27, 1950
                  p. 33, May 4, 1950
                  II, p. 3, May 21, 1950
   New York Times Magazine p. 14, Jan 29, 1950
   New Yorker 25:47, Jan 28, 1950
              26:26-9, Apr 1, 1950
   Newsweek 35:66, Jan 30, 1950
   Saturday Review 53:28-30, Feb 4, 1950
                   33:48, Feb 11, 1950
                   33:23, Feb 25, 1950
   School and Society 72:180, Sep 16, 1950
   Theatre Arts 34:8, May 1950
                34:10, Apr 1950
   Time 54:58, Sep 5, 1949
        55:37, Jan 30, 1950

The Confidential Clerk
Productions:
   Opened February 11, 1954 for 117 performances.
Reviews:
   America 90:608, Mar 6, 1954
   Catholic World 179:68, Apr 1954
   Commentary 17:367-72, Apr 1954
   Commonweal 59:475-6, Feb 12, 1954
              59:599, Mar 19, 1954
   Life 36:58, Feb 1, 1954
   Nation 178:184, Feb 27, 1954
   New Republic 129:17-18, Sep 21, 1953
                130:22, Feb 22, 1954
                131:124-5, Nov 22, 1954
   New York Theatre Critics' Reviews 1954:370
   New York Times p. 22, Feb 12, 1954
                  II, p. 1, Feb 21, 1954
   New York Times Magazine p. 16, Feb 21, 1954
   New Yorker 30:62, Feb 20, 1954

The Confidential Clerk (cont.)
    Newsweek 43:94, Feb 22, 1954
    Saturday Review 36:26-8, Aug 29, 1953
                   36:44-6, Sep 12, 1953
                   37:26-8, Feb 27, 1954
    Theatre Arts 37:81-2, Nov 1953
                 38:22-3, Apr 1954
    Time 63:80, Feb 22, 1954
    Vogue 123:130-1, Mar 1954
The Family Reunion
 Productions:
    Opened October 20, 1958 for 32 performances.
 Reviews:
    America 100:174, Nov 8, 1958
    Catholic World 188:331, Jan 1959
    Christian Century 75:1380-2, Nov 26, 1958
    Commonweal 69:232-4, Nov 28, 1958
    Nation 187:347, Nov 8, 1958
    New York Theatre Critics' Reviews 1958:255
    New York Times p. 39, Oct 21, 1958
                   II, p. 1, Oct 26, 1958
                   p. 26, Dec 10, 1960
    New Yorker 34:99-101, Nov 1, 1958
    Reporter 19:35, Nov 27, 1958
    Saturday Review 19:12, Apr 1, 1939
                    41:25, Nov 8, 1958
    Theatre Arts 41:23-4, May 1957
                 42:64, Dec 1958
    Time 72:48, Nov 3, 1958
Murder in the Cathedral
 Productions:
    Opened March 20, 1936 for 38 performances.
    Opened February 16, 1938 for 21 performances.
 Reviews:
    Catholic World 143:209, May 1936
    Christian Century 52:1636, Dec 18, 1935
    Commonweal 23:636, Apr 3, 1936
               27:524, Mar 4, 1938
    Forum 95:346, Jun 1936
    Life 19:123-7, Oct 1, 1945
    Nation 141:417, Oct 9, 1935
           142:459-60, Apr 8, 1936
    New Republic 86:253, Apr 8, 1936
                 94:101, Mar 2, 1938
    New York Times p. 13, Mar 21, 1936
                   IX, p. 1, Mar 29, 1936
                   p. 16, Feb 17, 1938

Newsweek 7:26, Mar 28, 1936
One Act Play Magazine 1:952, Feb 1938
                   1:1028, Mar 1938
Saturday Review 12:10, Oct 12, 1935
Stage 13:97, Nov 1935
Theatre Arts 20:21+, Jan 1936
            22:255, Apr 1938
Time 31:34, Feb 28, 1938
Yale Review 25:427, Winter 1936

Ervine, St. John
 Boyd's Daughter
  Productions:
    Opened October 11, 1940 for three performances.
  Reviews:
    American Mercury 51:485-6, Dec 1940
    New York Theatre Critics' Reviews 1940:256
    New York Times p. 20, Oct 12, 1940
    Time 36:71, Oct 21, 1940
 The First Mrs. Fraser
  Productions:
    Opened December 28, 1929 for 352 performances.
    Opened November 5, 1947 for 38 performances.
  Reviews:
    American Mercury 19:245-7, Feb 1930
    Commonweal 120:593, Feb 1930
              166:266, Dec 1947
    Life (NY) 95:20, Jan 17, 1930
           95:18, Jun 6, 1930
    Nation 165:603, Nov 29, 1947
    New Republic 117:35, Nov 24, 1947
    New York Theatre Critics' Reviews 1947:267
    New York Times p. 36, Nov 6, 1947
    New Yorker 23:54, Nov 15, 1947
    Newsweek 30:84, Nov 17, 1947
    Saturday Review 148:13, Jul 6, 1929
    School and Society 66:422, Nov 29, 1947
    Theatre Arts 14:114-15, Feb 1930
            14:200, Mar 1930
    Theatre Magazine 51:8, Mar 1930
              52:32+, Jul 1930
    Time 50:87, Nov 17, 1947
    Vogue 75:118, Feb 15, 1930
Jane Clegg
  Productions:
    Opened February 23, 1920 for 112 performances.
  Reviews:

Jane Clegg (cont.)
  Dial 60:472, May 11, 1916
  Dramatic Mirror 76:15, Aug 5, 1916
                       82:363, Feb 28, 1920
  Forum 63:489, Apr-May 1920
  Independent 101:382, Mar 13, 1920
  Life (NY) 75:462, Mar 11, 1920
  Nation 101:755-6, Dec 23, 1915
         110:376-7, Mar 20, 1920
  New Republic 22:61, Mar 10, 1920
  New York Clipper 68:19, Mar 3, 1920
  New York Times p. 14, Feb 25, 1920
                 V, p. 5, Feb 29, 1920
                 V, p. 6, Mar 28, 1920
  Outlook 126:182, Sep 29, 1920
  Theatre Magazine 31:265+, Apr 1920
  Weekly Review 2:289, Mar 20, 1920
John Ferguson
  Productions:
    Opened May 13, 1919 for 177 performances.
    Opened July 10, 1933 for 54 performances.
  Reviews:
    Bookman 53:527+, Aug 1921
    Catholic World 137:593-4, Aug 1933
    Commonweal 18:309, Jul 21, 1933
    Current Opinion 67:24-8, Jul 1919
    Dial 60:472, May 11, 1916
    Drama 23:466-7, Aug 1916
    Forum 62:375-6, Sep 1919
    Life (NY) 73:948, May 29, 1919
    Nation 102:202, Feb 17, 1916
           108:842-3, May 24, 1919
    New York Times p. 18, May 13, 1919
                   IV, p. 2, May 18, 1919
                   p. 15, Jul 11, 1933
    Touchstone 5:304-8, Jul 1919
    Theatre Magazine 30:13+, Jul 1919
    Weekly Review 1:87, Jun 7, 1919
The Magnanimous Lover
  Productions:
    Opened February 4, 1913 in repertory.
  Reviews:
    Dramatic Mirror 69:7, Feb 12, 1913
    Everybody's Magazine 28:679, May 1913
    Munsey 49:149-50, Apr 1913
Mary, Mary, Quite Contrary
  Productions:

94

Opened September 11, 1923 for 86 performances.
Reviews:
    Canadian Magazine 61:428-9, Sep 1923
    Current Opinion 75:573-86, Nov 1923
    Dramatist 14:1181-2, Oct 1923
    Nation 117:331, Sep 26, 1923
    New York Times p.14, Sep 12, 1923
                  VII,p.1, Sep 16, 1923
    Overland Monthly 85:115, Apr 1927
    Theatre Magazine 38:17+, Nov 1923

Mixed Marriage
  Productions:
    Opened February 4, 1913 in repertory.
    Opened December 14, 1920 for 124 performances.
  Reviews:
    Bookman 52:564, Feb 1921
    Collier's 67:19, Jan 15, 1921
    Dramatic Mirror 66:6, Dec 20, 1911
                  p.1192, Dec 18, 1920
    Everybody's Magazine 28:678-9, May 1913
    Life (NY) 77:24, Jan 6, 1921
    Nation 112:21, Jan 5, 1921
    New York Clipper 68:30, Dec 29, 1930
    New York Times p.18, Dec 15, 1920
    Outlook 127:49-50, Jan 12, 1921
    Theatre Magazine 33:107, Feb 1921
    Touchstone 8:355-60, Feb 1921
    Weekly Review 3:658-9, Dec 29, 1920
                4:55, Jan 19, 1921

The Wonderful Visit (with H. G. Wells)
  Productions:
    Opened February 12, 1924 for 56 performances.
  Reviews:
    American Mercury 1:502-3, Apr 1924
    Dramatist 15:1207-8, Apr 1924
    Living Age 308:789-92, Mar 26, 1921
    New York Times p.17, Feb 13, 1924
    Theatre Magazine 39:19, May 1924

Feydeau, Georges
  Breakfast in Bed
    Productions:
      Adapted by Willard Mack and Howard Booth. Opened
        February 3, 1920 for 75 performances.
    Reviews:
      Dramatic Mirror 82:258, Feb 14, 1920
      Dramatist 12:1043, Jan 1921

Breakfast in Bed (cont.)
New York Clipper 68:21, Feb 11, 1920
New York Times p. 12, Feb 4, 1920
Hotel Paradiso (with Maurice Desvallieres)
Productions:
Adapted by Peter Glenville. Opened April 11, 1957 for
108 performances.
Reviews:
Catholic World 185:228, Jun 1957
Commonweal 66:154, May 10, 1957
Life 42:122-4, May 13, 1957
Nation 184:377, Apr 27, 1957
New York Theatre Critics' Reviews 1957:298
New York Times p. 22, Apr 12, 1957
II, p. 1, Apr 21, 1957
New Yorker 33:81, Apr 20, 1957
Newsweek 49:69, Apr 22, 1957
Saturday Review 39:30, Oct 13, 1956
40:26, Apr 6, 1957
Theatre Arts 41:17, Jun 1957
Time 69:90, Apr 22, 1957
Vogue 129:85, Apr 15, 1957
The Lady from Lobster Square
Productions:
Opened April 4, 1910 for 24 performances.
Reviews:
Dramatic Mirror 63:5, Apr 16, 1910
Life (NY) 55:681, Apr 14, 1910
Occupe-toi d'Amelie (Keep Your Eyes On Emily) (see also
Noel Coward's Look After Lulu)
Productions:
Opened November 24, 1952 for four performances.
Reviews:
Nation 175:562, Dec 13, 1952
New York Theatre Critics' Reviews 1952:183
New York Times p. 35, Nov 25, 1952
Saturday Review 35:26, Dec 13, 1952

Frank, Bruno
Storm Over Patsy
Productions:
Adapted by James Bridie. Opened March 8, 1937 for
48 performances.
Reviews:
Catholic World 148:86, Apr 1937
Commonweal 25:584, Mar 19, 1937
Literary Digest 123:28, Mar 20, 1938

Nation 144:333, Mar 20, 1937
New Republic 90:210, Mar 24, 1937
New York Times p. 26, Mar 9, 1937
Newsweek 9:21, Mar 20, 1937
Theatre Arts 21:340+, May 1937
Time 29:59, Mar 22, 1937

Twelve Thousand
  Productions:
    Adapted by William A. Drake.   Opened May 12, 1928
      for 64 performances.
  Reviews:
    American Mercury 121-2, May 1928
    Outlook 149:23, May 2, 1928
    Nation 126:356, Mar 28, 1928
    New York Times p. 23, Mar 13, 1928
                   IX, p. 1, Mar 18, 1928
    Theatre Arts 12:318, May 1928
    Theatre Magazine 47:76, May 1928
    Vogue 71:136, May 1, 1928

Young Madame Conti
  Productions:
    Adapted by Hubert Griffith and Benn W. Levy.
      Opened March 31, 1937 for 22 performances.
  Reviews:
    Catholic World 145:213, May 1937
    Commonweal 25:726, Apr 23, 1937
    Literary Digest 123:21, Apr 17, 1937
    New York Times p. 18, Apr 1, 1937
    Newsweek p. 25, Apr 10, 1937
    Theatre Arts 21:348-9, May 1937
    Time 29:27, Apr 12, 1937

Friel, Brian
  Philadelphia, Here I Come!
    Productions:
      Opened February 16, 1966 for 119 performances.
    Reviews:
      America 114:364, Mar 12, 1966
      Catholic World 203:319-20, Aug 1966
      Commonweal 83:668-9, Mar 11, 1966
      Nation 202:309-10, Mar 14, 1966
      New York Theatre Critics' Reviews 1966:367
      New York Times p. 28, Feb 17, 1966
      New Yorker 42:71, Feb 26, 1966
      Newsweek 67:87, Feb 28, 1966
      Saturday Review 49:54, Mar 5, 1966
      Time 87:101, Feb 25, 1966

<u>Philadelphia, Here I Come!</u> (cont.)
    Vogue 147:109, Apr 1, 1966

Frisch, Max
<u>Andorra</u>
  Productions:
    English version by George Tabori. Opened February
    9, 1963 for nine performances.
  Reviews:
    Christian Century 79:1098, Sep 12, 1962
    New Republic 148:28-9, Mar 9, 1963
    New York Theatre Critics' Reviews 1963:380
    New York Times p.5, Feb 11, 1963
              p.7, Feb 25, 1963
    New Yorker 38:114, Feb 16, 1963
    Newsweek 61:60, Feb 25, 1963
    Saturday Review 46:29, Mar 2, 1963
    Time 81:75, Feb 22, 1963
<u>The Firebugs</u>
  Productions:
    (Off Broadway) Adapted by Mordecai Gorelik. Opened
    February 11, 1963 for eight performances.
  Reviews:
    New Republic 148:29, Mar 9, 1963
    New York Times p.7, Feb 13, 1963
              p.41, Nov 22, 1963
    New Yorker 39:114, Feb 23, 1963
    Newsweek 61:60, Feb 25, 1963
    Saturday Review 46:29, Mar 2, 1963
    Time 81:75, Feb 22, 1963

Fry, Christopher
<u>The Dark is Light Enough</u>
  Productions:
    Opened February 23, 1955 for 69 performances.
  Reviews:
    America 922:657+, Mar 19, 1955
    Catholic World 181:65, Apr 1955
    Commonweal 62:78, Apr 22, 1955
    Life 38:105-6, Apr 11, 1955
    Nation 180:226, Mar 12, 1955
    New York Theatre Critics' Reviews, 1955:357
    New York Times p.20, Feb 24, 1955
             II,p.1, Mar 16, 1955
    New Yorker 30:58+, May 29, 1954
           31:67, Mar 5, 1955
    Newsweek 45:85, Mar 7, 1955

Saturday Review 37:39, Apr 3, 1954
38:26, Mar 12, 1955
Theatre Arts 39:72-5, Feb 1955
39:26+, Mar 1955
39:17+, May 1955
Time 65:92, Mar 7, 1955

The Firstborn
Productions:
Opened April 30, 1958 for 38 performances.
Reviews:
America 99:243-4, May 17, 1958
Catholic World 187:310, Jul 1958
Christian Century 74:201, Feb 13, 1957
75:646, May 28, 1958
Commonweal 68:205-6, May 23, 1958
Nation 186:456, May 17, 1958
New York Theatre Critics' Reviews 1958:303
New York Times p.35, May 1, 1958
II,p.1, May 11, 1958
New Yorker 34:83-4, May 10, 1958
Saturday Review 41:29, May 17, 1958
Time 71:66, May 12, 1958

The Lady's Not for Burning
Productions:
Opened November 8, 1950 for 151 performances.
Reviews:
America 96:656, Mar 9, 1951
Catholic World 172:306, Jan 1951
Christian Science Monitor Magazine p.4, Nov 18, 1950
Commonweal 53:196, Dec 1, 1956
Life 29:141-2+, Nov 27. 1950   1950
Nation 171:466, Nov 18, 1950
New Republic 123:22, Nov 27, 1950
New York Theatre Critics' Reviews 1950:213
New York Times p.42, Nov 9, 1950
II,p.1, Nov 26, 1950
p.34, Apr 4, 1951
New Yorker 26:77, Nov 18, 1950
Newsweek 36:96, Nov 20, 1950
Saturday Review 33:46+, Dec 2, 1950
School and Society 73:180-1, Mar 24, 1951
Theatre Arts 35:13, Jan 1951
Time 56:58, Nov 20, 1950

A Phoenix Too Frequent
Productions:
Opened April 26, 1950 for 5 performances.
Reviews:
Catholic World 171:227, Jun 1950

A Phoenix Too Frequent (cont.)
 Christian Science Monitor Magazine p. 9, May 6, 1950
 Commonweal 52:152, May 19, 1950
 Nation 170:457, May 13, 1950
 New Republic 122:21, May 15, 1950
 New York Theatre Critics' Reviews 1950:303
 New York Times p. 36, Apr 27, 1950
 New Yorker 26:52, May 6, 1950
 Newsweek 35:80, May 8, 1950
 Theatre Arts 34:15, Jul 1950
A Sleep of Prisoners
 Productions:
 Opened October 16, 1951 for 31 performances.
 Reviews:
 Catholic World 174:226, Dec 1951
 Commonweal 55:92, Nov 2, 1951
 Life 31:73-5+, Nov 12, 1951
 Nation 173:381, Nov 3, 1951
 New Republic 124:23, Jun 11, 1951
 125:22, Nov 12, 1951
 New York Theatre Critics' Reviews 1951:207
 New York Times p. 36, Oct 17, 1951
 II, p. 1, Oct 28, 1951
 New York Times Magazine pp. 58-9, May 20, 1951
 New Yorker 27:66, Oct 27, 1951
 Newsweek 38:84, Oct 29, 1951
 Saturday Review 34:60+, Nov 17, 1951
 35:22, Mar 1, 1952
 School and Society 74:406-7, Dec 22, 1951
 Survey 87:527, Dec 1951
 Theatre Arts 35:3, Dec 1951
 36:20, Jan 1952
 Time 57:70-1, May 28, 1951
 58:38, Oct 29, 1951
Venus Observed
 Productions:
 Opened February 13, 1952 for 86 performances.
 Reviews:
 Catholic World 175:69, Apr 1952
 Commonweal 55:543, Mar 7, 1952
 Nation 174:237, Mar 8, 1952
 New Republic 122:21-2, Jun 5, 1950
 126:23, Mar 3, 1952
 New York Theatre Critics' Reviews 1952:364
 New York Times p. 24, Feb 14, 1952
 II, p. 1, Feb 14, 1952
 New Yorker 25:85, Feb 11, 1950

100

26:58+, Feb 23, 1952
Newsweek 39:95, Feb 25, 1952
Saturday Review 35:20-2, Mar 1, 1952
35:26, May 10, 1952
School and Society 75:183-4, Mar 22, 1952
Theatre Arts 34:29, Dec 1950
36:18-19, Apr 1952
Time 59:80, Feb 25, 1952

Galsworthy, John
A Bit of Love
Productions:
Opened May 12, 1925 for 4 performances.
Reviews:
Dial 59:328, Oct 14, 1915
Dramatic Mirror 73:5, Jun 23, 1915
Nation 101:298, Jun 5, 1915
101:25, Jul 1, 1915
120:635-6, Jun 3, 1925
New Republic 3:210, Jun 26, 1915
New York Times p. 24, May 13, 1925
Escape
Productions:
Opened October 26, 1927 for 173 performances.
Reviews:
American Mercury 13:118-20, Jan 1928
Catholic World 126:379-80, Dec 1927
Dial 84:82, Jan 1928
Dramatist 19:1363, Jan 1928
Independent 119:606, Dec 17, 1927
Life (NY) 90:25, Nov 17, 1927
Living Age 330:673-6, Sep 25, 1926
331:340-5, Nov 15, 1926
Nation 125:311-12, Nov 16, 1927
New Republic 52:311-12, Nov 9, 1927
New York Times p. 33, Oct 27, 1927
IX, p. 1, Nov 6, 1927
Outlook 147:308, Nov 9, 1927
Saturday Review 4:299-300, Nov 12, 1927
Theatre Arts 12:14-15, Jan 1928
Vogue 70:66, Dec 15, 1927
The Fugitive
Productions:
Opened May 19, 1917 for 56 performances.
Reviews:
Book News 35:257, May 1917
Dramatic Mirror 77:7, Mar 14, 1917

The Fugitive (cont.)
    Dramatist 5:459, Apr 1914
    Green Book 17:971-5, Jun 1917
    Harper's Weekly 61:263, Sep 11, 1915
    Life (NY) 69:526, Mar 29, 1917
    Nation 104:380, Mar 29, 1917
    New York Times VIII,p.5, Apr 1, 1917
    Theatre Magazine 25:277+, May 1917
    Yale Review 11:298-303, Jan 1922
Justice
 Productions:
    Opened April 3, 1916 for 104 performances.
 Reviews
    American Mercury 70:585-99, Sep 1910
                       70:819-31, Oct 1910
    Book News 34:432-3, Jun 1916
    Bookman 43:340-2, Jun 1916
    Current Opinion 60:324-8, May 1916
    Dramatic Mirror 75:8, Apr 8, 1916
    Dramatist 2:128, Jun 1911
             7:676, Apr 1916
    Everybody's Magazine 35:122-4, Jul 1916
    Green Book 15:969-77, Jun 1916
    Harper's Weekly 62:440, Apr 22, 1916
    Hearst 30:165-7+, Sep 1916
    Literary Digest 52:1220-1, Apr 29, 1916
    Nation 102:419-20, Apr 13, 1916
          122:429-30, Apr 30, 1916
    New Republic 6:294, Apr 15, 1916
    New York Dramatic News 62:17, Apr 8, 1916
    New York Times p.11, Apr 4, 1916
                II,p.8, Apr 9, 1916
                II,p.7, Apr 16, 1916
                II,p.8, Apr 23, 1916
    Outlook 132:246-8, May 31, 1916
    Stage 14:72, Aug 1937
    Theatre Arts 19:415, Jun 1935
    Theatre Magazine 14:89-90, Sep 1911
                   23:273, May 1916
                   23:296-7+, May 1916
                   24:77, Aug 1916
The Little Man
 Productions:
    Opened February 12, 1917 for 56 performances.
 Reviews:
    Dramatic Mirror 77:7, Feb 24, 1917
    New Republic 10:106, Feb 24, 1917

New York Times p. 9, Feb 13, 1917
Theatre Magazine 25:215+, Apr 1917
Loyalties
Productions:
Opened September 27, 1922 for 220 performances.
Reviews:
Bookman 56:477-8, Dec 1922
         63:161-5, Apr 1926
Catholic World 116:507-9, Jan 1923
Current Opinion 73:750-5+, Dec 1922
Dramatist 13:1134-8, Oct 1922
Everybody's Magazine 48:96-103, Feb 1923
Fortnightly Review 118:349-52, Aug 1922
Forum 68:975-6, Nov 1922
      68:1039-41, Dec 1922
Hearst 42:85+, Dec 1922
Independent 110:32-4, Jan 6, 1923
Life (NY) 80:18, Oct 19, 1922
Nation 115:420, Oct 18, 1922
New Republic 32:277-8, Nov 8, 1922
New York Clipper 70:21, Oct 4, 1922
New York Times p. 18, Sep 28, 1922
        VI,p. 1, Oct 8, 1922
        III,p. 4, Jan 14, 1923
Theatre Magazine 36:370-1+, Dec 1922
        37:28+, Jan 1923

Mob
Productions:
Opened October 1920.
Reviews:
Bookman 53:274-5, May 1921
Dramatic Mirror p. 683, Oct 16, 1920
Dramatist 6:510-12, Oct 1914
New Republic 1:27-8, Nov 7, 1914
New York Clipper 68:29, Oct 27, 1920
New York Times p. 18, Oct 11, 1920
Theatre Magazine 32:422, Dec 1920
Weekly Review 3:426-7, Nov 3, 1920
Yale Review 4:623, Apr 1915

Old English
Productions:
Opened December 23, 1924 for 183 performances.
Reviews:
American Mercury 4:244, Feb 1925
Current Opinion 78:316-23, Mar 1925
Dramatist 16:1249-50, Jan 1925
Nation 120:49-50, Jan 14, 1925

Old English (cont.)
New York Times p. 11, Dec 24, 1924
p. 21, Feb 10, 1925
Theatre Magazine 40:16+, Mar 1925
42:26+, Jul 1925
The Pigeon
Productions:
Opened March 12, 1912 for 64 performances.
Opened February 2, 1922 for 92 performances.
Reviews:
Blue Book 15:478-80, Jul 1912
Book News 31:287, Dec 1912
Bookman 35:243, May 1912
Dramatic Mirror 67:6, Mar 13, 1912
Green Book 7:970, May 1912
Independent 72:617-19, Mar 21, 1912
Life (NY) 59:588, Mar 21, 1912
Munsey 47:283, May 1912
Nation 114:196, Feb 15, 1922
New York Clipper 70:20, Feb 8, 1922
New York Dramatic News 55:14-15, Mar 16, 1912
New York Times p. 13, Feb 3, 1922
Red Book 19:370+, Jun 1912
Theatre Magazine 15:106-7, Apr 1912
Yale Review 1:690-3, Jul 1912
The Roof
Productions:
Opened October 30, 1931 for 28 performances.
Reviews:
Catholic World 134:333, Dec 1931
New York Times p. 22, Oct 31, 1931
Theatre Arts 16:19, Jan 1932
The Silver Box
Productions:
Opened January 17, 1928 for 23 performances.
Reviews:
Dramatist 2:158, Apr 1911
Life (NY) 91:21, Feb 2, 1928
New York Times p. 23, Jan 18, 1928
Theatre Magazine 7:114+, May 1907
Vogue 71:94+, Mar 15, 1928
The Skin Game
Productions:
Opened October 20, 1920 for 176 performances.
Reviews:
Bookman 51:659, Aug 1920
53:275, May 1921

Current Opinion 69:649-56, Nov 1920
Drama 12:122+, Jan 1922
Dramatic Mirror p. 795, Oct 30, 1920
Dramatist 11:1011-12, Jul 1920
Fortnightly Review 113:961-5, Jun 1920
Forum 65:242-4, Feb 1921
Independent 104:213, Nov 13, 1920
Life (NY) 76:872-3, Nov 11, 1920
Literary Digest 67:30, Nov 6, 1920
Living Age 305:494-5, May 22, 1920
Nation 111:539, Nov 10, 1920
New York Clipper 68:29, Oct 27, 1920
New York Times p. 11, Oct 21, 1920
           VI, p. 1, Oct 31, 1920
Theatre Magazine 33:7+, Jan 1921
Weekly Review 3:454-5, Nov 10, 1920

Strife
Productions:
Opened November 17, 1909 in repertory.
Reviews:
Bookman 30:461, Feb 1910
Current Literature 48:81-3, Jan 1910
           48:537-45, May 1910
Dramatic Mirror 62:5, Nov 27, 1909
Forum 43:70, Jan 1910
Green Book 3:391-2, Feb 1910
Hampton 24:272, Feb 1910
Life (NY) 54:855, Dec 9, 1909
Literary Digest 39:1013, Dec 4, 1909
Metropolitan Magazine 31:816-17, Mar 1910
Nation 89:520, Nov 25, 1909
Pearson 22:229-31, Aug 1909
Theatre Magazine 11:2+, Jan 1910

Windows
Productions:
Opened October 8, 1923 for 48 performances.
Reviews:
Bookman 58:441, Dec 1923
Dramatist 14:1167-8, Jul 1923
Freeman 8:186, Oct 31, 1923
Life (NY) 82:18, Oct 25, 1923
Nation 117:469-70, Oct 24, 1923
New York Times p. 17, Oct 9, 1923
           VIII, p. 1, Oct 24, 1923
Theatre Magazine 38:16-17, Dec 1923

García Lorca, Federico

Blood Wedding (Bitter Oleander)
  Productions:
    Translated by José A. Weissman. Opened February
      11, 1935 for 24 performances.
    (Off Broadway) Season of 1948-1949.
  Reviews:
    Catholic World 169: 65, Apr 1949
    Commonweal 49:542-3, Mar 11, 1949
                 62:473, Aug 12, 1955
    Forum 111:164, Mar 1949
    Nation 168:221, Feb 19, 1949
    New Republic 82:78, Feb 27, 1935
                 120:27, Feb 21, 1949
    New York Times p. 24, Feb 12, 1935
                   II, p. 1, Jan 30, 1949
                   p. 16, Feb 7, 1949
    Saturday Review 21:21, Jan 15, 1940
    School and Society 69:155, Feb 26, 1949
    Theatre Arts 19:248+, Apr 1935
                 33:24, May 1949
    Vanity Fair 44:43, Apr 1935
The House of Bernarda Alba
  Productions:
    Translated by James Graham Lujan and Richard L.
      O'Connell. Opened January 7, 1951 for 17
      performances.
  Reviews:
    Christian Science Monitor Magazine p. 8, May 20, 1950
    Commonweal 53:398, Jan 26, 1951
                62:475, Aug 12, 1955
    Nation 172:66, Jan 20, 1951
    New Republic 124:22, Feb 5, 1951
    New York Theatre Critics' Reviews 1951:395
    New York Times p. 14, Jan 8, 1951
    New Yorker 26:54+, Jan 20, 1951
    School and Society 73:100-1, Feb 17, 1951
    Theatre Arts 35:17, Mar 1951
If Five Years Pass
  Productions:
    (Off Broadway) Opened April 6, 1945.
    (Off Broadway) Opened May 10, 1962 for 22 perform-
      ances.
  Reviews:
    Commonweal 42:17, Apr 20, 1945
                42:71, May 4, 1945
    New York Times p. 37, May 11, 1962
    Theatre Arts 46:57, Aug 1962

Genét, Jean
  The Balcony
    Productions:
      (Off Broadway) Translated by Bernard Frechtman.
      Opened March 30, 1960 for 672 performances.
    Reviews:
      Christian Century 77:546-8, May 4, 1960
      Nation 185:18, Jul 6, 1957
              190:282-3, Mar 26, 1960
      New Republic 142:21-2, Mar 28, 1960
      New York Times p. 21, Mar 4, 1960
                     II, p. 1, Mar 20, 1960
      New Yorker 36:116+, Mar 12, 1960
      Saturday Review 43:34, Mar 26, 1960
      Time 75:54+, Apr 18, 1960
  The Blacks
    Productions:
      (Off Broadway) Translated by Bernard Frechtman.
      Opened May 4, 1961 for 1,408 performances.
    Reviews:
      America 105:671, Aug 26, 1961
      Catholic World 194:62-4, Oct 1961
      Christian Century 78:744-5, Jun 14, 1961
      Ebony 17:47-8+, Sep 1962
      Nation 192:447-8, May 20, 1961
      New Republic 144:21-2, May 29, 1961
      New York Times p. 23, May 5, 1961
                     II, p. 1, May 14, 1961
                     p. 37, Sep 25, 1963
      New Yorker 37:93-4, May 13, 1961
      Newsweek 57:68, May 15, 1961
      Saturday Review 44:29, Jun 3, 1961
      Theatre Arts 45:8-9, Jul 1961
      Time 77:64, May 12, 1961
      Yale Review 55:209-26, Dec 1965
  Deathwatch
    Productions:
      (Off Broadway) Season of 1958-1959.
      (Off Broadway) Opened February 11, 1962 in repertory.
    Reviews:
      New York Times p. 34, Oct 10, 1958
      Saturday Review 41:28, Nov 1, 1958
  The Maids
    Productions:
      (Off Broadway) Translated by Bernard Frechtman.
      Opened November 14, 1963 for 62 performances.
    Reviews:

The Maids (cont.)
    Commonweal 62:398-9, Jul 22, 1955
    Nation 180:469-70, May 28, 1955
    New York Times p. 29, Nov 15, 1963
    New Yorker 39:143-4+, Nov 23, 1963

Geraldy, Paul
  Aimer (see To Love)

  The Nest (Les Noces d'Argent)
    Productions:
      Adapted by Grace George.   Opened January 28, 1922
        for 161 performances.
    Reviews:
      Bookman 55:180, Apr 1922
      Independent 108:265, Mar 11, 1922
      Life (NY) 79:18, Mar 2, 1922
      New York Clipper 70:20, Feb 8, 1922
      New York Times p. 20, Feb 2, 1922
      Theatre Magazine 35:215+, Apr 1922
  She Had To Know
    Productions:
      Adapted by Grace George.   Opened February 2, 1925
        for 80 performances.
    Reviews:
      Life (NY) 85:18, Feb 26, 1925
      Nation 120:192-3, Feb 18, 1925
      New York Times p. 25, Feb 3, 1925
      Theatre Magazine 41:16, Apr 1925
  To Love (Aimer)
    Productions:
      Translated by Grace George.   Opened October 17, 1922
        for 55 performances.
    Reviews:
      Dramatist 13:1135-6, Oct 1922
      Forum 68:1041-3, Dec 1922
      Nation 115:506-7, Nov 8, 1922
      New York Clipper 70:20, Oct 25, 1922
      New York Times p. 16, Oct 18, 1922
      Theatre Magazine 36:371, Dec 1922

Gide, Andre
  The Trial (Le Proces) (with Jean-Louis Barrault)
    Productions:
      Based on Kafka's novel.   Opened November 17, 1952
        for 4 performances.
      (Off Broadway) Season of 1963-1964 for 9 perform-
        ances.

Reviews:
    Christian Science Monitor Magazine p. 9, May 6, 1950
    Nation 175:500, Nov 29, 1952
    New York Theatre Critics' Reviews 1952:194
    New York Times p. 36, Nov 18, 1952
    Saturday Review 35:41, Dec 6, 1952

Giraudoux, Jean
  Amphitryon 38
    Productions:
      Adapted by S. N. Behrman.   Opened November 1,
      1937 for 153 performances.
    Reviews:
      Catholic World 146:338-9, Dec 1937
      Commonweal 27:78, Nov 12, 1937
      Life 3:70, Jul 1937
      Literary Digest 1:35, Nov 20, 1935
      Nation 145:539, Nov 13, 1937
      New Republic 93:44, Nov 17, 1937
                 94:132, Mar 9, 1938
      New York Times p. 32, November 2, 1937
                   XI,p. 1, Nov 7, 1937
      Newsweek 10:20-1, Jul 3, 1937
              10:22, Nov 8, 1937
      Scribner's Magazine 102:66+, Oct 1937
      Stage 15:46-9, Oct 1937
          15:94, Nov 1937
          15:44-5, Jan 1938
      Theatre Arts 21:924, Dec 1937
      Time 30:25, Nov 8, 1937
  Duel of Angels
    Productions:
      Adapted by Christopher Fry.   Opened April 19, 1960
      for 51 performances.
    Reviews:
      America 103:266, May 14, 1960
      Christian Century 77:672-3, Jun 1, 1960
      Life 48:95, May 16, 1960
      Nation 190:411-12, May 7, 1960
      New York Theatre Critics' Reviews 1960:287
      New York Times p. 42, Apr 20, 1960
                II,p. 1, May 1, 1960
                p. 24, Jul 14, 1960
      New Yorker 36:83, Apr 30, 1960
      Newsweek 55:54, May 2, 1960
      Saturday Review 43:26, May 7, 1960
      Time 75:78, May 2, 1960

The Enchanted (see also Intermezzo)
  Productions:
    Adapted by Maurice Valency.   Opened January 18,
      1950 for 45 performances.
  Reviews:
    Catholic World 170:469, Mar 1950
    Commonweal 51:486, Feb 10, 1950
    New Republic 122:30, Feb 13, 1950
    New York Theatre Critics' Reviews 1950:387
    New York Times p. 34, Jan 19, 1950
                   p. 41, Apr 23, 1958
    New Yorker 25:50, Jan 28, 1950
    Newsweek 35:67, Jan 30, 1950
    School and Society 71:118-19, Feb 25, 1950
    Theatre Arts 34:17+, Mar 1950
    Time 55:37, Jan 30, 1950
Intermezzo (see also The Enchanted)
  Productions:
    Opened January 30, 1957 in repertory.
  Reviews:
    Catholic World 185:68, Apr 1957
    Commonweal 136:21, Mar 18, 1957
    New York Theatre Critics' Reviews 1957:345
    New York Times p. 20, February 15, 1957
    Theatre Arts 41:82, Apr 1957
Judith
  Productions:
    (Off Broadway) English version by John K. Savacool.
      Opened March 24, 1965 for 79 performances.
  Reviews:
    Nation 200:403-4, Apr 12, 1965
    New Republic 152:23-4, Apr 10, 1965
    New York Times p. 42, Mar 25, 1965
                   II, p. 1, Apr 4, 1965
    New Yorker 41:86, Apr 3, 1965
    Reporter 32:38-40, May 6, 1965
    Saturday Review 48:58, Apr 10, 1965
    Time 85:79, Apr 9, 1965
    Vogue 145:68, Jun 1965
The Madwoman of Chaillot
  Productions:
    Adapted by Maurice Valency.   Opened December 27,
      1948 for 368 performances.
    Adapted by Maurice Valency.   Opened June 13, 1950
      for 17 performances.
  Reviews:
    Catholic World 168:401, Feb 1949

Commonweal 49:351, Jan 14, 1949
Forum 111:93-4, Feb 1949
House and Garden 95:186, Apr 1949
Life 26:64+, Jan 24, 1949
Nation 168:53, Jan 8, 1949
New Republic 120:28, Jan 17, 1949
New York Theatre Critics' Reviews 1948:104
New York Times p. 18, Dec 28, 1948
               II, p. 1, Jan 9, 1949
               VI, p. 6, Mar 13, 1949
               II, p. 1, Sep 11, 1949
               p. 41, Jun 14, 1950
New Yorker 21:46-8, Feb 9, 1946
           24:48+, Jan 8, 1949
Newsweek 33:72, Jan 10, 1949
Saturday Review 32:32-4, Jan 15, 1949
School and Society 69:82-4, Jan 29, 1949
Theatre Arts 33:14-17, Mar 1949
             41:67-8+, Mar 1957
Time 53:36, Jan 10, 1949
Vogue 107:168, Mar 1, 1946
      112:150-51, Mar 1, 1949

Ondine
  Productions:
    Adapted by Maurice Valency.   Opened February 18,
      1954 for 157 performances.
  Reviews:
    America 90:664+, Mar 20, 1954
    Catholic World 179:67-8, Apr 2, 1954
    Commonweal 59:649-50, Apr 2, 1954
    Life 36:60-2+, Mar 8, 1954
    Look 18:88+, Apr 20, 1954
    Nation 178:206, Mar 6, 1954
    New Republic 130:21, Mar 8, 1954
    New Yorker 30:74+, Feb 27, 1954
    Newsweek 43:71, Mar 1, 1954
    New York Theatre Critics' Reviews 1954:362
    New York Times p. 23, Feb 19, 1954
                  II, p. 1, Feb 28, 1954
    Saturday Review 37:26-7, Mar 13, 1954
    Theatre Arts 38:18-20, May 1954
    Time 63:76, Mar 1, 1954

Siegfried
  Productions:
    Translated by Philip Carr. Opened October 20, 1930
      for 23 performances.
  Reviews:

Siegfried (cont.)
 Bookman 72:513-14, Jan 1931
 Catholic World 132:337, Dec 1930
 Commonweal 13:49, Nov 12, 1930
 Nation 131:506, Nov 5, 1930
 New York Times p. 34, Oct 21, 1930
 Vogue 76:134+, Dec 8, 1930
 Yale Review 20:816-17, Summer 1931
Tiger at the Gates
 Productions:
 Translation by Christopher Fry. Opened by
 October 3, 1955 for 217 performances.
 Reviews:
 America 94:258+, Nov 26, 1955
 Catholic World 182:223-4, Dec 1955
 Commonweal 63:200-1, Nov 25, 1955
 Life 39:164-5, Oct 17, 1955
 Nation 181:348, Oct 22, 1955
 New Republic 133:22, Oct 24, 1955
 New York Theatre Critics' Reviews 1955:264
 New York Times p. 40, Oct 4, 1955
 II, p. 1, Oct 23, 1955
 New York Times Magazine p. 20, Sep 11, 1955
 New Yorker 31:61, Jul 30, 1955
 31:76+, Oct 15, 1955
 Newsweek 46:103, Oct 17, 1955
 Reporter 13:42, Oct 20, 1955
 Saturday Review 38:27, Oct 22, 1955
 Theatre Arts 39:22, Dec 1955
 Time 66:51-2, Oct 17, 1955
 Vogue 125:136-7+, Mar 1, 1955

Gorki, Maxim
 At the Bottom (also see Night Lodging and The Lower
 Depths)
 Productions:
 Adapted by William L. Lawrence. Opened January 9,
 1930 for 72 performances.
 Reviews:
 New York Times p. 24, Jan 10, 1930
 Outlook 154:229, Feb 5, 1930
 Theatre Arts 14:190+, Mar 1930
 Theatre Magazine 51:48, Mar 1930
 Vogue 75:70+, Mar 1, 1930
 The Lower Depths (also see Night Lodging and At the Bottom)
 Productions:
 Opened January 1923 in repertory.

Opened November 1923 in repertory (Moscow Art
Theatre).
(Off Broadway) Translated by Alex Szogyi.   Opened
March 30, 1964 for 52 performances.
Reviews:
Arts and Decoration 32:75, Mar 1930
Commonweal 11:342, Jan 22, 1930
Nation 198:404, Apr 20, 1964
New York Times p. 16, Jan 16, 1923
               p. 30, Mar 31, 1964
               II, p. 1, Apr 12, 1964
New Yorker 40:95-7, Apr 11, 1964
Outlook 154:229, Feb 5, 1930
Night Lodging (see also The Lower Depths and At the Bottom)
Productions:
Opened December 22, 1919 for 14 performances.
Reviews:
Current Opinion 68:195-7, Feb 1920
Nation 110:49-50, Jan 1920
New Republic 21:173, Jan 7, 1920
New York Times p. 12, Dec 23, 1919
               VIII, p. 2, Dec 28, 1919

Greene, Graham
The Complaisant Lover
Productions:
Opened November 1, 1961 for 101 performances.
Reviews:
Christian Century 78:1532, Dec 20, 1961
Commonweal 75:233-4, Nov 24, 1961
Nation 193:437, Nov 25, 1961
New York Theatre Critics' Reviews 1961:184
New York Times p. 43, Nov 2, 1961
New Yorker 37:117-18, Nov 11, 1961
Newsweek 58:95, Nov 13, 1961
Reporter 25:62, Dec 7, 1961
Saturday Review 44:36, Dec 2, 1961
Theatre Arts 46:15+, Jan 1962
Time 78:66, Nov 10, 1961
The Living Room
Productions:
Opened November 17, 1954 for 22 performances.
(Off Broadway) Opened November 21, 1962 for 23
performances.
Reviews:
America 90:600-2, Mar 6, 1954
          92:386-7, Jan 8, 1955

The Living Room (cont.)
        93:433-5, Jul 30, 1955
    Catholic World 177:406-10, Sep 1953
    Commonweal 59:477-8, Feb 12, 1954
            61:278, Dec 10, 1954
            61:333, Dec 24, 1954
            61:354-5, Dec 31, 1954
            71:123-4, Oct 30, 1959
            77:316-17, Dec 14, 1962
    Nation 177:138, Aug 15, 1953
        179:496-7, Dec 4, 1954
    New Republic 131:22, Dec 13, 1954
    New York Theatre Critics' Reviews 1954:251
    New York Times p. 41, Nov 18, 1954
            II, p. 1, Nov 28, 1954
            p. 43, Nov 22, 1962
    New Yorker 29:69, Jul 18, 1953
            30:156+, Oct 23, 1954
            30:86, Nov 27, 1954
    Newsweek 44:92, Nov 29, 1954
    Saturday Review 36:24, Aug 1, 1953
            37:24-5, Dec 18, 1954
    Theatre Arts 39:12+, Feb 1955
    Time 64:50, Nov 29, 1954
        64:55, Dec 20, 1954
The Potting Shed
  Productions:
    Opened January 29, 1957 for 143 performances.
    (Off Broadway) Opened October 19, 1962 for nine
    performances.
  Reviews:
    America 96:594-5, Feb 23, 1957
            97:168-70, May 4, 1957
            97:293, Jun 8, 1957
    Catholic World 185:66, Apr 1957
            186:210-13, Dec 1957
    Christian Century 74:262, Feb 27, 1957
    Commonweal 65:613-14, Mar 15, 1957
    Life 42:65-6+, Apr 1, 1957
    Nation 184:146, Feb 16, 1957
    New York Theatre Critics' Reviews 1957:372
    New York Times p. 32, Jan 30, 1957
                II, p. 1, Feb 10, 1957
    New Yorker 32:70+, Feb 9, 1957
    Newsweek 49:67, Feb 11, 1957
    Reporter 16:41, Mar 7, 1957
    Saturday Review 40:26-7, Feb 16, 1957

Theatre Arts 41:15, Apr 1957
Time 69:70, Feb 11, 1957

Gregory, Lady
Coats
    Productions:
        Opened February 4, 1913 in repertory (The Irish
            Players).
    Reviews:
        Dramatic Mirror 69:7, Mar 5, 1913
        New York Times p. 13, Mar 4, 1913
Damer's Gold
    Productions:
        Opened February 4, 1913 in repertory (The Irish
            Players).
    Reviews:
        Dramatic Mirror 69:6-7, Feb 19, 1913
The Dragon
    Productions:
        Opened March 25, 1929 for five performances.
    Reviews:
        New York Times p. 34, Mar 26, 1929
        Weekly Review 3:321, Oct 13, 1920
The Gaol Gate (The Jail Gate)
    Productions:
        Opened November 20, 1911 in repertory (The Irish
            Players).
        Opened February 4, 1913 in repertory (The Irish
            Players).
    Reviews:
        Dramatic Mirror 66:6, Dec 6, 1911
Hyacinth Halvey
    Productions:
        Opened November 20, 1911 in repertory (The Irish
            Players).
    Reviews:
        Dramatic Mirror 66:7, Dec 20, 1911
The Image
    Productions:
        Opened November 20, 1911 in repertory (The Irish
            Players).
    Reviews:
        Dramatic Mirror 66:6, Dec 27, 1911
The Jackdaw
    Productions:
        Opened November 20, 1911 in repertory (The Irish
            Players)

The Jackdaw (cont.)
  Opened February 4, 1913 in repertory (The Irish
    Players).
Reviews:
  Dramatic Mirror 69:7, Feb 12, 1913
The Rising of the Moon
  Productions:
  Opened November 20, 1911 in repertory (The Irish
    Players).
  Opened February 4, 1913 in repertory (The Irish
    Players).
  Opened October 21, 1932 in repertory (Irish
    Repertory Company).
Reviews:
  American Playwright 1:24, Jan 1912
  Dramatic Mirror 66:7, Nov 22, 1911
  New York Times p. 25, Oct 21, 1932
Spreading the News
  Productions:
  Opened November 20, 1911 in repertory (The Irish
    Players).
  Opened February 4, 1913 in repertory (The Irish
    Players).
Reviews:
  Dramatic Mirror 66:7, Nov 22, 1911
  Green Book 7:636, Mar 1912
The Travelling Man
  Productions:
  Opened December 26, 1916 for two performances.
Reviews:
  Dramatic Mirror 77:7, Jan 6, 1917
The Workhouse Ward
  Productions:
  Opened November 20, 1911 in repertory (The Irish
    Players).
  Opened February 4, 1913 in repertory (The Irish
    Players).
Reviews:
  Catholic World 189:243, Jun 1959
  Dramatic Mirror 66:6, Dec 6, 1911
  New Yorker 35:82-3, Apr 18, 1959

Guitry, Sacha
  The Comedian
  Productions:
  Adapted by David Belasco. Opened March 13, 1923
    for 87 performances.

Reviews:
    Dial 74:635-6, Jun 1923
    Hearst 44:85-7+, Jul 1923
    Life (NY) 81:20, Apr 5, 1923
    New York Clipper 71:14, Mar 21, 1923
    New York Times p. 14, Mar 14, 1923
                    VIII,p. 1, Mar 25, 1923
    Theatre Magazine 37:14+, May 1923
Deburau
  Productions:
    Adapted by Harley Granville-Barker. Opened
      December 23, 1920 for 189 performances.
  Reviews:
    Bookman 52:566-7, Feb 1921
    Collier's 67:19, Jan 22, 1921
    Dramatic Mirror 83:11, Jan 1, 1921
    Dramatist 12:1070-1, Jul 1921
    Fortune 116:1034-44, Dec 1921
    Hearst 39:21-3+, Apr 1921
    Life (NY) 77:64, Jan 13, 1921
    New Republic 27:51, Jan 8, 1921
    New York Clipper 68:18, Dec 29, 1920
    New York Times VI,p. 1, Dec 19, 1920
                    p. 14, Dec 14, 1920
                    VI,p. 3, Jan 2, 1921
                    VI,p. 9, Jan 9, 1921
                    VI,p. 1, Jan 16, 1921
                    VI,p. 1, Jan 30, 1921
    Outlook 127:249-50, Feb 16, 1921
    Theatre Magazine 33:81-2+, Feb 1921
                      33:172-3+, Mar 1921
    Weekly Review 4:39-40, Jan 12, 1921
Don't Listen, Ladies
  Productions:
    Translated by Stephen Powys. Opened December 28,
      1948 for 15 performances.
  Reviews:
    New York Theatre Critics' Reviews 1948:100
    New York Times p. 16, Dec 29, 1948
    New Yorker 24:52, Jan 8, 1949
    Newsweek 33:72, Jan 10, 1949
    Theatre Arts 33:17, Mar 1949
    Time 53:36, Jan 10, 1949
The Grand Duke
  Productions:
    Translated by A. Abdullah. Opened November 1,
      1921 for 131 performances.

Reviews:
Dramatic Mirror 84:665, Nov 5, 1921
Dramatist 13:1087-8, Jan 1922
Hearst 41:17-19+, Feb 1922
Independent 107:165, Nov 12, 1921
Life (NY) 78:18, Nov 24, 1921
New Republic 28:352, Nov 16, 1921
New York Clipper 69:20, Nov 9, 1921
New York Times p. 20, Nov 2, 1921
VI,p. 1, Nov 17, 1921
Theatre Magazine 35:25+, Jan 1922
Mozart (Music by Reynaldo Hahn)
Productions:
English version by Ashley Dukes. Prologue by Brian
Hooker. Opened November 22, 1926 for 32 per-
formances.
Reviews:
Arts and Decoration 24:55, Apr 1926
Nation 124:46, Jan 12, 1927
New York Times p. 26, Nov 23, 1926
p. 16, Dec 28, 1926
Vogue 69:122, Jan 15, 1927
Pasteur   69:126, Feb 1927
Productions:
Adapted by Arthur Hornblow, Jr. Opened March 12,
1923 for 16 performances.
Reviews:
New York Clipper 71:14, Mar 14, 1923
New York Times p. 19, Mar 13, 1923
VII,p. 1, Mar 18, 1923
Science ns56:12, Jul 7, 1922
Theatre Magazine 37:5+, May 1923
Sleeping Partners
Productions:
Opened October 5, 1918 for 161 performances.
Reviews:
Dramatic Mirror 79:579, Oct 19, 1918
Life (NY) 72:562, Oct 17, 1918
New York Dramatic News 65:7, Oct 12, 1918
New York Times p. 11, Oct 7, 1918
IV,p. 2, Oct 13, 1918
Theatre Magazine 28:347, Dec 1918

Hamilton, Patrick
Angel Street (Gas Light)
Productions:
Opened December 5, 1941 for 1,295 performances.

118

Opened January 22, 1948 for 14 performances.
Reviews:
Commonweal 47:424, Feb 6, 1948
Nation 153:649, Dec 20, 1941
New Republic 118:34, Feb 9, 1948
New York Theatre Critics' Reviews 1941:182
New York Times p. 15, Dec 6, 1941
p. 26, Jan 23, 1948
New Yorker 23:40, Jan 31, 1948
Newsweek 18:72, Dec 15, 1941
Theatre Arts 26:77, 87 Feb 1942
Time 38:73, Dec 15, 1941
Vogue 99:60-61, Feb 15, 1942
The Duke in Darkness
Productions:
Opened January 24, 1944 for 24 performances.
Reviews:
Commonweal 39:420, Feb 11, 1944
New York Theatre Critics' Reviews 1944:279
New York Times p. 15, Jan 25, 1944
Theatre Arts 28:208, Apr 1944
Rope's End (Rope)
Productions:
Opened September 19, 1929 for 100 performances.
Reviews:
Catholic World 120:467-8, Jan 1930
Literary Digest 103:18-19, Oct 19, 1929
New York Times p. 34, Sep 20, 1929
Review of Reviews 80:158, Dec 1929
Theatre Magazine 50:74, Nov 1929
Vogue 74:154, Nov 9, 1929

de Hartog, Jan
The Fourposter
Productions:
Opened October 24, 1951 for 632 performances.
Opened January 5, 1955 for 15 performances.
Reviews:
America 92:463, Jan 29, 1955
Catholic World 174:227, Dec 1951
180:468, Mar 1955
Commonweal 55:118, Nov 9, 1951
Life 31:125-6, Nov 26, 1951
New Republic 132:22, Feb 7, 1955
New York Theatre Critics' Reviews 1951:190
New York Times p. 34, Oct 25, 1951
II, p. 1, Nov 25, 1951

The Fourposter (cont.)
                          p. 33, Apr 7, 1953
                          p. 23, Jan 6, 1955
      New Yorker 27:91, Nov 3, 1951
      Newsweek 38:64, Nov 5, 1951
      Saturday Review 35:27, Jul 5, 1952
      Theatre Arts 35:3, Dec 1951
                      36:21+, Jan 1952
                      39:91, Mar 1955
      Time 58:66, Nov 5, 1951
Skipper Next To God
   Productions:
      Opened January 4, 1948 for 6 performances.
   Reviews:
      Catholic World 166:458, Feb 1948
      Commonweal 47:372-3, Jan 23, 1948
      Life 24:86+, Mar 29, 1948
      New Republic 118:33, Jan 19, 1948
      New York Times p. 14, Jan 5, 1948
                      II, p. 1, Feb 1, 1948
      New Yorker 23:40, Feb 7, 1948
      School and Society 67:244-5, Mar 27, 1948
This Time Tomorrow
   Productions:
      Opened November 3, 1947 for 32 performances.
   Reviews:
      Catholic World 166:266-7, Dec 1947
      Commonweal 47:143, Nov 21, 1947
      Nation 165:568, Nov 22, 1947
      New Republic 117:32, Nov 17, 1947
      New York Theatre Critics' Reviews 1947:274
      New York Times p. 31, Nov 4, 1947
      New Yorker 23:57, Nov 15, 1947
      Newsweek 30:85, Nov 17, 1947
      School and Society 66:420-1, Nov 29, 1947
      Theatre Arts 31:17, Nov 1947
      Time 50:87, November 17, 1947

Harwood, H. M.
   Billeted (with F. Tennyson Jesse)
   Productions:
      Opened December 25, 1917 for 79 performances.
      Opened May 9, 1922 for 23 performances.
   Reviews:
      Dramatic Mirror 78:7, Jan 5, 1918
      Green Book 19:393+, Mar 1918
      Nation 105:379, Oct 4, 1917

New York Times p. 7, Dec 26, 1917
          IV, p. 8, Jan 6, 1918
Theatre Magazine 27:73+, Feb 1918
          36:32, Jul 1922
The Black Mask (with F. Tennyson Jesse)
  Productions:
    Opened September 27, 1913 in repertory (The Princess
      Players).
  Reviews:
    Bookman 38:364, Dec 1913
    Dramatic Mirror 70:6, Oct 15, 1913
    Green Book 10:1062-3, Dec 1913
    Theatre Magazine 18:143, Nov 1913
Cynara (with R. F. Gore-Browne)
  Productions:
    Opened November 2, 1931 for 210 performances.
  Reviews:
    Arts and Decoration 36:62, Jan 1932
    Catholic World 134:333-4, Dec 1931
    Commonweal 15:270, Jan 6, 1932
    New York Times p. 31, Nov 3, 1931
    Outlook 159:376, Nov 18, 1931
    Sketch Book 9:20, Jan 1932
    Theatre Arts 16:21, Jan 1932
    Theatre Guild Magazine 9:3-4, Dec 1931
                          9:2, Jan 1932
    Town and Country 86:46-7, Dec 1931
    Vanity Fair 37:74, Jan 1932
    Vogue 79:82, Jan 15, 1932
A Kiss of Importance (with Andre Picard)
  Productions:
    Adapted by Arthur Hornblow, Jr. Opened
      December 1, 1930 for 24 performances.
  Reviews:
    Life (NY) 96:18-19, Dec 19, 1930
    New York Times p. 31, Dec 2, 1930
Lady Jane (The Old Folks At Home)
  Productions:
    Opened September 10, 1934 for 40 performances.
  Reviews:
    Catholic World 140:90-1, Oct 1934
    Golden Book 20:506+, Nov 1934
    Literary Digest 118:20, Sep 22, 1934
    Nation 139:364, Sep 26, 1934
    New York Times p. 24, Sep 11, 1934
    Theatre Arts 18:817, Nov 1934
    Vanity Fair 43:49-50, Nov 1934

The Man In Possession
  Productions:
    Opened November 1, 1930 for 98 performances.
  Reviews:
    Catholic World 132:338-9, Dec 1930
    Commonweal 13:329, Jan 21, 1931
    Life (NY) 96:15, Nov 21, 1930
    New York Times VIII,p.4, Oct 12, 1930
                    p.19, Nov 3, 1930
    Theatre Magazine 53:25-6, Jan 1931
    Vogue 77:88, Jan 1, 1931
The Old Folks At Home (see Lady Jane)

The Pelican (with F. Tennyson Jesse)
  Productions:
    Opened September 21, 1925 for 65 performances.
  Reviews:
    Bookman 62:320, Nov 1925
    New York Times p.23, Sep 22, 1925
                    VII,p.1, Sep 27, 1925
    Theatre Magazine 42:18, Nov 1925
A Pin to See the Peepshow (with F. Tennyson Jesse)
  Productions:
    Opened September 27, 1953 for one performance.
  Reviews:
    New York Theatre Critics' Reviews 1953:278
    New York Times p.17, Sep 18, 1953
                    II,p.1, Nov 8, 1953
    New Yorker 29:79, Sep 26, 1953
    Newsweek 42:90, Sep 28, 1953
    Theatre Arts 37:19, Nov 1953
A Pinch Hitter
  Productions:
    Opened January 1, 1922 for 17 performances.
  Reviews:
    Life (NY) 79:18, Jun 22, 1922
    New York Clipper 70:24, Jun 7, 1922
    Theatre Magazine 36:71+, Aug 1922
Please Help Emily
  Productions:
    Opened August 14, 1916 for 40 performances.
  Reviews:
    Dramatic Mirror 76:8-9, Aug 19, 1916
    Dramatist 8:741-2, Oct 1916
    Nation 103:183, Aug 24, 1916
    New York Dramatic News 63:3+, Aug 19, 1916
    New York Times p.7, Aug 15, 1916
    Theatre Magazine 24:138, Sep 1916

Hauptmann, Gerhart
  Before Sundown (Before Sunset)
    Productions:
      (Off Broadway) Opened March 6, 1962 for 14 perform-
        ances.
    Reviews:
      New York Times p. 43, Mar 14, 1962
  Hannele (The Assumption of Hannele)
    Productions:
      Opened April 11, 1910 for 16 performances.
      Opened February 15, 1924 for three performances.
    Reviews:
      American Mercury 1:503, Apr 1924
      Bookman 31:417-18, Jun 1910
      Dramatic Mirror 63:7, Apr 23, 1910
      Green Book 2:1245-6, Jun 1910
      Hampton 24:829-30, Jun 1910
      Independent 112:106, Feb 16, 1924
      Life (NY) 55:766, Apr 28, 1910
      New Republic 38:21, Feb 27, 1924
      New York Times p. 16, Feb 16, 1924
      Theatre Magazine 11:139-41, May 1910
  Rose Bernd
    Productions:
      Opened September 26, 1922 for 87 performances.
    Reviews:
      Dial 73:584-5, Nov 1922
      Forum 68:974-5, Nov 1922
      Life (NY) 80:18, Oct 19, 1922
      Nation 115:392-4, Oct 11, 1922
            115:440, Oct 25, 1922
      New Republic 32:251-2, Nov 1, 1922
      New York Times p. 17, Sep 27, 1922
      Theatre Arts 17:27-8, Jan 1933
      Theatre Magazine 36:375, Dec 1922
  The Weavers
    Productions:
      Translated by Mary Morrison.   Opened December 14,
        1915 for 87 performances.
    Reviews:
      Book News 34:323-4, Mar 1916
      Bookman 42:647,650, Feb 1916
      Collier's 57:24, May 13, 1916
      Craftsman 20:531, Aug 1911
      Current Opinion 60:178-9, Mar 1916
      Dramatic Mirror 74:8, Dec 25, 1915
      Dramatist 7:654-6, Jan 1916

The Weavers (cont.)
    Harper's Weekly 62:16, Jun 1, 1916
    Hearst 29:372-4,386, May 1916
    Life (NY) 66:1282, Dec 30, 1915
    Nation 101:786, Dec 30, 1915
            115:392-4, Oct 11, 1922
    New Republic 5:200, Dec 25, 1915
    New York Times p.15, Dec 15, 1915
    North American Review 203:289, Feb 1916
    Survey 35:372, Jan 1, 1916
    Theatre Magazine 23:64, Feb 1916

Hiejermans, Herman
  The Devil to Pay
    Productions:
      Translated by Caroline Heijermans-Houwink and
        Lilian Saunders. Opened December 3, 1925 for
        11 performances.
    Reviews:
      New York Times p.26, Dec 4, 1925
                      IX,p.4, Dec 13, 1925
  The Good Hope
    Productions:
      Translated by Lilian Saunders and Caroline
        Heijermans-Houwink. Opened October 18, 1927 for
        49 performances.
    Reviews:
      Canadian Forum 12:198, Feb 1932
      Nation 125:185, Nov 2, 1927
      New Republic 52:285, Nov 2, 1927
      New York Times p.24, Oct 19, 1927
                      VIII,p.1, Oct 23, 1927
      Outlook 147:340, Nov 16, 1927
      Saturday Review 4:275-6, Nov 5, 1927
      Theatre Arts 11:895+, Dec 1927
      Theatre Magazine 47:70, Jan 1928
      Vogue 70:116, Dec 15, 1927

Hochhuth, Rolf
  The Deputy
    Productions:
      Adapted by Jerome Rothenberg. Opened February 26,
        1964 for 316 performances.
    Reviews:
      America 108:730-1, May 25, 1963
              109:70, Jul 20, 1963
              109:187, Aug 24, 1963

Houghton, Stanley
Fancy Free
  Productions:
    Opened March 14, 1913 in repertory for 115
    performances.

Fancy Free (cont.)
  Reviews:
      Blue Book 17:438-9, Jul 1913
      Bookman 37:310-11, May 1913
      Dramatic Mirror 69:6, Mar 19, 1913
Hindle Wakes (Fanny Hawthorne)
  Productions:
      Opened December 9, 1912 for 32 performances.
      Opened May 11, 1922 for 36 performances.
  Reviews:
      American Playwright 2:5, Jan 1913
      Bookman 36:641, Feb 1913
      Colliers 50:7, Dec 28, 1912
      Current Opinion 55:169-72, Sep 1913
      Dramatist 4:323, Jan 1913
      Everybody's Magazine 28:394-7, Mar 1913
      Green Book 9:249, Feb 1913
      Life (NY) 60:2492-3, Dec 19, 1912
      McClure's Magazine 40:64-5+, Mar 1913
      New York Times p. 22, May 12, 1922
      Red Book 21:115, May 1913
      Theatre Magazine 17:2-3, Jan 1913
Phipps
  Productions:
      Opened September 27, 1913 in repertory.
      Opened October 17, 1914 in repertory.
  Reviews:
      Dramatic Mirror 72:8, Oct 28, 1914
      Green Book 13:125, Jan 1915
      Theatre Magazine 20:267, Dec 1914
The Younger Generation
  Productions:
      Opened September 25, 1913 for 60 performances.
  Reviews:
      Bookman 38:266, Nov 1913
      Dramatic Mirror 70:6, Oct 1, 1913
      Dramatist 5:396, Oct 1913
      Everybody's 29:809, Dec 1913
      Life (NY) 62:612, Oct 9, 1913
      New York Times p. 11, Sep 26, 1913
      Theatre Magazine 18:145, Nov 1913

Housman, Laurence
  Prunella (with Harley Granville-Barker and J. Moorat)
  Productions:
      Opened October 27, 1913 for 104 performances.
  Reviews:

American Mercury 77:33-4, Mar 1914
Bookman 38:363, Dec 1913
Current Opinion 56:24-8, Jan 14, 1914
Dramatic Mirror 70:6, Oct 29, 1913
Everybody's 30:264, Feb 1914
Green Book 11:71-2, Jan 1914
                 11:165-6, Jan 1914
Harper's Bazaar 49:37+, Mar 1914
International 7:364+, Dec 1913
Leslie's Weekly 117:495, Nov 20, 1913
Life (NY) 62:790-1, Nov 6, 1913
Literary Digest 47:944-5, Nov 15, 1913
Munsey 50:726-7, Jan 1914
New York Times p. 9, Oct 27, 1913
Theatre Magazine 18:174-5+, Dec 1913

Victoria Regina
  Productions:
    Opened December 26, 1935 for 517 performances.
    Opened October 3, 1938 for 87 performances.
  Reviews:
    Catholic World 142:598-9, Feb 1936
    Commonweal 23:301, Jan 10, 1936
    Harper's 172:1-2, Apr 1936
    Literary Digest 121:19, Jan 11, 1936
    Life 4:62-4, Apr 11, 1938
    Nation 142:83-4, Jan 15, 1936
    New Republic 85:286, Jan 15, 1936
    New York Times p. 25, Sep 5, 1935
                  p. 30, Dec 13, 1935
                   p. 15, Dec 27, 1935
                   IX, p. 1, Jan 5, 1936
                   p. 20, Oct 4, 1938
    Newsweek 6:25, Dec 28, 1935
    Pictorial Review 37: 50, Apr 1936
    Stage 13:41-3, Jan 1936
         13:6, Feb 1936
    Theatre Arts 20:86+, Feb 1936
              20:467, Dec 1936
              22:386, May 1938
    Time 26:22, Dec 30, 1935
    Vogue 89:70-1+, May 15, 1937

Huxley, Aldous
  Genius and the Goddess (with Beth Wendel in collaboration
    with Alec Coppell)
    Productions:
      Opened December 10, 1957 for seven performances.

Genius and the Goddess (cont.)
  Reviews:
    New York Theatre Critics' Reviews 1957:153
    New York Times p.41, Dec 11, 1957
    New Yorker 33:42-3, Dec 21, 1957
    Saturday Review 40:22, Dec 28, 1957
    Theatre Arts 42:24, Feb 1958

Ibsen, Henrik
A Doll's House
  Productions:
    Opened April 29, 1918 for 32 performances.
    Adapted by Thornton Wilder. Opened December 27,
      1937 for 144 performances.
    (Off Broadway) Adapted by Carmel Ross. Translated
      by R. Farquharson Sharpe. Opened February 2,
      1963 for 66 performances.
  Reviews:
    Catholic World 146:596-7, Feb 1938
    Dramatic Mirror 78:656, May 11, 1918
    Green Book 20:11-13, Jul 1918
    Literary Digest 125:22-3, Jan 15, 1938
    Living Age 320:415-16, Mar 1, 1924
    Nation 146:53-4, Jan 8, 1938
    New Republic 93:338, Jan 26, 1938
    New York Times p.13, Apr 30, 1918
                    IV,p.8, May 5, 1918
                    p.28, Dec 28, 1937
                    p.5, Feb 4, 1963
    New Yorker 38:68+, Feb 9, 1963
    Newsweek 11:28, Jan 10, 1938
             61:56, Feb 18, 1963
    One Act Play Magazine 1:845-7, Jan 1938
    Player's Magazine 14:12, Sep-Oct 1937
    Scribner's Magazine 103:71, Mar 1938
    Stage 15:55, Feb 1938
    Theatre Arts 20:170, Mar 1936
                 22:92+, Feb 1938
                 22:384, May 1938
                 47:12-13, Apr 1963
    Theatre Magazine 12:41-4, Aug 1910
                     27:358, Jun 1918
    Time 31:32, Jan 10, 1938
An Enemy of the People
  Productions:
    November 1923 in repertory (Moscow Art Theatre).
    Opened October 3, 1927 for 127 performances.

Opened November 5, 1928 for 16 performances.
Opened February 15, 1937 for 16 performances.
Adapted by Arthur Miller. Opened December 28, 1950
   for 36 performances.
Reviews:
   Catholic World 172:387, Feb 1951
   Christian Science Monitor Magazine p. 6, Jan 6, 1951
   Commonweal 53:374, Jan 19, 1951
   Commonweal 53:374, Jan 19, 1951
   Independent 104:1, Oct 2, 1920
   Nation 125:430-1, Oct 19, 1927
            144:249, Feb 27, 1937
            172:18, Jan 6, 1951
   New Republic 90:139, Mar 10, 1937
                124:22, Jan 22, 1951
   New York Theatre Critics' Reviews 1950:154
   New York Times p. 25, Dec 4, 1923
                  p. 32, Oct 4, 1927
                  p. 19, Feb 16, 1937
                  p. 14, Dec 29, 1950
                  II, p. 1, Jan 7, 1951
   New Yorker 26:44, Jan 13, 1951
              34:68+, Feb 14, 1959
   Newsweek 37:67, Jan 8, 1951
   Outlook 147:279, Nov 2, 1927
   Saturday Review 42:34, Feb 21, 1959
   School and Society 73:105, Feb 17, 1951
   Theatre Arts 11:884+, Dec 1927
                35:15, Mar 1951
   Theatre Magazine 46:42, Dec 1927
   Time 57:31, Jan 8, 1951
   Vogue 70:172, Dec 1, 1927
   Weekly Review 3:274, Sep 29, 1920
Ghosts
 Productions:
   Opened March 4, 1912 for 4 performances.
   Opened April 20, 1915 for 2 performances.
   Translated by William Archer. May 7, 1917 in
      repertory (Washington Square Players).
   Opened February 7, 1919 for 1 performance.
   Opened Winter 1922 for 21 performances.
   November 29, 1923 in repertory for 2 performances.
   Opened March 16, 1926 for 34 performances.
   Translated by William Archer, revised by Harrison
      Grey Fishe. Opened January 10, 1927 for 24 per-
      formances.
   Opened May 23, 1933 for 6 performances.

<u>Ghosts</u> (cont.)
Opened December 12, 1935 for 81 performances.
Translated by Eva Le Gallienne. Opened February 24, 1948 for 10 performances.
(Off Broadway) Adapted by Carmel Ross. Translated by R. Farquharson Sharpe. Opened September 21, 1961 for 216 performances.
Reviews:
America 106:29, Oct 7, 1961
American Mercury 10:376, Mar 1927
Bookman 65:205, Apr 1927
Catholic World 142:601, Feb 1936
Commonweal 23:244, Dec 27, 1935
            75:94, Oct 20, 1961
Dramatic Mirror 73:8, Apr 1, 1915
                 77:7, May 19, 1917
                 80:304, Mar 1, 1919
Dramatist 17:1322, Oct 1926
Life (NY) 69:892, May 17, 1917
Nation 166:256, Feb 28, 1948
       193:459, Dec 2, 1961
New Republic 11:83, May 19, 1917
              85:230, Jan 1, 1936
              145:30-1, Oct 9, 1961
New York Theatre Critics' Reviews 1948:343
New York Times p. 4, Apr 16, 1915
                   p. 9, May 8, 1917
                   p. 13, Feb 8, 1919
                   p. 12, Feb 7, 1922
                   p. 14, Nov 7, 1923
                   VII,p. 1, Jan 16, 1927
                   p. 24, May 24, 1933
                   p. 30, Dec 13, 1935
                   p. 28, May 12, 1936
                   p. 31, Feb 17, 1948
                   p. 29, Sep 22, 1961
New Yorker 37:120+, Sep 30, 1961
Newsweek 6:39, Dec 21, 1935
Theatre Arts 20:97-8, Feb 1936
            45:59-60, Nov 1961
Theatre Magazine 25:340, Jun 1917
                29:144, Mar 1919
Time 26:32, Dec 23, 1935
       78:88, Oct 6, 1961
<u>Hedda Gabler</u>
Productions:
Opened April 8, 1918 for 24 performances.

Opened May 16, 1924 for 8 performances.
Translated by William Archer. Opened January 26,
   1926 for 59 performances.
Translated by Julie Le Gallienne and Paul Leyssac.
   Opened March 26, 1928 for 15 performances.
Opened February 2, 1929 for 25 performances.
Opened November 16, 1936 for 32 performances.
Translated by Ethel Borden and Mary Cass Canfield.
   Opened January 29, 1942 for 12 performances.
Translated by Eva Le Gallienne. Opened February 24,
   1948 for 15 performances.
(Off Broadway) Translated by Michael Meyer.
   Opened November 9, 1960 for 340 performances.
Reviews:
Catholic World 144:469, Jan 1937
Commonweal 9:460, Feb 20, 1929
            21:207, Dec 14, 1934
            25:134, Nov 27, 1936
            35:417, Feb 13, 1942
            74:304-5, Jun 16, 1961
Dramatic Mirror 78:585, Apr 17, 1918
                78:548, Apr 20, 1918
                p.635, Oct 9, 1920
Forum 52:765-9, Nov 1914
Green Book 6:1211-18, Dec 1911
Nation 139:720, Dec 19, 1934
       143:641-2, Nov 28, 1936
       154:202, Feb 14, 1942
       191:462-3, Dec 10, 1960
New Republic 14:359, Apr 20, 1918
             39:49, Jun 4, 1924
             45:356-7, Feb 17, 1926
             106:204, Feb 9, 1942
             106:238, Feb 16, 1942
             143:39, Nov 28, 1960
New York Theatre Critics' Reviews 1942:358+
                                  1948:327
New York Times IV,p.6, Apr 14, 1918
               p.18, May 17, 1924
               p.30, Mar 27, 1928
               p.20, Feb 4, 1929
               p.34, Nov 17, 1936
               p.22, Jan 30, 1942
               p.27, Feb 25, 1948
               p.61, Nov 10, 1960
               p.24, Nov 25, 1960
New Yorker 36:94+, Nov 19, 1960

Hedda Gabler (cont.)
        38:175-6, Dec 15, 1962
     Newsweek 8:19, Nov 28, 1936
     Outlook 151:299, Feb 20, 1929
     Review 1:525-6, Oct 25, 1919
     Saturday Review 44:27, Jan 28, 1961
     Theatre Arts 21:11, Jan 1937
               26:226, Apr 1942
               27:50-1, Jan 1943
               45:72, Jan 1961
     Theatre Magazine 27:287, May 1918
                   27:349, Jun 1918
                   43:14-15, Apr 1926
                   47:65, Jun 1928
     Vogue 73:104, Mar 30, 1929
     Weekly Review 3:427-8, Nov 3, 1920
John Gabriel Borkman
  Productions:
     Opened April 1, 1915 for 3 performances.
     Translated by Eva Le Gallienne. Opened January 29,
       1926 for 7 performances.
     Opened November 9, 1926 for 15 performances.
     Opened November 12, 1946 for 21 performances.
  Reviews:
     Catholic World 164:360, Jan 1947
     Commonweal 45:167, Nov 29, 1946
     Current Opinion 58:408-9, Jun 1915
     Dramatic Mirror 73:8, Apr 21, 1915
     Harper's Weekly 60:419, May 1, 1915
     Life 21:109, Dec 21, 1946
     Nation 163:629, Nov 30, 1946
     New Republic 2:285, Apr 17, 1915
                 115:726, Dec 2, 1946
     New York Theatre Critics' Reviews 1946:263
     New York Times p. 13, Apr 14, 1915
                 p. 13, Jan 30, 1926
                 p. 24, Nov 10, 1926
                 p. 33, Nov 13, 1946
     New Yorker 22:57, Nov 23, 1946
     Newsweek 29:94, Nov 25, 1946
     Review 2:494+, May 8, 1920
     Saturday Review 29:30, Nov 30, 1946
     Theatre Arts 31:23+, Jan 1947
     Theatre Magazine 21:281, Jun 1915
     Time 48:55, Nov 25, 1946
The Lady from the Sea
  Productions:

November 6, 1911 in repertory.
Opened March 18, 1929 for 24 performances.
Opened May 1, 1934 for 15 performances.
Opened August 7, 1950 for 16 performances.
Reviews:
    Bookman 35:362+, Dec 1911
    Catholic World 139:344-5, Jun 1934
               172:69-70, Oct 1950
    Commonweal 9:626-7, Apr 3, 1929
    Dramatic Mirror 66:7, Nov 15, 1911
    Life (NY) 58:902, Nov 23, 1911
    Nation 171:174, Aug 19, 1950
    New Republic 36:309-11, Nov 14, 1923
              79:22, May 16, 1934
            123:23, Aug 28, 1950
    New York Times p. 36, Mar 19, 1929
              p. 25, May 2, 1934
              p. 23, Aug 8, 1950
    Theatre Magazine 14:186, Dec 1911

Little Eyolf

Productions:
Opened April 18, 1910 for 48 performances.
Opened February 2, 1926 for 8 performances.
(Off Broadway) Translated by R. V. Forslund.
    Opened March 16, 1964 for 33 performances.
Reviews:
    Bookman 31:416-17, Jun 1910
    Collier's 45:34, May 7, 1910
    Dramatic Mirror 63:8, Apr 30, 1910
    Hampton 24:828, Jun 1910
    Harper's Weekly 54:24, May 21, 1910
    Life (NY) 55:766, Apr 28, 1910
    Metropolitan Magazine 32:532-3, Jul 1910
    Nation 198:355-6, Apr 6, 1964
    New Republic 45:356-7, Feb 17, 1926
    New York Times p. 22, Feb 3, 1926
              p. 31, Mar 17, 1964
    New Yorker 40:138, Mar 28, 1964
    Theatre Magazine 11:201, Jun 1910

The Master Builder

Productions:
Opened November 10, 1925 for 76 performances (Eva
    Le Gallienne).
Opened November 1, 1926 for 29 performances.
Week of September 16, 1929 in repertory.
Adapted by Max Faber. Opened March 1, 1955 for
    40 performances.

The Master Builder (cont.)
 Reviews:
     America 93:25-6, Apr 2, 1955
     Catholic World 122:663-4, Feb 1926
                    181:68, Apr 1955
     Commonweal 62:127, May 6, 1955
     Nation 123:513-14, Nov 17, 1926
            180:246, Mar 19, 1955
     New Republic 132:27-8, Mar 14, 1955
     New York Theatre Critics' Reviews 1955:349
     New York Times p. 27, Nov 11, 1925
                    VIII,p. 1, Nov 15, 1925
                    p. 35, Nov 2, 1926
                    p. 23, Mar 2, 1955
                    II,p. 1, Mar 20, 1955
     New Yorker 31:64+, Mar 12, 1955
     North American Review 196:254-63, Aug 1912
     Review 2:65, Jun 17, 1920
     Saturday Review 38:30, Apr 2, 1955
     Theatre Arts 39:87, May 1955
Peer Gynt
 Productions:
     Translated by William Archer and Charles Archer.
     Opened February 5, 1923 for 120 performances.
     English version by Paul Green. Opened January 28,
     1951 for 32 performances.
     English version by Norman Ginsburg. Opened
     January 12, 1960 for 32 performances.
 Reviews:
     Bookman 57:192-3, Apr 1923
     Catholic World 172:464, Mar 1951
     Commonweal 53:468-9, Feb 16, 1951
     Dial 74:420-1, Apr 1923
     Dramatist 13:1120-21, Jul 1922
     Freeman 7:16-17, Mar 14, 1923
     Independent 110:141-2, Feb 17, 1923
     Literary Digest 76:30-1, Mar 3, 1923
     Modern Language Notes 29:233-9, Dec 1914
     Nation 116:258, Feb 28, 1923
            172:139-40, Feb 10, 1951
            190:106, Jan 30, 1960
     New Republic 34:46-7, Mar 7, 1923
                  124:22-3, Mar 5, 1951
                  142:21, Feb 1, 1960
     New York Clipper 71:14, Feb 14, 1923
     New York Theatre Critics' Reviews 1951:373
                                       1960:393

134

New York Times p. 14, Feb 6, 1923
                VII, p. 1, Feb 11, 1923
                p. 15, Jan 29, 1951
                II, p. 1, Feb 4, 1951
                p. 21, Jan 13, 1960
                II, p. 1, Jan 24, 1960
New Yorker 26:61, Feb 10, 1951
           35:72+, Jan 23, 1960
School and Society 73:184, Mar 24, 1951
Theatre Arts 19:908-9, Dec 1935
           29:147, Mar 1945
           35:14, Apr 1951
Theatre Magazine 37:15+, Apr 1923
Time 44:70, Sep 18, 1944

Pillars of Society

Productions:
Opened March 28, 1910 for 16 performances.
Opened October 14, 1931 for 2 performances.

Reviews:
Bookman 31:414-17, Jun 1910
Commonweal 14:639-40, Oct 28, 1931
Dramatic Mirror 63:6, Apr 9, 1910
           69:6-7, Feb 12, 1913
Everybody's 22:849-50, Jun 1910
Green Book 3:1244-5, Jun 1910
Life (NY) 55:680-1, Apr 14, 1910
Metropolitan Magazine 32:401, Jun 1910
New York Times p. 17, Oct 15, 1931
Theatre Arts 15:989-90, Dec 1931
Theatre Magazine 11:129-33+, May 1910

Rosmersholm

Productions:
Translated by Charles Archer. Opened May 5, 1925
for 30 performances.
Translated by Eva Le Gallienne. Opened December 2,
1935 for 8 performances.
(Off Broadway) Translated by Carmel Ross. Opened
April 11, 1962 for 119 performances.

Reviews:
Bookman 61:578-9, Jul 1925
Commonweal 23:218, Dec 20, 1935
           76:175+, May 11, 1962
Nation 120:579-80, May 20, 1925
          194:407-8, May 5, 1962
New Republic 146:20-2, Apr 30, 1962
New York Times p. 27, May 6, 1925
           p. 32, Dec 3, 1935

Rosmersholm (cont.)
                        p. 42, Apr 12, 1962
                        II, p. 1, Apr 22, 1962
        New Yorker 38:85-7, Apr 21, 1962
        Theatre Arts 46:59+, Jun 1962
        Yale Review 5:120-1, Oct 1915
The Vikings of Helgeland (Vikings)
    Productions:
        Opened May 12, 1930 for 8 performances.
    Reviews:
        Commonweal 12:109, May 28, 1930
        Nation 130:633, May 28, 1930
        New Republic 63:42-3, May 28, 1930
        New York Times p. 27, May 13, 1930
        Theatre Arts 12:638-41, Sep 1928
        Theatre Magazine 52:42, Jul 1930
When We Dead Awaken
    Productions:
        (Off Broadway) Opened April 18, 1966 for 8
        performances.
    Reviews:
        New York Times p. 37, Apr 19, 1966
        Review 1:568, Nov 8, 1919
The Wild Duck
    Productions:
        Opened March 11, 1918 for 32 performances.
        Opened February 24, 1925 for 103 performances.
        Translated by William Archer. Opened November 19,
        1928 for 80 performances.
        Opened April 16, 1938 for 3 performances.
        Adapted by Max Faber. Opened December 26, 1951
        for 15 performances.
    Reviews:
        Bellman 24:604-6, Jun 1, 1918
        Bookman 61:337, May 1925
                62:678-81, Feb 1926
        Catholic World 174:464, Mar 1952
        Commonweal 55:349, Jan 11, 1952
        Dial 78:430-3, May 1925
        Dramatic Mirror 78:5, Mar 23, 1918
        Green Book 19:969+, Jun 1918
        Life (NY) 71:474-5, Mar 21, 1918
                85:18, Mar 19, 1925
                92:13, Dec 14, 1928
        Nation 106:328-9, Mar 21, 1918
                120:299, Mar 18, 1925
        New Republic 9:356, Jan 27, 1917

               14:238, Mar 23, 1918
               42:70-1, Mar 11, 1925
               126:23, Jan 21, 1952
     New York Theatre Critics' Reviews 1951:128
     New York Times p. 11, Mar 12, 1918
                    IV,p. 12, Mar 17, 1918
                    IX,p. 2, Apr 19, 1925
                    p. 17, Nov 17, 1928
                    p. 16, Apr 16, 1938
                    p. 17, Dec 27, 1951
     Theatre Arts 15:634-7, Aug 1931
                  36:70, Mar 1952
     Theatre Magazine 27:217, Apr 1918
     Time 59:44, Jan 7, 1952

Ionesco, Eugene
  The Bald Soprano
    Productions:
      (Off Broadway) Season of 1958-59.
      (Off Broadway) Translated by Donald M. Allen.
      Opened September 17, 1963, for 40 performances.
    Reviews:
      Catholic World 187:387, Aug 1958
      Nation 187:59, Aug 2, 1958
      New York Times p. 39, Jun 3, 1958
                     p. 35, Sep 18, 1963
      New Yorker 39:94+, Sep 28, 1963
      Newsweek 62:60, Sep 30, 1963
  The Chairs
    Productions:
      Translated by Donald T. Watson.   Opened January 9,
        1958 for 22 performances.
    Reviews:
      Catholic World 186:469, Mar 1958
      Christian Century 75:137, Jan 29, 1958
      Nation 195:17, Jul 6, 1957
      New York Theatre Critics' Reviews 1958:397
      New York Times p. 20, Jan 10, 1958
      New Yorker 33:68, Jan 18, 1958
      Newsweek 51:84, Jan 20, 1958
      Saturday Review 41:26, Jan 25, 1958
      Theatre Arts 42:14, Mar 1958
      Time 71:42, Jan 20, 1958
  Jack
    Productions:
      (Off Broadway) Season of 1958-1959.
    Reviews:

Jack (cont.)
    Nation 187:59, Aug 2, 1958
    New York Times p. 39, Jun 4, 1958
The Killer
    Productions:
        (Off Broadway) Translated by Donald Watson. Opened
            March 22, 1960 for 16 performances.
        (Off Broadway) Opened February 11, 1962 in repertory.
    Reviews:
        New York Times p. 33, Mar 23, 1960
                        II, p. 1, Apr 3, 1960
        New Yorker 36:82+, Apr 2, 1960
        Saturday Review 43:37, Apr 9, 1960
The Lesson
    Productions:
        Translated by Donald Watson. Opened January 9,
            1958 for 22 performances.
        (Off Broadway) Translated by Donald M. Allen.
            Opened September 17, 1963 for 40 performances.
    Reviews:
        Catholic World 186:468-9, Mar 1958
        Christian Century 75:137, Jan 29, 1958
        Nation 196:87, Jan 25, 1958
        New York Theatre Critics' Reviews 1958:397
        New York Times p. 20, Jan 10, 1958
                        p. 35, Sep 18, 1963
        New Yorker 33:68, Jan 18, 1958
                   39:96, Sep 28, 1963
        Newsweek 51:84, Jan 20, 1958
        Saturday Review 41:26, Jan 25, 1958
        Theatre Arts 42:14, Mar 1958
        Time 71:42, Jan 20, 1958
The New Tenant
    Productions:
        (Off Broadway) Season of 1959-1960.
        (Off Broadway) Translated by Donald Watson. Opened
            May 24, 1964 for 32 performances.
    Reviews:
        Nation 185:439, Dec 7, 1957
        New York Times p. 40, May 28, 1964
Rhinoceros
    Productions:
        Translated by Derth Prouse. Opened January 9,
            1961 for 240 performances.
        Translated by Derth Prouse. Opened September 18,
            1961 for 16 performances.
    Reviews:

America 104:576-7, Jan 28, 1961
        104:593-5, Feb 4, 1961
Americás 17:6-10, Feb 1965
Catholic World 192:380-1, Mar 1961
Christian Century 78:274, Mar 1, 1961
Nation 192:85-6, Jan 28, 1961
National Review 10:157-8, Mar 11, 1961
New Republic 144:22-3, Jan 30, 1961
New York Theatre Critics' Reviews 1961:397
New York Times p. 27, Jan 10, 1961
              II, p. 1, Jan 22, 1961
New Yorker 36:103, May 28, 1960
        36:66+, Jan 21, 1961
Newsweek 57:57, Jan 23, 1961
Saturday Review 44:51, Jan 21, 1961
Theatre Arts 45:9-10, Mar 1961
Time 75:56, May 23, 1960
     77:77, Jan 20, 1961

Victims of Duty
  Productions:
    (Off Broadway) Season of 1959-1960.
    (Off Broadway) Translated by Donald Watson. Opened
      May 24, 1964 for 32 performances.
  Reviews:
    New York Times p. 40, May 28, 1964
    New Yorker 40:88-9, Jun 6, 1964

Jerome, Helen
  Pride and Prejudice
    Productions:
      Opened November 5, 1935 for 219 performances.
    Reviews:
      Catholic World 144:469-71, Jan 1937
      Commonweal 25:220, Dec 18, 1936
      Literary Digest 120:20, Nov 16, 1935
      Nation 141:603-4, Nov 20, 1935
      New Republic 85:134, Dec 11, 1935
      New York Times p. 19, Oct 23, 1935
                X, p. 1, Nov 3, 1935
                p. 32, Nov 6, 1935
                IX, p. 2, Nov 10, 1935
                IX, p. 1, Nov 17, 1935
      Newsweek 6:19, Nov 16, 1935
      Stage 13:7-8, Dec 1935
      Theatre Arts 20:7-9+, Jan 1936
      Time 26:40, Nov 18, 1935
      Vanity Fair 45:44+, Jan 1937

Job, Thomas
  Barchester Towers
    Productions:
      Opened November 30, 1937 for 40 performances.
    Reviews:
      Catholic World 146:469-70, Jan 1938
      Commonweal 27:220, Dec 17, 1937
      New Republic 93:170-1, Dec 15, 1937
      New York Times p.26, Nov 19, 1937
                    XI,p.3, Nov 28, 1937
                    p.27, Dec 1, 1937
      Newsweek 10:31, Dec 13, 1937
      Stage 15:54+, Jan 1938
      Theatre Arts 22:8+, Jan 1938
      Time 30:57, Dec 13, 1937
  Land's End
    Productions:
      Opened December 11, 1946 for 5 performances.
    Reviews:
      New York Theatre Critics' Reviews 1946:222
      New York Times p.37, Dec 12, 1946
      New Yorker 22:41, Dec 21, 1946
      Theatre Arts 31:16, Feb 1947
  Therese (Guilty)
    Productions:
      Opened October 9, 1945 for 96 performances.
    Reviews:
      Catholic World 162:168, Nov 1945
      Commonweal 43:45, Oct 26, 1945
      Life 19:57-60, Oct 22, 1945
      Nation 161:413, Oct 20, 1945
      New Republic 113:573, Oct 29, 1945
      New York Theatre Critics' Reviews 1945:146
      New York Times p.24, Oct 10, 1945
                    II,p.1, Oct 28, 1945
      New Yorker 21:46, Oct 20, 1945
      Newsweek 26:93, Oct 22, 1945
      Saturday Review 28:22-4, Oct 20, 1945
      Theatre Arts 29:683-4, Dec 1945
      Time 46:70, Oct 22, 1945
  Uncle Harry
    Productions:
      Opened May 20, 1942 for 430 performances.
    Reviews:
      Catholic World 155:471-2, Jul 1942
      Independent Woman 21:378, Dec 1942
      Life 12:45-6+, Jun 29, 1942
      New York Theatre Critics' Reviews 1942:284

New York Times p. 24, May 21, 1942
New Republic 106:798, Jun 8, 1942
Newsweek 17:67, Jun 1, 1942
Theatre Arts 26:421-2, Jul 1942
Time 39:34, Jun 1, 1942

Johnston, Denis
  The Moon in the Yellow River
    Productions:
      Opened February 29, 1932 for 40 performances.
      (Off Broadway) Opened February 6, 1961 for 48
        performances.
    Reviews:
      Arts and Decoration 37:46, May 1932
      America 104:768, Mar 11, 1961
      Bookman 74:665, Mar 1932
      Catholic World 135:74, Apr 1932
      Commonweal 15:550, Mar 16, 1932
      Nation 134:319, Mar 16, 1932
             192:193-4, Mar 4, 1961
      New Republic 70:127, Mar 16, 1932
      New York Times p. 19, Mar 1, 1932
                     VIII, p. 1, Mar 13, 1932
                     II, p. 3, Feb 5, 1961
                     p. 40, Feb 7, 1961
      New Yorker 37:93-4, Feb 18, 1961
      Outlook 160:229, Apr 1932
      Theatre Arts 16:354, May 1932
                   45:84, Apr 1961
      Theatre Guild Magazine 9:36-8, Apr 1932
      Vanity Fair 38:26, 66, Jun 1932
      Vogue 79:61, 88, May 1, 1932
  The Old Lady Says "No!"
    Productions:
      Opened February 17, 1948 for 8 performances.
    Reviews:
      Catholic World 167:72, Apr 1948
      Commonweal 47:520, Mar 5, 1948
      New Republic 118:24, Mar 1, 1948
      New York Theatre Critics Reviews 1948:342
      New York Times p. 35, Feb 18, 1948
                     II, p. 1, Feb 22, 1948
      New Yorker 24:49, Feb 28, 1948
      Time 51:63, Mar 1, 1948

Jones, Henry Arthur
  Cock O' the Walk

Cock O' the Walk (cont.)
    Productions:
    Opened December 27, 1915 for 72 performances.
    Reviews:
    American Mercury 81:90, May 1916
    Bookman 42:651, Feb 1916
    Collier's 57:24, May 13, 1916
    Dramatic Mirror 74:11, Oct 16, 1915
                    75:8, Jan 1, 1916
    Dramatist 7:614, Oct 1915
    Green Book 15:442-3, Mar 1916
    Harper's Weekly, 61:427, Oct 30, 1915
    Nation 102:26-7, Jan 6, 1916
    New York Dramatic News 62:19, Jan 1, 1916
    Theatre Magazine 23:64, 67, Feb 1916
The Goal
    Productions:
    In repertory beginning October 17, 1914. (Princess
        Players).
    Reviews:
    Bookman 40:416, Dec 1914
    Dramatic Mirror 72:8, Oct 28, 1914
    Green Book 13:124, Jan 1915
The Liars
    Productions:
    Opened November 9, 1915 in repertory.
    Reviews:
    Dramatic Mirror 74:8, Nov 20, 1915
    Harper's Weekly 61:515, Nov 27, 1915
    Life (NY) 66:1008-9, Nov 25, 1915
    Nation 101:605, Nov 18, 1915
    New York Times p. 13, Nov 10, 1915

The Lie
    Productions:
    Opened December 24, 1914 for 172 performances.
    Reviews:
    Bookman 40:638-9, Feb 1915
    Book News 33:303-4, Feb 1915
    Current Opinion 58:99, Feb 1915
    Dramatic Mirror 73:8, Jan 6, 1915
    Dramatist 6:552-5, Apr 1915
    Green Book 13:567-8, Mar 1915
    Hearst 28:126-9, Aug 1915
    Life (NY) 65:68-9, Jan 14, 1915
    Munsey 54:324+, Mar 1915
    Nation 99:783, Dec 31, 1914

New Republic 1:25, Jan 16, 1915
New York Times p. 11, Dec 25, 1914
Theatre Magazine 21:56, 59, Feb 1915

Lydia Gilmore

Productions:
Opened February 1, 1912 for 12 performances.
Reviews:
American Playwright 1:42, Feb 1912
Bookman 35:170, Apr 1912
Dramatic Mirror 67:6-7, Feb 7, 1912
Everybody's 26:681, Mar 1912
Green Book 7:799, Apr 1912
Life (NY) 59:348, Feb 15, 1912
Munsey 47:126-7, Apr 1912
Theatre Magazine 15:74+, Mar 1912

Mary Goes First

Productions:
Opened November 2, 1914 for 32 performances.
Reviews:
American Playwright 3:392, Dec 1914
Bookman 40:414, Dec 1914
Dramatic Mirror 72:8, Nov 11, 1914
Dramatist 6:515, Oct 1914
Life (NY) 64:904, Nov 19, 1914
Nation 99:530, Oct 29, 1914
99:587, Nov 12, 1914
New York Times I, p. 7, Nov 4, 1914
Theatre Magazine 20:300, Dec 1914

Mrs. Dane's Defense

Productions:
Opened February 6, 1928 for 16 performances.
Reviews:
Green Book 7:305-10, Feb 1912
New York Times p. 30, Feb 7, 1928
Theatre Arts 31:28+, Mar 1947
Theatre Magazine 47:48, Apr 1928

We Can't Be As Bad As That

Productions:
Opened December 30, 1910 for 19 performances.
Reviews:
Bookman 23:607, Feb 1911
Canadian Magazine 36:476-8, Mar 1911
Columbian 3:1079-81, Mar 1911
Dramatic Mirror 65:11, Jan 4, 1911
Life (NY) 57:124, Jan 12, 1911
Munsey 44:710, Feb 1911
Red Book 16:949-52, Mar 1911

We Can't Be As Bad As That (cont.)
    Theatre Magazine 13:35-7, Feb 1911

Joyce, James
Exiles
    Productions:
        Opened February 19, 1925 for 41 performances.
    Reviews:
        American Mercury 4:501, Apr 1925
        Life (NY) 85:20, Mar 12, 1925
        Nation 107:430-1, Oct 12, 1918
                120:272, Mar 11, 1925
        New Republic 16:318-19, Oct 12, 1918
        New York Times p. 20, Feb 20, 1925

Kaiser, Georg
From Morn to Midnight
    Productions:
        Translated by Ashley Dukes. Opened May 14, 1922
        in repertory.
        Opened June 26, 1922 for 24 performances.
    Reviews:
        Bookman 55:598, Aug 1922
        Dial 73:116-17, Jul 1922
        Dramatist 14:1141, Jan 1923
        Nation 114:726, Jun 14, 1922
        New Republic 31:189, Jul 12, 1922
        Theatre Magazine 36:71, 94, Aug 1922
The Phantom Lover (Oktobertag)
    Productions:
        Translated by Herman Bernstein and Adolph E. Meyer.
        Opened September 4, 1928 for 15 performances.
    Reviews:
        Life (NY) 92:11, Sep 21, 1928
        New York Times p. 25, Sep 5, 1928

Kapek, Karel (see Capek, Karel)

Katayev, Valentin
Squaring the Circle
    Productions:
        Adapted by Dimitri Ostrow. Translated by Charles
        Malamuth and Eugene Lyons. Opened October 3,
        1935 for 108 performances.
    Reviews:
        Catholic World 142:213, Nov 1935
        Literary Digest 120:23, Aug 31, 1935

Nation 141:490, Oct 23, 1935
      141:590, Nov 20, 1935
Newsweek 6:29, Oct 12, 1935
New York Times X, p. 3, Sep 22, 1935
      X, p. 3, Sep 29, 1935
Saturday Review 12:16, Oct 12, 1935
Theatre Arts 18:418, Jun 1934
      19:900, Dec 1935
Time 26:45, Oct 14, 1935
Vanity Fair 45:68, Dec 1935

Knott, Frederick
Dial "M" for Murder
  Productions:
    Opened October 29, 1952 for 522 performances.
  Reviews:
    Catholic World 176:229, Dec 1952
    Commonweal 57:164, Nov 21, 1952
    Life 33:73-6, Nov 10, 1952
    Nation 175:454, Nov 15, 1952
    New York Theatre Critics' Reviews 1952:215
    New York Times p. 41, Oct 30, 1952
           II, p. 1, Nov 30, 1952
           II, p. 1, Nov 8, 1953
           II, p. 3, Nov 15, 1953
    Newsweek 40:94, Nov 10, 1952
    Saturday Review 35:30, Nov 15, 1952
      36:5, Aug 1, 1953
    Theatre Arts 37:22-3, Jan 1953
      37:66-7, Jun 1953
    Time 60:71, Nov 10, 1952
Wait Until Dark
  Productions:
    Opened February 2, 1966 for 373 performances.
  Reviews:
    Look 30:112-13+, May 17, 1966
    New York Theatre Critics' Reviews 1966:376
    New York Times p. 21, Feb 3, 1966
    Newsweek 67:88, Feb 14, 1966
    Saturday Review 49:52-3, Feb 19, 1966
    Time 87:66, Feb 11, 1966
Write Me A Murder
  Productions:
    Opened October 26, 1961 for 196 performances.
  Reviews:
    America 106:375, Dec 9, 1961
    New York Theatre Critics' Reviews 1961:194

Write Me A Murder (cont.)
New York Times p.28, Oct 27, 1961
New Yorker 37:126+, Nov 4, 1961
Newsweek 58:69, Nov 6, 1961
Saturday Review 44:39, Nov 18, 1961
Theatre Arts 46:12-13, Jan 1962
Time 78:44, Nov 3, 1961

Lawler, Ray
Summer of the 17th Doll
Productions:
Opened January 22, 1958 for 29 performances.
Reviews:
Commonweal 67:540, Feb 21, 1958
Nation 185:19, Jul 6, 1957
186:126, Feb 8, 1958
New York Theatre Critics' Reviews: 1958:389
New York Times p.23, Jan 23, 1958
New York Times Magazine p.32, Jan 12, 1958
New Yorker 33:53, Jul 13, 1957
33:53, Feb 1, 1958
Newsweek 51:54, Feb 3, 1958
Reporter 18:36-7, Mar 6, 1958
Saturday Review 41:27, Feb 8, 1958
Theatre Arts 42:18-19, Apr 1958
Time 71:76+, Feb 3, 1958

Lenormand, Henri Rene
The Failures
Productions:
Translated by Winifred Katzin. Opened November 19,
1923 for 40 performances.
Reviews:
American Mercury 1:116, Jan 1924
Drama 14:133, Jan 1924
Freeman 8:376, Dec 26, 1923
Life (NY) 82:18, Dec 13, 1923
Nation 117:692, Dec 12, 1923
New Republic 37:46, Dec 5, 1923
New York Times p.20, Nov 23, 1923
VIII,p.1, Dec 2, 1923
Theatre Magazine 39:16, Feb 1924
Fear (with Jean D'Augugan)
Productions:
Opened March 14, 1913 in repertory.
Opened September 27, 1913 in repertory.
Reviews:

146

Blue Book 17:436-7, Jul 1913
Bookman 37:312, May 1913
Dramatic Mirror 69:6, Mar 19, 1923
Red Book 21:310+, Jun 1913
Man and His Phantoms
    Productions:
    Opened November 10, 1924 in repertory.
    No Reviews.
Time Is A Dream
    Productions:
    Opened in the Fall of 1923 for nine performances.
    Reviews:
    Nation 118:540, May 7, 1924
    New Republic 38:287, May 7, 1924

Levy, Benn W.
  Art and Mrs. Bottle
    Productions:
    Opened November 18, 1930 for 50 performances.
    Reviews:
        Arts and Decoration 34:80, Feb 1931
        Catholic World 132:462, Jan 1931
        Commonweal 13:159, Dec 10, 1930
        Drama 21:12, Feb 1931
        Life (NY) 96:18, Dec 19, 1930
        New York Times p. 19, Nov 19, 1930
        Theatre Magazine 53:26, Jan 1931
        Vogue 77:82, Feb 1, 1931
  Clutterbuck
    Productions:
    Opened December 3, 1949 for 218 performances.
    Reviews:
        Catholic World 170:386, Feb 1950
        Nation 169:629, Dec 24, 1949
        New Republic 122:21, Jan 2, 1950
        New York Theatre Critics' Reviews 1949:205
        New York Times p. 29, Dec 5, 1949
                        p. 34, Aug 9, 1950
        New Yorker 25:54, Dec 10, 1949
        Newsweek 34:79, Dec 12, 1949
        Theatre Arts 34:11, Feb 1950
        Time 54:83, Dec 12, 1949
  The Devil Passes
    Productions:
    Opened January 4, 1932 for 96 performances.
    Reviews:
        Catholic World 134:589-90, Feb 1932

147

The Devil Passes (cont.)
  Commonweal 15:329-30, Jan 20, 1932
  Literary Digest 112:15, Jan 23, 1932
  Nation 134:126, Jan 1927
  New York Times p. 20, Jan 5, 1932
  Outlook 160:86, Jan 20, 1932
  Theatre Arts 16:193-4, Mar 1936
  Theatre Guild Magazine 9:35, Feb 1932
If I Were You (with Paul Hervey Fox)
  Productions:
  Opened January 24, 1938 for 8 performances.
  Reviews:
  Nation 146:162, Feb 5, 1938
  New York Times p. 24, Jan 25, 1938
A Man With Red Hair
  Productions:
  Adapted from Hugh Walpole's novel. Opened November
    8, 1928 for 20 performances.
  Reviews:
  Life (NY) 91:31, Apr 5, 1928
  New York Times p. 22, Nov 9, 1928
Mrs. Moonlight
  Productions:
  Opened September 29, 1930 for 321 performances.
  Reviews:
  Catholic World 133:204, Nov 1930
  Commonweal 13:274, Jan 7, 1931
  New York Times p. 24, Sep 30, 1930
Rape of the Belt
  Productions:
  Opened November 5, 1960 for 5 performances.
  Reviews:
  New York Theatre Critics' Reviews 1960:179
  New York Times p. 46, Nov 7, 1960
  New Yorker 36:104, Nov 12, 1960
Springtime for Henry
  Productions:
  Opened December 9, 1931 for 199 performances.
  Opened May 1, 1933 for 16 performances.
  Opened March 14, 1951 for 53 performances.
  Reviews:
  Arts and Decoration 36:56, Feb 1932
  Bookman 74:563, Jan-Feb 1932
  Catholic World 134:588, Feb 1932
            173:147, May 1951
  Commonweal 15:215, Dec 23, 1931
            53:646, Apr 6, 1951

Life 21:86, Aug 5, 1946
Nation 133:732, 734 Dec 30, 1931
        172:285, Mar 24, 1951
New Republic 69:189-90, Dec 30, 1931
New York Theatre Critics' Reviews 1951:315
New York Times p. 29, Dec 10, 1931
              p. 20, May 2, 1933
              p. 36, Mar 15, 1951
New Yorker 27:56, Mar 24, 1951
Outlook 159:535, Dec 23, 1931
Theatre Arts 35:21, May 1951
Time 36:62, Jul 22, 1940
      57:67, Mar 26, 1951
Vogue 79:58-9, Feb 1, 1932

This Woman Business
  Productions:
    Opened December 7, 1926 for 47 performances.
  Reviews:
    New York Times p. 25, Dec 8, 1926
Topaze (see entry under Pagnol, Marcel)

The Tumbler
  Productions:
    Opened February 24, 1960 for 5 performances.
  Reviews:
    New York Theatre Critics Reviews 1960:349
    New York Times p. 32, Feb 25, 1960
    New Yorker 36:123-4, Mar 1960
Young Madame Conti (see entry under Frank, Bruno)

Lonsdale, Frederick
  Another Love Story
    Productions:
      Opened October 12, 1943 for 104 performances.
    Reviews:
      New York Theatre Critics' Reviews 1943:260
      New York Times p. 29, Oct 13, 1929
      New Yorker 19:34, Oct 23, 1943
      Newsweek 22:110, Oct 25, 1923
      Theatre Arts 27:707, Dec 1943
  Aren't We All?
    Productions:
      Opened May 21, 1923 for 32 performances.
      Opened April 13, 1925 for 16 performances.
    Reviews:
      New York Clipper 71:14, May 30, 1923
      New York Times p. 14, May 22, 1923

Aren't We All? (cont.)
    Theatre Magazine 38:14-15, Aug 1923
                        38:26+, Sep 1923
Canaries Sometime Sing
  Productions:
    Opened October 20, 1930 for 24 performances.
  Reviews:
    Life (NY) 96:17, Nov 7, 1930
    New York Times p. 34, Oct 21, 1930
    Nation 131:506, Nov 5, 1930
The Day After Tomorrow
  Productions:
    Opened October 26, 1950 for 12 performances.
  Reviews:
    Christian Science Monitor Magazine p. 6, Nov 4, 1950
    Commonweal 53:140, Nov 17, 1950
    New York Theatre Critics' Reviews 1950:227
    New York Times p. 25, Oct 27, 1950
    New Yorker 26:76, Nov 4, 1950
    Newsweek 36:89, Nov 6, 1950
    Theatre Arts 35:10, Jan 1951
    Time 56:57, Nov 6, 1950
The Fake
  Productions:
    Opened October 6, 1924 for 88 performances.
  Reviews:
    Life (NY) 84:18, Oct 23, 1924
    New York Times p. 26, Oct 7, 1924
    Theatre Magazine 39:62, Dec 1924
Foreigners
  Productions:
    Opened December 5, 1939 for seven performances.
  Reviews:
    Nation 149:688, Dec 16, 1939
    New York Times p. 30, Dec 6, 1939
    Newsweek 14:35, Dec 18, 1939
The High Road
  Productions:
    Opened September 10, 1928 for 144 performances.
  Reviews:
    American Mercury 15:375-6, Nov 1928
    Catholic World 128:213-14, Nov 1928
    Life (NY) 92:17, Sep 28, 1928
    Nation 127:328, Oct 3, 1928
    New York Times p. 31, Sep 11, 1928
    Outlook 150:864, Sep 26, 1928
    Theatre Magazine 48:46-8, Nov 1928

Vogue 72:108+, Oct 27, 1928
The Last of Mrs. Cheyney
Productions:
Opened November 9, 1925 for 385 performances.
Reviews:
Dial 80:166, Feb 1926
New York Times p. 23, Nov 10, 1925
Theatre Magazine 43:15, Jan 1926
Vogue 67:63, Jan 1, 1926
On Approval
Productions:
Opened October 18, 1926 for 96 performances.
Reviews:
Life (NY) 88:23, Nov 11, 1926
New York Times p. 27, Oct 19, 1926
Theatre Magazine 44:74, Dec 1926
Once Is Enough
Productions:
Opened February 15, 1938 for 105 performances.
Reviews:
Catholic World 147:83-4, Apr 1938
Commonweal 27:524, Mar 4, 1938
Nation 146:253, Feb 26, 1938
New Republic 94:101, Mar 2, 1938
New York Times p. 17, Jan 28, 1938
                p. 16, Feb 16, 1938
Newsweek 11:32, Feb 28, 1938
One Act Play Magazine 1:1025, Mar 1938
Theatre Arts 22:250+, Apr 1938
Time 31:35, Feb 28, 1938
Spring Cleaning
Productions:
Opened November 9, 1923 for 251 performances.
Reviews:
Life (NY) 82:18, Nov 29, 1923
Nation 117:615, Nov 28, 1923
New York Times p. 16, Nov 10, 1923
                VIII, p. 1, Nov 18, 1923
Theatre Magazine 39:17+, Jan 1924
                39:26+, Jan 1924
The Woman of It
Productions:
Opened January 14, 1913 for 15 performances.
Reviews:
Dramatic Mirror 69:6, Jan 22, 1913
Life (NY) 61:240, Jan 30, 1913
Munsey 48:1017, Mar 1913

The Woman of It (cont.)
  New York Dramatic News 57:22, Jan 25, 1913
  New York Times p. 13, Jan 15, 1913

Lorca, Federico García (see García-Lorca, Federico)

Maeterlinck, Maurice
The Betrothal
  Productions:
    Translated by Alexander Teixeira de Mattos.   Opened
      November 18, 1918 for 120 performances.
  Reviews:
    Canadian Magazine 53:438, Sep 1919
    Current Opinion 66:23-6, Jan 1919
    Dramatic Mirror 79:831, Dec 7, 1918
    Dramatist 10:927, Jan 1919
    Independent 96:210, Nov 16, 1918
    Life (NY) 72:900, Dec 12, 1918
    Literary Digest 59:28-9, Dec 7, 1918
    Nation 107:671-2, Nov 10, 1918
    New Republic 17:313, Jan 11, 1919
    New American 209:117, Jan 1919
    New York Times p. 11, Nov 19, 1918
                  VIII, p. 8, Dec 1, 1918
    Theatre Magazine 29:17, 21, Jan 1919
The Blue Bird
  Productions:
    Opened October 1, 1910 in repertory.
    Opened September 15, 1911 for 19 performances.
    Opened December 24, 1923 for 33 performances.
  Reviews:
    Blue Book 12:631-4, Jan 1911
    Bookman 33:137, Apr 1911
    Canadian Magazine 36:288, Jan 1911
    Collier's 46:24+, Oct 22, 1910
    Current Literature 49: 548-50, Nov 1910
    Dramatic Mirror 64:8, Oct 5, 1910
                    65:7, Feb 8, 1911
                    66:11, Sep 20, 1911
    Everybody's 24:119-20, Jan 1911
    Green Book 4:1218, Dec 1910
    Harper's 54:20, Oct 29, 1910
    Independent 71:1300, Dec 14, 1911
    Literary Digest 41:645, Oct 15, 1910
    Life (NY) 56:616, Oct 13, 1910
    New England Magazine 43:36-42, Sep 1910
    New York Times p. 13, Dec 26, 1923

VII, p. 1, Dec 30, 1923
Pearson 24:522-7, Oct 1910
Play Book 1:3-6, Sep 1913
Review of Reviews 42:689, Dec 1910
Theatre Arts 7:29-40, Jan 1923
Theatre Magazine 12:130, Nov 1910

The Burgomaster of Belgium
Productions:
Opened March 24, 1919 for 32 performances.
Reviews:
Dramatist 10:942, Apr 1919
Forum 61:627-8, May 1919
Life (NY) 73:614, Apr 10, 1919
Nation 108:511, Apr 5, 1919
108:578, Apr 12, 1919
Theatre Magazine 29:200, Apr 1919
29:273-4, May 1919

The Death of Tintagiles
Productions:
Translated by Philip Moeller. Opened August 30, 1916 in repertory (Washington Square Players).
Reviews:
Dramatic Mirror 59:20, Mar 21, 1914
77:7, Feb 24, 1917
Theatre Magazine 25:213, 223, Apr 1917

Interior
Productions:
Opened February 19, 1915 in repertory.
Opened October 4, 1915 in repertory.
Reviews:
Dramatic Mirror 73:8, Feb 24, 1915
New York Times p. 11, Oct 19, 1915

The Intruder
Productions:
Opened September 26, 1916 for 31 performances.
Reviews:
Dramatic Mirror 76:7, Oct 7, 1916
Life (NY) 68:626-7, Oct 12, 1916
Nation 103:330, Oct 5, 1916
Theatre Magazine 24:283, Nov 1916
Vogue 72:156, Sep 15, 1928
Yale Review 5:122-3, Oct 1915

Mary Magdalene
Productions:
Opened December 5, 1910 for 16 performances.
Reviews:
Bookman 23:602-4, Feb 1911

153

Mary Magdalene (cont.)
    Collier's 46:24, Jan 7, 1911
    Current Literature 49:667-9, Dec 1910
    Dramatist 2:121, Jan 1911
    Dramatic Mirror 64:7, Dec 7, 1910
    Everybody's 24:408-13, Mar 1911
    Independent 70:150, Jan 19, 1911
    Life (NY) 56:1108, Dec 15, 1910
    Literary Digest 41:1202-3, Dec 24, 1910
    Nation 91:374, Oct 20, 1910
    New England Magazine 43:485-91, Jan 1911
    Red Book 16:753-8, Feb 1911
    Theatre Magazine 13:2-3, Jan 1911
A Miracle Of Saint Anthony
  Productions:
    Opened February 19, 1915 in repertory (Washington
      Square Players).
    Translated by Ralph Roeder. Opened August 30,
      1916 in repertory (Washington Square Players).
  Reviews:
    Nation 107:131, Aug 3, 1918
    New York Times p. 15, May 8, 1915
    Theatre Magazine 21: 282+, Jun 1915
Pelleas and Melisande
  Productions:
    Opened December 4, 1923 for 13 performances.
  Reviews:
    Life (NY) 82:18, Dec 27, 1923
    Nation 117:747, Dec 26, 1923
    New Republic 37:123, Dec 26, 1923
    New York Times p. 23, Dec 5, 1923
                      IX, p. 1, Dec 16, 1923
    Theatre Magazine 39:14-15, Feb 1924
Sister Beatrice
  Productions:
    Opened March 14, 1910 in repertory.
    Opened June 19, 1911 for 1 performance in repertory.
  Reviews:
    Blue Book 13:926-7, Sep 1911
    Bookman 31:412-14, Jun 1910
    Cosmopolitan 49:77-8, Jun 1910
    Dramatic Mirror 63:7, Mar 26, 1910
                     65:7, Jun 21, 1911
    Everybody's 22:841-9, Jun 1910
    Green Book 3:1243-4, Jun 1910
    Life (NY) 55:516, Mar 24, 1910
    Pearson 23:692-4, May 1910

Theatre Magazine 11:186, 188, Jun 1910
11:98-9, Apr 1910

Marceau, Felicien
The Egg
Productions:
Translated by Robert Schlitt.   Opened January 8, 1962
for eight performances.
Reviews:
New Republic 146:20+, Jan 29, 1962
New York Theatre Critics' Reviews 1962:384
New York Times p. 23, Jan 9, 1962
New Yorker 37:63, Jan 20, 1962
Newsweek 59:50, Jan 22, 1962
Saturday Review 45:29, Jan 27, 1962
Time 79:68, Jan 19, 1962
The Good Soup
Productions:
Adapted by Garson Kanin.   Opened March 2, 1960 for
21 performances.
Reviews:
America 103:27, Apr 2, 1960
Nation 190:262, Mar 19, 1960
New York Theatre Critics' Reviews 1960:330
New York Times p. 26, Mar 3, 1960
New Yorker 36:113-14, Mar 12, 1960
Saturday Review 43:26-7, Mar 19, 1960
Theatre Arts 43:14, Jul 1959
Time 75:73, Mar 14, 1960

Martinez-Sierra, Gregorio
The Cradle Song
Productions:
Translated by John G. Underhill.   Opened January 24,
1927 for 57 performances.
Opened the week of September 16, 1929 in repertory.
Opened October 6, 1930 in repertory.
Off Broadway 1955-56.
Reviews:
America 94:342, Dec 17, 1955
Bookman 65:207, Apr 1927
Catholic World 124:812-13, Mar 1927
182:385, Feb 1956
Commonweal 63:457-8, Feb 3, 1956
Dramatic Mirror 83:427,   Mar 5, 1921
Independent 105:281, Mar 19, 1921
Nation 112:411, Mar 16, 1921

The Cradle Song (cont.)
    124:243-4, Mar 2, 1927
   New Republic 50:274, Apr 27, 1927
             51:18, May 25, 1927
            134:20, Jun 2, 1956
   New York Clipper 69: Mar 16, 1921
   New York Times p. 18, Jan 25, 1927
              VIII,p. 1, Jan 30, 1927
              p. 32, Dec 2, 1955
   Outlook 145:231-2, Feb 23, 1927
   Theatre Arts 28:342, Jun 1944
   Theatre Magazine 33:340, May 1921
   Vogue 69:138,140, Mar 15, 1927
   Weekly Review 4:280, Mar 23, 1921

The Kingdom of God
 Productions:
   English version by Helen and Harley Granville-Barker.
    Opened December 20, 1928 for 92 performances.
 Reviews:
   Dial 86:350-51, Apr 1929
   Life (NY) 93:23, Jan 18, 1929
   Literary Digest 100:21-2, Jan 12, 1929
   Nation 128:52, Jan 7, 1929
   New Republic 57:245-7, Jan 16, 1929
   New York Times X,p. 1, Oct 14, 1928
              IX,p. 2, Oct 21, 1928
             VIII,p. 1, Dec 30, 1928
   Theatre Magazine 49:49, Mar 1929
   Vogue 73:71,106, Feb 16, 1929

The Road to Happiness (with Eduardo Marquina)
 Productions:
   Opened May 2, 1927 for 16 performances in repertory.
 Reviews:
   New Republic 50:354-5, May 18, 1927

The Romantic Young Lady
 Productions:
   English version by Helen and Harley Granville-Barker.
    Opened May 4, 1926 for 25 performances.
 Reviews:
   Bookman 63:589-90, Jul 1926
   Nation 122:561, May 9, 1926
   New Republic 47:59-60, Jun 2, 1926
   New York Times p. 24, May 5, 1926
   Theatre Magazine 44:5,15, Jul 1926
   Vogue 68:69, Jul 1, 1926

Spring in Autumn
 Productions:

Adapted by Blanche Yurka and Nene Belmonte.   Opened
October 24, 1933 for 41 performances.
Reviews:
Commonweal 19:75, Nov 17, 1933
New Outlook 162:46, Dec 1933
New York Times p. 22, Oct 25, 1933

Masefield, John
 The Faithful
  Productions:
  Opened October 13, 1919 for 49 performances.
  Reviews:
  Dial 60:77, Jan 20, 1916
  Drama 21:155, Feb 1916
  Dramatist 10:968, Oct 1919
  Living Age 301:719, Jun221, 1919
  Nation 101:604, Nov 18, 1915
          109:591, Nov 8, 1919
  New Republic 4:312, Oct 23, 1915
                20:326, Nov 12, 1919
  New York Times p. 14, Oct 14, 1919
  Review 1:545, Nov 1, 1919
  Saturday Review 120:139, Aug 7, 1915
  Theatre Arts 4:67, Jan 1920
 The Tragedy of Nan (Nan)
  Productions:
  Opened January 13, 1913 for one performance.
  Opened February 17, 1919 for four performances.
  Reviews:
  Dramatic Mirror 69:67, Jan 22, 1913
                  77:4, Aug 25, 1917
                  77:28, Sep 22, 1917
                  82:362, Feb 28, 1920
  Dramatist 7:687-8, Apr 1916
  Independent 72:1158-60, May 30, 1912
  Life (NY) 75:414, Mar 4, 1920
  Living Age 274:778, Sep 28, 1912
  New York Dramatic Mirror 69:67, Jan 22, 1913
  Theatre Magazine 31:271-2, Apr 1920

Maugham, W. Somerset
 The Breadwinner
  Productions:
  Opened September 22, 1931 for 55 performances.
  Reviews:
  Commonweal 134:209, Nov 1931
  Life (NY) 98:19, Oct 9, 1931

157

The Breadwinner (cont.)
  New Republic 68:209, Oct 7, 1931
  New York Times p.19, Sep 23, 1931
  Outlook 159:182, Oct 7, 1931
  Theatre Arts 15:990, Dec 1931
  Theatre Magazine 53:30, Feb 1931
Caesar's Wife
  Productions:
  Opened November 24, 1919 for 81 performances.
  Reviews:
    Dramatic Mirror 80:1861, 1863, Dec 4, 1919
    Independent 101:86, Jan 17, 1920
    New York Times p.9, Nov 25, 1919
    Review 1:688, Dec 20, 1919
    Theatre Magazine 31:19, Jan 1920
The Camel's Back
  Productions:
  Opened November 13, 1923 for 15 performances.
  Reviews:
    Life (NY) 82:50, Dec 6, 1923
    Nation 117:615, Nov 20, 1923
    New York Times p.19, Nov 14, 1923
                     VIII,p.1, Nov 18, 1923
Caroline
  Productions:
  Opened September 29, 1916 for 45 performances.
  Reviews:
    Dramatic Mirror 76:7, Sep 30, 1916
    Nation: 102:364, Mar 30, 1916
            103:331, Oct 5, 1916
    New York Times p.11, Feb 27, 1916
                    p.9, Sep 21, 1916
                    II,p.4, Sep 24, 1916
    Theatre Magazine 24:273, 283, Nov 1916
The Circle
  Productions:
  Opened September 12, 1921 for 175 performances.
  Opened April 18, 1938 for 72 performances.
  Reviews:
    Bookman 54:232, Nov 1921
    Catholic World 147:346-7, Jun 1938
    Commonweal 28:48, May 6, 1938
    Current Opinion 71:463-72, Oct 1921
    Dramatic Mirror 84:412, Sep 17, 1921
    Dramatist 12:1079, Oct 1921
    Everybody's Magazine 46:91, Jan 1922
    Hearst 40:61, Dec 1921

Independent 106:137, Sep 24, 1921
Nation 113:356, Sep 28, 1921
146:512-3, Apr 30, 1938
New Republic 28:161, Oct 5, 1921
New York Clipper 69:17, Sep 21, 1921
New York Times VI, p. 1, Aug 14, 1921
p. 12, Sep 13, 1921
p. 24, Apr 19, 1938
Newsweek 11:26, Apr 25, 1938
Review 5:275, Sep 24, 1921
Theatre Magazine 34:300+, Nov 1921
34:316, Nov 1921
Time 31:26, May 2, 1938

The Constant Wife

Productions:
Opened November 29, 1926 for 233 performances.
Opened December 8, 1951 for 138 performances.

Reviews:
Bookman 64:733, Feb 1927
Catholic World 174:392, Feb 1952
Commonweal 55:299, Dec 28, 1951
Dial 82:169, Feb 1927
Dramatist 18:1339, Apr 1907
Life (NY) 88:19, Dec 16, 1926
Nation 124:21, Jan 5, 1927
New Republic 49:108, Dec 15, 1926
126:22, Jan 7, 1952
New York Theatre Critics' Reviews 1951:149
New York Times p. 11, Dec 31, 1926
p. 34, Dec 10, 1951
II, p. 3, Dec 16, 1957
New Yorker 27:22, Dec 15, 1951
Newsweek 38:69, Dec 17, 1951
Saturday Review 34:18-19, Dec 29, 1951
School and Society 75:326, May 24, 1952
Theatre Magazine 45:16, Feb 1927
45:26+, Mar 1927
Time 58:76, Dec 17, 1951
Vogue 69:118, Feb 1, 1927

East of Suez

Productions:
Opened September 21, 1922 for 100 performances.
Reviews:
Dramatist 14:1140, Jan 1923
New York Clipper 70:21, Oct 4, 1922
New York Times p. 16, Sep 22, 1922
Theatre Magazine 36:380+, Dec 1922
36:299, Nov 1922

The Explorer
  Productions:
    Opened May 7, 1912 for 23 performances.
  Reviews:
    American Playwright 1:190, Jun 1912
    Green Book Album 8:123, Jul 1912
    Life (NY) 59:1073, May 23, 1912
    Theatre Magazine 15:171, Jun 1912
For Services Rendered
  Productions:
    Opened April 12, 1923 for 21 performances.
  Reviews:
    Catholic World 137:208-10, May 1933
    Commonweal 17:719, Apr 26, 1933
    New Outlook 161:46, May 1933
    Nation 136:511-12, May 3, 1933
    New York Times p. 15, Apr 13, 1933
    Newsweek 1:28, Apr 22, 1933
    Stage 10:7, May 1933
          10:16, May 1933
    Theatre Arts 17:416, Jun 1933
    Time 21:21, Apr 24, 1933
The Land Of Promise
  Productions:
    Opened December 25, 1913 for 76 performances.
  Reviews:
    American Playwright 3:39-42, Feb 1914
    Bookman 38:609, Feb 1914
    Dramatist 5:419, Jun 1914
    Green Book Album 11:414, Mar 1914
The Letter
  Productions:
    Opened September 26, 1927 for 104 performances.
  Reviews:
    Dial 84:166-7, Feb 1928
    Dramatist 19:1361-2, Jan 1927
    Independent 119:482, Nov 12, 1927
    Life (NY) 90:23, Oct 13, 1927
    New Republic 52:207-8, Oct 12, 1927
    New York Times p. 30, Sep 27, 1927
    Outlook 147:181-2, Oct 12, 1927
    Saturday Review 4:193-4, Oct 15, 1927
    Theatre Magazine 46:28, 30, 56, Nov 1927
    Vogue 70:166, Nov 15, 1927
The Mask and the Face (see entry under Chiarelli, Luigi)

Mrs. Dot

Productions:
    Opened January 24, 1910 for 72 performances.
Reviews:
    Collier's 44:34, Feb 12, 1910
    Dramatic Mirror 63:6, Feb 5, 1910
    Dramatist 1:89, Jul 1910
    Life (NY) 55:245, Feb 10, 1910

The Noble Spaniard
Productions:
    Opened September 20, 1909 for 40 performances.
Reviews:
    Forum 42:439, Nov 1909
    Life (NY) 54:476, Oct 7, 1909
    New York Dramatic Mirror 62:7, Oct 2, 1909
    Theatre Magazine 10:137, 160, Nov 1909
Our Betters
Productions:
    Opened May 12, 1917 for 112 performances.
    Opened February 20, 1928 for 128 performances.
Reviews:
    Dial 84:439-40, May 1928
    Green Book 17:964-71, Jun 1917
    Life 91:19, Mar 15, 1928
        69:486, Mar 22, 1917
    Nation 104:350, Mar 22, 1917
    New Republic 10:200, Mar 17, 1917
    New York Times p.9, Mar 13, 1917
                    VIII,p.5, Mar 25, 1917
                    p.18, Feb 21, 1928
                    IX,p.1, Mar 4, 1928
    Outlook 148:383, Mar 7, 1928
    Vogue 71:94-5, Apr 15, 1928
Penelope
Productions:
    Opened December 13, 1909 for 48 performances.
Reviews:
    Collier's 44:34, Feb 23, 1910
    Dramatic Mirror 62:5, Dec 25, 1909
    Forum 43:189, Feb 1910
    Theatre Magazine 11:12, Jan 1910
The Sacred Flame
Productions:
    Opened November 19, 1928 for 24 performances.
    Opened October 6, 1952 for 24 performances.
Reviews:
    Life (NY) 92:9, Dec 28, 1928

The Sacred Flame (cont.)
Nation 175:365, Oct 18, 1952
New York Theatre Critics' Reviews 1952:249
New York Times p. 28, Nov 20, 1928
                p. 35, Oct 8, 1952
New Yorker 28:82, Oct 18, 1952
Outlook 150:1275, Dec 5, 1928
Saturday Review 35:28-9, Oct 25, 1952
Time 60:56, Oct 20, 1952
Sheppey
Productions:
Opened April 18, 1944 for 23 performances.
Reviews:
Commonweal 40:60-1, May 5, 1944
Nation 158:521, Apr 29, 1940
New York Theatre Critics' Reviews 1944:209
New York Times p. 27, Apr 19, 1944
New Yorker 20:44, Apr 29, 1944
Saturday Review 156:327-8, Sep 23, 1933
Theatre Arts 18:101, Feb 1934
             28:335-6, Jun 1944
Time 43:58, May 1, 1944
Smith
Productions:
Opened September 5, 1910 for 112 performances.
Reviews:
Bookman 32:349, Dec 1910
Harper's Weekly 54:13, Nov 19, 1910
Life (NY) 56:434, Sep 15, 1910
New York Dramatic Mirror 64: 11, Sep 14, 1910
Theatre Magazine 12:98, 107, Oct 1920
Theatre (with Guy Bolton)
Productions:
Opened November 12, 1941 for 69 performances.
Reviews:
Catholic World 154:473, Jan 1942
Commonweal 35:144, Nov 28, 1941
New Republic 105:762, Dec 8, 1941
New York Theatre Critics' Reviews 1941:226
New York Times p. 34, Nov 13, 1941
Theatre Arts 26:15, Jan 1942
Too Many Husbands
Productions:
Opened October 8, 1919 for 102 performances.
Reviews:
Dramatic Mirror 80:1654, Oct 23, 1919
Nation 109:548, Oct 25, 1919

162

New York Times p.16, Oct 19, 1919
VIII,p.3, Oct 19, 1919

Mayor, Osborne H. (see Bridie, James)

Milne, A. A.
 Ariadne (Business First)
  Productions:
   Opened February 23, 1925 for 48 performances.
  Reviews:
   Living Age 324:562-71, Mar 7, 1925
   New York Times p.17, Feb 27, 1925
 Belinda
  Productions:
   Opened May 6, 1918 for 32 performances.
  Reviews:
   Dramatic Mirror 78:692, May 18, 1918
   Green Book 20:6-9, Jul 1918
   Life (NY) 71:802, May 16, 1918
   New York Dramatic News 65:6, May 11, 1918
   New York Times p.11, May 7, 1918
   Theatre Magazine 27:355+, Jun 1918
 Business First (see Ariadne)

 The Dover Road
  Productions:
   Opened December 23, 1921 for 204 performances.
  Reviews:
   Arts and Decoration 16:278, Feb 1922
   Bookman 55:61, Mar 1922
   Everybody's 46:157, May 1922
   Fortune 118:339, Aug 1922
   Independent 108:41-3, Jan 14, 1922
   Life (NY) 79:18, Jan 12, 1922
   New York Clipper 69:20, Dec 28, 1921
   New York Times p.7, Dec 24, 1921
   Theatre Magazine 35:360, Jun 1922
                    35:143+, Mar 1922
 Give Me Yesterday (Success)
  Productions:
   Opened March 4, 1931 for 72 performances.
  Reviews:
   Arts and Decoration 35:57, May 1931
   Catholic World 133:80-1, Apr 1931
   Commonweal 13:694, Apr 22, 1931
   Life (NY) 97:25, Mar 21, 1931
   Nation (NY) 132:306, Mar 18, 1931

Give Me Yesterday (Success) (cont.)

    New York Times p. 39, Mar 3, 1931
                   p. 32, Mar 5, 1931
                   IX,p. 1, Mar 15, 1931
    Outlook 157:411, Mar 18, 1931
    Theatre Arts 15:372-3, May 1931
    Vogue 77:59+, May 1, 1931

The Great Broxopp
  Productions:
    Opened November 15, 1921 for 66 performances.
  Reviews:
    Dramatic Mirror 84:736, Nov 19, 1921
    Independent 108:43, Jan 14, 1922
    New York Clipper 69:20, Nov 23, 1921
    New York Times p. 22, Nov 16, 1921
                   VI,p. 1, Nov 27, 1921
    Theatre Magazine 35:128, Feb 1922

The Ivory Door
  Productions:
    Opened October 18, 1927 for 310 performances.
  Reviews:
    Life (NY) 90:23, Nov 10, 1927
    New York Times p. 24, Oct 19, 1927
    Outlook 147:465, Dec 14, 1927
    Saturday Review 4:320, Nov 19, 1927
    Theatre Magazine 47:38, Jan 1928

The Lucky One
  Productions:
    Opened November 20, 1922 for 40 performances.
  Reviews:
    Life (NY) 80:18, Dec 14, 1922
    Nation 115:671, Dec 13, 1922
    New York Clipper 70:20, Nov 29, 1922
    New York Times p. 15, Nov 21, 1922
                 VIII,p. 1, Dec 3, 1922
    Theatre Magazine 37:19, Jan 1923

Meet The Prince (To Have the Honor)
  Productions:
    Opened February 25, 1929 for 96 performances.
  Reviews:
    Catholic World 129:85, Apr 1929
    Commonweal 9:544-5, Mar 13, 1929
    New York Times p. 30, Feb 26, 1929
                 X,p. 1, Mar 10, 1929
    Outlook 151:423, Mar 13, 1929

Michael and Mary
  Productions:
    Opened December 13, 1929 for 246 performances.
  Reviews:
    Drama 20:138, Feb 1930
    Life (NY) 95:20, Jan 3, 1930
    New York Times p. 23, Dec 14, 1929
    Outlook 154:32, Jan 1, 1930
    Nation 130:52, Jan 8, 1930
    Theatre Magazine 51:45-6, Feb 1930
    Vogue 75:118, Feb 15, 1930
Mr. Pim Passes By
  Productions:
    Opened February 28, 1921 for 124 performances.
    Opened April 18, 1927 for 36 performances.
  Reviews:
    Bookman 65:573, Jul 1927
    Current Opinion 70:755-84, Jun 1921
    Dramatic Mirror 83:428, Mar 5, 1921
    Independent 105:281, Mar 19, 1921
    Life (NY) 77:390, Mar 17, 1921
    Nation 112:411, Mar 16, 1921
    New York Clipper 69:23, Mar 9, 1921
    New York Times p. 18, Mar 1, 1921
                   p. 24, Apr 19, 1927
                   VIII, p. 1, May 22, 1927
    Outlook 127:627, Apr 20, 1921
    Theatre Magazine 33:319+, May 1921
                     34:152+, Sep 1921
    Weekly Review 4:280, Mar 23, 1921
The Perfect Alibi
  Productions:
    Opened November 27, 1928 for 255 performances.
  Reviews:
    Bookman 68:685, Feb 1929
    Commonweal 10:104, May 29, 1929
    Life (NY) 92:9, Dec 28, 1928
    New York Times p. 24, Nov 28, 1928
    Outlook 150:1355, Dec 19, 1928
The Romantic Age
  Productions:
    Opened November 14, 1922 for 31 performances.
  Reviews:
    Life (NY) 80:18, Dec 14, 1922
    New York Clipper 70:20, Nov 22, 1922
    New York Times II, p. 1, Mar 19, 1922
    Weekly Review 3:603, Dec 15, 1920

Success (see Give Me Yesterday)

They Don't Mean Any Harm
  Productions:
    Opened February 23, 1932 for 15 performances.
  Reviews:
    New York Times p. 25, Feb 24, 1932
    Theatre Arts 16:363-4, May 1932
    Theatre Guild 9:9, Apr 1932
To Have the Honor (see Meet the Prince)

The Truth About Blayds
  Productions:
    Opened March 14, 1922 for 108 performances.
    Opened April 11, 1932 for 24 performances.
  Reviews:
    Bookman 55:387-8, Jun 1922
    Catholic World 135:210, May 1932
    Commonweal 16:49-50, May 11, 1922
    Current Opinion 72:629-39, May 1922
    Dramatist 13:1101-2, Apr 1922
    Everybody's 47:76-82, Aug 1922
    Independent 108:462-3, May 13, 1922
    Life (NY) 79:20, Apr 6, 1922
    Literary Digest 73:30-1, May 13, 1922
    Nation 114:376, Mar 29, 1922
          134:497-8, Apr 27, 1932
    New Republic 30:198-9, Apr 12, 1922
    New York Clipper 70:22, Mar 22, 1922
    New York Times p. 22, Mar 15, 1922
                   VI,p. 1, Mar 26, 1922
                   p. 25, Apr 12, 1932
    Theatre Magazine 35:306-7, May 1922
                     36:156+, Sep 1922

Molnar, Ferenc
  Carnival
    Productions:
      Translated by Melville Baker.   Opened December 29,
        1924 for 32 performances.
    Reviews:
      Drama 15:97, Feb 1925
      Life (NY) 85:18, Jan 22, 1925
      Nation 120:75, Jan 21, 1925
      New York Times VIII,p. 2, Nov 30, 1924
                     p. 15, Dec 30, 1924
      Theatre Magazine 40:15, Mar 1925

Delicate Story
    Productions:
        English text by Gilbert Miller.   Opened December 4,
            1940 for 29 performances.
    Reviews:
        Catholic World 152:470-1, Jan 1941
        Nation 151:641, Dec 21, 1940
        New York Theatre Critics' Reviews 1940:199
        New York Times p. 32, Dec 5, 1940
        Newsweek 16:66, Dec 16, 1940
        Stage 1:9, Dec 1940
        Theatre Arts 25:97, Feb 1941
        Time 36:72, Dec 16, 1940
Fashions for Men
    Productions:
        English version by Benjamin Glazer.   Opened
            December 5, 1922 for 86 performances.
    Reviews:
        Bookman 56:747-9, Feb 1923
        Dramatist 14:1161, Apr 1923
        Life (NY) 80:18, Dec 28, 1922
        New York Clipper 70:20, Dec 13, 1922
        New York Times p. 22, Dec 6, 1922
                        VII, p. 1, Dec 24, 1922
                        III, p. 4, Jan 14, 1923
The Glass Slipper
    Productions:
        Opened October 19, 1925 for 65 performances.
    Reviews:
        Bookman 62:594, Jan 1926
        Life (NY) 86:20, Nov 12, 1925
        Nation 121:550-51, Nov 11, 1925
        New York Times p. 29, Oct 20, 1925
                        VIII, p. 2, Oct 25, 1925
The Good Fairy
    Productions:
        English text by Jane Hinton.   Opened November 24,
            1931 for 151 performances.
        English text by Jane Hinton.   Opened November 17,
            1932 for 68 performances.
    Reviews:
        Arts and Decoration 36:56, Feb 1932
        Bookman 74:565, Jan 1932
        Catholic World 134:469, Jan 1932
        Commonweal 15:187-8, Dec 16, 1931
        Nation 133:678, Dec 16, 1931
        New York Times p. 17, Nov 25, 1931

The Good Fairy (cont.)
                    p. 22, Nov 18, 1932
      Outlook 159:470, Dec 9, 1931
      Theatre Arts 16:97-8, Feb 1932
      Theatre Guild Magazine 9:3-4, Jan 1932
      Vogue 79:82, Jan 15, 1932
The Guardsman (also see Where Ignorance Is Bliss)
   Productions:
      Opened October 13, 1924 for 248 performances.
   Reviews:
      American Mercury 3:501-2, Dec 1924
      Dial 77:440-41, Nov 1924
      Living Age 323:68-78, Oct 4, 1924
      Nation 119:501, Nov 5, 1924
      New York Times p. 23, Oct 14, 1924
      Theatre Magazine 39:15, Dec 1924
Launzi
   Productions:
      Adapted by Edna St. Vincent Millay. Opened
      October 10, 1923 for 13 performances.
   Reviews:
      Life (NY) 82:20, Nov 1, 1923
      Nation 117:470, Oct 24, 1923
      New Republic 36:230-1, Oct 24, 1923
      New York Times p. 16, Oct 11, 1923
      Theatre Magazine 38:16, Dec 1923
Liliom
   Productions:
      Opened April 20, 1921 for 83 performances.
      Adapted by Benjamin Glazer. Opened October 26,
      1932 for 35 performances.
      Adapted by Benjamin Glazer. Opened March 25, 1940
      for 56 performances.
   Reviews:
      Bookman 53:414-15, Jul 1921
      Catholic World 136:463-4, Jan 1933
                    151:210-11, May 1940
      Commonweal 17:75, Nov 16, 1932
                    31:514, Apr 5, 1940
      Current Opinion 71:187-97, Aug 1921
      Drama 11:308-10, Jun 1921
      Dramatic Mirror 83:733, Apr 30, 1921
                    84:485, Oct 1, 1921
      Everybody's 45:57-64, Oct 1921
      Hearst 40:25-7+, Aug 1921
      Life (NY) 77:   May 5, 1921
      Literary Digest 69:24-5, May 21, 1921

Nation 112:695, May 11, 1921
       150:497, Apr 6, 1940
National Magazine 50:519, Mar-Apr 1922
New Republic 26:299, May 4, 1921
              102:473, Apr 8, 1940
New York Clipper 69:19, Apr 27, 1921
New York Theatre Critics' Reviews 1940:354
New York Times p. 18, Apr 21, 1921
              VI,p. 1, Apr 21, 1921
              VII,p. 1, May 1, 1921
              VI,p. 1, May 27, 1921
              p. 23, Oct 27, 1932
              p. 17, Mar 26, 1940
New Yorker 16:30, Apr 6, 1940
Newsweek 15:34, Apr 8, 1940
Outlook 128:153-4, May 25, 1921
Player's Magazine 16:20-3, Jan 1940
Poet Lore 35:43-7, Mar 1924
Theatre Arts 17:14-15+, Jan 1933
             24:315-16, May 1940
Theatre Magazine 34:5+, Jul 1921
                 34:220-6, Oct 1921
Time 35:38, Apr 8, 1940
Vogue 95:66, May 1, 1940
Weekly Review 4:444-5, May 7, 1921
Mima
  Productions:
    Adapted by David Belasco from Molnar's The Red Mill.
    Opened December 12, 1928 for 180 performances.
  Reviews:
    American Mercury 16:249, Feb 1929
    Bookman 68:686, Feb 1929
    Catholic World 128:593-4, Feb 1929
    Life (NY) 93:23, Jan 18, 1929
    New York Times p. 24, Dec 13, 1928
                   VIII,p. 1, Dec 23, 1928
    Scientific American 140:244-5, Mar 1929
    Theatre Magazine 49:49, Feb 1929
    Vogue 73:118, Feb 2, 1929
Miracle in the Mountains
  Productions:
    Opened April 25, 1947 for 3 performances.
  Reviews:
    New York Theatre Critics' Reviews: 1947:387
    New York Times p. 10, Apr 26, 1947
    New Yorker 23:54+, May 3, 1927
    Newsweek 29:86, May 5, 1947
    Time 49:76, May 5, 1947

169

Olympia
    Productions:
        English version by Sidney Howard. Opened
        October 16, 1928 for 39 performances.
    Reviews:
        Dial 85:534-5, Dec 1928
        Life (NY) 92:17, Nov 9, 1928
        New York Times p. 26, Oct 17, 1928
        Theatre Magazine 48:47+, Dec 1928
        Vogue 72:146, Dec 8, 1928
One, Two, Three
    Productions:
        Opened September 29, 1930 for 40 performances.
    Reviews:
        Catholic World 132:209, Nov 1930
        Commonweal 12:610, Oct 15, 1930
        Life (NY) 96:19, Oct 17, 1930
        New York Times p. 24, Sep 30, 1930
        Vanity Fair 35:90, Dec 1930
The Phantom Rival (see also Tale of the Wolf)
    Productions:
        Opened October 6, 1914 for 127 performances.
    Reviews:
        American Playwright 3:363-6, Nov 1914
        American Mercury 79:84, Feb 1915
        Bookman 40:255-6, Nov 1914
        Book News 33:127-8, Nov 1914
        Collier's 54:9, Jan 2, 1915
        Current Opinion 57:400-404, Dec 1914
        Dramatic Mirror 72:8, Oct 14, 1914
        Green Book 12:1059-60, Dec 1914
        McClure's 44:23-6, Jan 1915
        Nation 99:476-7, Oct 15, 1914
        New York Dramatic News 60:18, Oct 17, 1914
        North American Review 200:934-6, Dec 1914
        Theatre Magazine 20:209+, Nov 1914
The Play's the Thing
    Productions:
        Adapted by P. G. Wodehouse. Opened November 3,
        1926 for 260 performances.
        Adapted by P. G. Wodehouse. Opened April 9, 1928
        for 24 performances.
        Adapted by P. G. Wodehouse. Opened April 28, 1948
        for 244 performances.
    Reviews:
        Catholic World 167:264-5, Jun 1948
        Dial 82:76, Jan 1927

170

Life 24:85-6+, May 24, 1948
Life (NY) 88:22, Nov 25, 1926
Nation 123:540, Nov 24, 1926
         166:557-8, May 15, 1948
New Republic 118:34, May 17, 1948
New York Theatre Critics' Reviews 1948:283
New York Times p. 25, Nov 4, 1926
              VIII,p. 1, Nov 14, 1926
              p. 32, Apr 16, 1928
              p. 19, Apr 29, 1948
              II,p. 1, May 9, 1948
New Yorker 24:54, May 8, 1948
Newsweek 31:77, May 10, 1948
Theatre Arts 32:13+, Jun 1948
Theatre Magazine 45:14-15, Jan 1927
                45:26+, Feb 1927
Time 51:81, May 10, 1948
Vanity Fair 27:42, Jan 1927
The Red Mill (see Mima)

The Swan
  Productions:
    Translated by Melville Baker.   Opened October 23,
      1923 for 255 performances.
  Reviews:
    Classic 18:46+, Jan 1924
    Current Opinion 76:58-64, Jan 1924
    Freeman 8:281-2, Nov 28, 1923
    Life (NY) 82:20, Nov 15, 1923
    New York Times p. 14, Aug 27, 1924
    Theatre Magazine 38:14-15, Dec 1923
A Tale of the Wolf (see also The Phantom Rival)
  Productions:
    Opened October 7, 1925 for 13 performances.
  Reviews:
    New York Times p. 31, Oct 8, 1925
                  IX,p. 1, Oct 18, 1925
The Violet
  Productions:
    Opened September 29, 1930 for 40 performances.
  Reviews:
    Catholic World 132:209, Nov 1930
    Commonweal 12:610, Oct 15, 1930
    Life (NY) 96:19, Oct 17, 1930
    New York Times p. 24, Sep 30, 1930
    Vanity Fair 35:90, Dec 1930
Where Ignorance Is Bliss

Where Ignorance Is Bliss (cont.)
  Productions:
    English version by Philip Littell. Opened September 3,
      1913 for 8 performances.
  Reviews:
    American Playwright 2:278-9, Sep 1913
    Bookman 38:136, Oct 1913
    Dramatic Mirror 70:6, Sep 10, 1913
    Everybody's Magazine 29:686, Nov 1913
    Harper's Weekly 58:26, Sep 20, 1913
    New York Dramatic News 58:18-19, Sep 13, 1913
    New York Times p. 9, Sep 4, 1913
    Smart Set 49:145-7, Nov 1913
    Theatre Magazine 18:115, Oct 1913

Morley, Robert
  Edward, My Son (with Noel Langley)
  Productions:
    Opened September 30, 1948 for 260 performances.
  Reviews:
    Catholic World 168:159, Nov 1948
    Commonweal 49:12-13, Oct 15, 1948
    Forum 110:351-2, Dec 1948
    Life 25:111-14, Oct 18, 1948
    Nation 167:501, Oct 30, 1948
    New Republic 119:26, Oct 18, 1948
    New York Theatre Critics' Reviews 1948:219
    New York Times p. 30, Oct 1, 1948
                    p. 39, Apr 13, 1949
    New York Times Magazine pp. 48-9, Oct 3, 1948
    New Yorker 24:60+, Oct 9, 1948
    Newsweek 32:84, Oct 11, 1948
    Saturday Review 31:26-8, Oct 16, 1948
    School and Society 68:303, Oct 30, 1948
    Theatre Arts 31:35-6, Oct 1947
                 33:14, Jan 1949
    Time 52:78, Oct 11, 1948
    Vogue 112:183, Dec 1948

Munro, C. K.
  At Mrs. Beam's
  Productions:
    Opened April 26, 1926 for 59 performances.
  Reviews:
    Bookman 63:587-8, Jul 1926
    Nation 122:540, May 12, 1926

New Republic 46:361-2, May 12, 1926
New York Times p. 24, Apr 26, 1926
Overland Monthly 85:115, Apr 1927
Theatre Magazine 44:16, Jul 1926
Vogue 68:68, Jul 1, 1926

Beau-Strings
  Productions:
    Opened April 26, 1926 for 24 performances.
  Reviews:
    Bookman 63:587-8, Jul 1926
    New York Times p. 22, Apr 27, 1926
    Theatre Magazine 44:16, Jul 1926
    Vogue 68:68, Jul 1, 1926

Murray, T. C.
 Autumn Fire
  Productions:
    Opened October 26, 1926 for 71 performances.
  Reviews:
    Independent 117:621, Nov 27, 1926
    New York Times p. 25, Oct 27, 1926
    Theatre Magazine 45:16+, Jan 1927
 Birthright
  Productions:
    Opened November 20, 1911 in repertory (Irish Players).
    Opened February 4, 1913 in repertory (Irish Players).
    Season of 1919-1920
    Opened October 21, 1932 in repertory (Irish Repertory
      Company).
  Reviews:
    American Playwright 1:25-6, Jan 1912
    Dramatic Mirror 66:7, Nov 22, 1911
                   69:7, Feb 12, 1913
                   82:1098, May 29, 1920
    Green Book 7:462-3+, Mar 1912
    Life (NY) 75:1089, Jun 10, 1920
    New York Times p. 14, May 25, 1920
                   p. 25, Nov 4, 1932
 Maurice Harte
  Productions:
    Opened February 4, 1913 in repertory (Irish Players).
  Reviews:
    Dramatic Mirror 69:6-7, Feb 19, 1913
    Everybody's 28:679-80, May 1913
    New York Times p. 5, Feb 14, 1913
 Spring
  Productions:

Spring (cont.)
> Opened in the Fall of 1934 for two performances in repertory (Abby Theatre Players).
No Reviews.

Nichols, Robert
  Wings Over Europe (with Maurice Browne)
    Productions:
      Opened December 10, 1928 for 90 performances.
    Reviews:
      American Mercury 16:247-8, Feb 1929
      Catholic World 128:589-90, Feb 1929
      Dial 86:170-71, Feb 1929
      Life (NY) 93:23, Jan 19, 1923
      Literary Digest 99:19-20, Dec 29, 1928
      Nation 127:721-2, Dec 26, 1928
      New Republic 57:163-4, Dec 26, 1928
      New York Times p. 35, Dec 11, 1928
                    III, p. 4, Dec 6, 1928
      Outlook 151:224, Feb 6, 1929
      Review of Reviews 79:158, Feb 1929
      Theatre Arts 13:84-7, Feb 1929
      Theatre Magazine 49:49-51, Feb 1929
                      49:30-31+, Mar 1929
      Vogue 73:58-9+, Feb 2, 1929

O'Casey, Sean
  Bedtime Story
    Productions:
      Opened April 15, 1959 for 37 performances.
    Reviews:
      New York Times p. 28, Apr 16, 1959
                    II, p. 1, Apr 26, 1959
      Theatre Arts 43:9, Jun 1959
  Cock-A-Doodle Dandy
    Productions:
      (Off Broadway) Season of 1958-1959.
    Reviews:
      Nation 187:416, Nov 29, 1958
      New York Times p. 40, Oct 7, 1958
                    II, p. 1, Nov 9, 1958
                    p. 39, Nov 13, 1958
                    II, p. 1, Nov 23, 1958
      New Yorker 34:100-2, Nov 22, 1958
      Newsweek 52:78, Nov 24, 1958
      Saturday Review 38:37, Nov 19, 1955
                      41:37, Dec 6, 1958

174

Theatre Arts 42:22-4, Nov 1958
             43:64, Jan 1959
Time 72:83, Nov 24, 1958
Figuro in the Night
Productions:
   (Off Broadway) Opened October 30, 1962 for one
   performance (ANTA Matinee).
Reviews:
New York Times p. 33, Oct 31, 1962
Juno and the Paycock
Productions:
   Opened March 15, 1926 for 74 performances.
   Opened December 19, 1927 for 40 performances.
   Opened October 21, 1932 in repertory (Irish Repertory
   Company).
   Opened November 23, 1934 for 9 performances.
   Opened December 6, 1937 for 8 performances.
   Opened January 16, 1940 for 105 performances.
Reviews:
   Arts and Decoration 25:64, May 1926
   Bookman 63:343-4, May 1926
   Catholic World 150:730-1, Mar 1940
   Commonweal 31:327, Feb 2, 1940
   Dial 84:259-60, Mar 1928
   Drama 18:67-70, Dec 1927
   Independent 116:580, May 15, 1926
   Living Age 321:869-70, May 3, 1924
   Nation 122:348, Mar 31, 1926
   New York Theatre Critics' Reviews 1940:415+
   New York Times p. 22, Mar 10, 1926
                  VIII, p. 1, Mar 21, 1926
                  p. 32, Dec 20, 1927
                  p. 24, Oct 20, 1932
                  p. 32, Dec 7, 1937
                  p. 24, Jan 17, 1940
   Theatre Arts 10:286+, May 1926
                24:154+, Mar 1940
   Theatre Magazine 43:15, May 1926
   Time 35:36, Jan 29, 1940
   Vogue 67:98+, May 15, 1926
         71:87+, Feb 15, 1928
The Moon Shines on Kylenamoe
Productions:
   (Off Broadway) Opened October 30, 1962 for one
   performance (ANTA Matinee).
Reviews:
New York Times p. 33, Oct 31, 1962

The Plough and the Stars
  Productions:
    Opened November 28, 1927 for 32 performances.
    Opened November 12, 1934 for 13 performances.
    Opened October 7, 1937 for four performances (Abbey
      Theatre Players).
    Opened December 6, 1960 for 32 performances.
  Reviews:
    America 91:481, Aug 14, 1954
    American Mercury 9:245-6, Oct 1926
    Catholic World 192:320, Feb 1961
    Commonweal 21:122, Nov 23, 1934
    Dial 84:58, Feb 28, 1958
    Literary Digest 95:20-1, Dec 24, 1927
                   123:23, Jan 16, 1937
    Living Age 328:693-4, Mar 27, 1926
               122:21-2, Sep 19, 1936
    Nation 125:718, Dec 21, 1927
           144:194, Feb 13, 1937
           176:353, Apr 25, 1953
           191:510, Dec 24, 1960
    New York Theatre Critics' Reviews 1960:147
    New York Times p. 30, Nov 29, 1927
                   X,p. 1, Dec 4, 1927
                   p. 32, Dec 20, 1927
                   p. 22, Nov 13, 1934
                   p. 26, Oct 8, 1937
                   p. 56, Dec 7, 1960
    New Yorker 36:96-8, Dec 17, 1950
    Newsweek 9:30, Jan 23, 1937
    Outlook 148:187, Feb 1, 1928
    Queen's Quarterly 34:420-9, Apr - Jun 1927
    Saturday Review 4:427, Dec 10, 1927
                    36:25, Jun 6, 1953
    Theatre Arts 12:91-3, Feb 1928
                 45:11, Feb 1961
    Theatre Magazine 47:58, Feb 1928
    Time 29:45, Feb 1, 1937
         76:63, Dec 19, 1960
    Vogue 71:100, Feb 1, 1928
Pound on Demand
  Productions:
    Opened December 19, 1946 for 40 performances.
    Opened April 15, 1959 for 37 performances.
  Reviews:
    New Republic 116:42, Jan 6, 1947
    New York Theatre Critics' Reviews 1946:217

New York Times p. 28, Apr 16, 1959
                 p. 1, Apr 26, 1959
Newsweek 28:71, Dec 30, 1946
Theatre Arts 43:9, Jun 1959

Purple Dust
Productions:
   (Off Broadway) Season of 1956-1957.
Reviews:
   Catholic World 184:469-70, Mar 1957
   Nation 184:65, Jan 19, 1957
   New York Times p. 15, Dec 28, 1956
                 II, p. 1, Jan 6, 1957
   Newsweek 49:67, Jan 21, 1957
   Saturday Review 40:48, Jan 19, 1957

Red Roses for Me
Productions:
   Opened December 28, 1955 for 29 performances.
   (Off Broadway) Opened November 27, 1961 for 176
      performances.
Reviews:
   America 94:459-60, Jan 21, 1956
   Commonweal 182:387, Feb 1956
   Nation 181:555-6, Dec 24, 1955
          182:39, Jan 14, 1956
   New Republic 134:21, Jan 30, 1956
   New York Theatre Critics' Reviews 1955:182
   New York Times p. 15, Dec 29, 1955
                 II, p. 1, Jan 8, 1956
                 p. 41, Nov 28, 1961
   New Yorker 31:62+, Jan 14, 1956
              37:162+, Dec 9, 1961
   Saturday Review 39:20, Jan 14, 1956
   Theatre Arts 28:256, Apr 1944
                30:355, Jun 1946
                40:15, Mar 1956
   Time 67:51, Jan 9, 1956

The Shadow of a Gunman
Productions:
   Opened November 20, 1958 for 52 performances.
   Opened January 12, 1959 for 48 performances.
Reviews:
   America 10:382, Dec 20, 1958
   Catholic World 188:417, Feb 1959
   Christian Century 75:1463, Dec 17, 1958
   New York Theatre Critics' Reviews 1958:200
   New York Times p. 26, Nov 21, 1958
                 II, p. 1, Nov 30, 1958

The Shadow of a Gunman (cont.)
    New Yorker 34:113, Dec 6, 1958
    Saturday Review 41:37, Dec 6, 1958
    Theatre Arts 43:22-3, Feb 1959
The Silver Tassie
  Productions:
    Opened October 24, 1929 for 51 performances.
  Reviews:
    Catholic World 130:334-5, Dec 1929
    Commonweal 50:631-2, Oct 7, 1949
    Fortune 132:851-3, Dec 1929
    Literary Digest 98:24-5, Aug 4, 1928
    Life (NY) 94:24, Nov 15, 1929
    New Republic 61:17-18, Nov 27, 1929
                121:21, Sep 19, 1949
    New York Times p. 26, Oct 25, 1929
                X,p. 1, Nov 10, 1929
    Theatre Arts 14:6, Jan 1930
                15:790-2, Oct 1931
Within the Gates
  Productions:
    Opened October 22, 1934 for 141 performances.
  Reviews:
    Catholic World 140:338-40, Dec 1934
    Commonweal 21:66, Nov 9, 1934
    Nation 139:546, Nov 7, 1934
    New Republic 80:369, Nov 7, 1934
    New York Times p. 23, Oct 23, 1934
                IX,p. 1, Oct 28, 1934
    Player's Magazine 11:10, Nov-Dec 1934
    Saturday Review 10:519, Mar 3, 1934
                11:256, Nov 3, 1934
    Stage 12:13, Dec 1934
          12:18-19, Dec 1934
    Theatre Arts 18:258-9, Apr 1934
                18:894, Dec 1934
    Time 24:30, Nov 5, 1934
    Vanity Fair 41:42+, Jan 1934
                43:31-2, Jan 1935
    Vogue 84:72, Dec 15, 1934

Osborne, John
  The Entertainer
    Productions:
      Opened February 12, 1958 for 97 performances.
    Reviews:
      America 98:736, Mar 22, 1958

114:54, Jan 8, 1966
Catholic World 187:68, Apr 1958
Life 44:118, Mar 10, 1958
Nation 186:192-3, Mar 1, 1958
New York Theatre Critics' Reviews 1958:357
New York Times p. 22, Feb 13, 1958
                    II, p. 1, Feb 23, 1958
New Yorker 33:153-4, Sep 28, 1957
              34:63, Feb 22, 1958
Newsweek 51:62, Feb 24, 1958
Reporter 18:39, Mar 20, 1958
Saturday Review 40:26, May 11, 1957
                  41:24, Mar 1, 1958
Theatre Arts 42:22-3, Apr 1958
Time 71:52, Feb 24, 1958

Epitaph for George Dillon (with Anthony Creighton)
Productions:
Opened November 4, 1958 for 23 performances.
Reviews:
America 100:299, Nov 29, 1958
Christian Century 75:1436, Dec 10, 1958
Nation 187:394-5, Nov 22, 1958
New York Theatre Critics' Reviews 1958:219
New York Times p. 44, Nov 5, 1958
                    II, p. 1, Nov 16, 1958
New Yorker 34:101-3, Nov 15, 1958
              36:68+, Jan 14, 1961
Newsweek 52:75, Nov 17, 1958
Saturday Review 41:24-5, Nov 22, 1958
Theatre Arts 43:21-3, Jan 1959
                45:68, Mar 1961
Time 72:62, Nov 17, 1958

Inadmissible Evidence
Productions:
Opened November 30, 1965 for 166 performances.
Reviews:
Christian Century 82:1066, Sep 1, 1965
Commentary 41:75, Mar 1966
Commonweal 83:375, Dec 24, 1965
Harper 232:125, Apr 1966
Life 60:17, Jan 14, 1966
Nation 201:508-9, Dec 20, 1965
National Review 18:325-7, Apr 5, 1966
New Republic 154:34-5, Jan 1, 1966
New York Theatre Critics' Reviews 1965:240
New York Times p. 52, Dec 1, 1965
New Yorker 41:176+, Apr 17, 1965

Inadmissible Evidence (cont.)
          41:142, Dec 11, 1965
          42:47, Oct 8, 1966
      Newsweek 66:90, Dec 13, 1965
      Reporter 33:38-40+, Nov 4, 1965
      Saturday Review 48:31, May 29, 1965
                      48:43, Dec 18, 1965
                      49:96, Jan 8, 1966
      Time 86:76+, Dec 10, 1965
      Vogue 146:51-2, Aug 15, 1965
            147:34, Jan 15, 1966
Look Back in Anger
  Productions:
    Opened October 1, 1957 for 407 performances.
  Reviews:
    America 98:146, Nov 2, 1957
    Catholic World 186:226, Dec 1957
                   188:122-8, Nov 1958
    Christian Century 74:1262-3, Oct 23, 1957
    Commonweal 67:232-3, Nov 29, 1957
    Life 43:141-2+, Oct 14, 1957
    Nation 185:272, Oct 19, 1957
    New Republic 137:16-17, Sep 9, 1957
                 137:19-21, Dec 23, 1957
                 138:23-4, Jan 20, 1958
                 138:22, Feb 10, 1958
    New York Theatre Critics' Reviews 1957:243
    New York Times p. 28, Oct 2, 1957
                   II, p. 1, Oct 13, 1957
    New Yorker 33:153-4, Sep 28, 1957
               33:93, Oct 12, 1957
    Newsweek 50:114, Oct 14, 1957
    Reporter 15:33-5, Oct 18, 1956
             17:38, Nov 14, 1957
    Saturday Review 39:30, Oct 13, 1957
                    40:30, Oct 12, 1957
    Theatre Arts 41:28, May 1957
                 41:18, Dec 1957
    Time 69:90+, Apr 22, 1957
         70:85+, Oct 14, 1957
Luther
  Productions:
    Opened September 25, 1963 for 211 performances.
  Reviews:
    America 107:533, Jul 21, 1962
            109:496-7, Oct 26, 1963
    Catholic World 194:99-105, Nov 1961

198:135-6, Nov 1963
Christian Century 80:1351, Oct 30, 1963
Commonweal 79:103-4, Oct 18, 1963
Nation 193:539-40, Dec 30, 1961
197:245-6, Oct 19, 1963
National Review 15:446-8+, Nov 19, 1963
New Republic 149:28+, Oct 19, 1963
New York Theatre Critics' Reviews 1963:276
New York Times p. 41, Sep 26, 1963
II, p. 1, Oct 6, 1963
New Yorker 37:200-201, Oct 14, 1961
39:133, Oct 5, 1963
Newsweek 62:96, Oct 7, 1963
Reporter 25:50+, Oct 12, 1961
19:54+, Oct 24, 1963
Saturday Review 46:30, Oct 12, 1963
Theatre Arts 47:12-13, Dec 1963
Time 77:58-9, Jun 30, 1961
82:63, Oct 4, 1963
Vogue 143:20, Jan 1, 1964

Pagnol, Marcel
Marseilles
Productions:
Adapted by Sidney Howard.   Opened November 17,
1930 for 16 performances.
Reviews:
Commonweal 13:160 Dec 10, 1930
New York Times II, p. 3, Nov 9, 1930
p. 28, Nov 18, 1930
Theatre Arts 15:18-19, Jan 1931
Merchants of Glory (with Paul Nivoix)
Productions:
Translated by Ralph Roeder.   Opened December 14,
1925 for 42 performances.
Reviews:
Dial 80:167-8, Feb 1926
Drama 16:166, Apr 1926
Nation 121:765, Dec 30, 1925
New York Times p. 28, Dec 15, 1925
VII, p. 1, Dec 27, 1925
Topaze
Productions:
Adapted by Benn W. Levy.   Opened February 12, 1930
for 159 performances.
Opened August 18, 1930 for 16 performances.
Opened February 16, 1931 for 8 performances.

Topaze (cont.)
    Opened December 17, 1947 for 1 performance.
    Reviews:
        Commonweal 11:659, Apr 9, 1930
        Life (NY) 95:18, Mar 7, 1930
        Nation 130:278, Mar 5, 1930
        New York Theatre Critics' Reviews 1947:226
        New York Times p. 25, Feb 13, 1930
                        IX,p.1, Mar 2, 1930
                        p. 21, Dec 29, 1947
        New Outlook 161:49, Mar 1933
                    23:45-7, Jan 10, 1948
        Outlook 154:353, Feb 26, 1930
        Theatre Arts 14:281, Apr 1930
        Theatre Magazine 51:44, Apr 1930
                         51:32-5, Jun 1930
        Vanity Fair 40:43, Apr 1933
                    75:132, Apr 12, 1930

Parker, Louis N.
  Beauty and the Barge (with W. W. Jacobs)
    Productions:
        Opened November 13, 1913 for six performances.
    Reviews:
        Dramatic Mirror 70:6, Nov 19, 1913
        New York Times p. 11, Nov 14, 1913
  Disraeli
    Productions:
        Opened September 18, 1911 for 280 performances.
        Opened for one matinee on April 25, 1912.
        Opened April 9, 1917 for 48 performances.
    Reviews:
        Blue Book 13:455-8, Jul 1911
        Bookman 34:244-5, Nov 1911
        Current Literature 51:663-9, Dec 1911
        Delineator 79:175, Mar 1912
        Dramatic Mirror 66:11, Sep 20, 1911
        Dramatist 3:241-2, Apr 1913
        Everybody's 25:825-6, Dec 1911
        Green Book 6:1208, Dec 1911
        Leslie's Weekly 113:383, Oct 5, 1911
        Life (NY) 58:524, Sep 28, 1911
        Munsey 46:280, Nov 1911
        New York Times p. 11, Apr 4, 1917
                        VIII,p.5, Apr 15, 1917
        Pearson 26:520-3+, Oct 1911
               26:650-2, Nov 1911

Red Book 18:380-1+, Dec 1911
Theatre Magazine 14:xiii-xiv, Nov 1911
The Highway of Life
  Productions:
    Opened October 26, 1914 for 24 performances.
  Reviews:
    Dramatic Mirror 72:8, Nov 4, 1914
    Green Book 13:121, Jan 1915
    Munsey 53:794-5, Jan 1915
    Nation 99:560-1, Nov 5, 1914
    New York Dramatic News 60:17, Oct 31, 1914
    New York Times p. 11, Oct 27, 1914
                  VIII, p. 8, Nov 1, 1914
Johannes Kreisler (Music by E. H. Von Reznich)
  Productions:
    Adapted from the German of Meinhard and Bernauer.
      Opened December 20, 1922 for 65 performances.
  Reviews:
    Bookman 57:54-5, Mar 1923
    Independent 110:73, Jan 20, 1923
    Life (NY) 81:18, Jan 10, 1923
    New York Clipper 70:20, Jan 3, 1923
    New York Times p. 20, Dec 25, 1922
                  VII, p. 3, Jan 21, 1923
    Scientific American 128:154-5, Mar 1923
    Theatre Magazine 37:15-16, Feb 1923
Joseph and His Brethren
  Productions:
    Opened January 11, 1913 for 121 performances.
  Reviews:
    Blue Book 16:1132-6, Apr 1913
    Bookman 37:63-4, Mar 1913
    Collier's 50:23, Feb 22, 1913
    Current Opinion 54:206-7, Mar 1913
    Dramatic Mirror 69:10, Jan 8, 1913
                     69:7, Jan 22, 1913
                     70:12, Sep 10, 1913
    Dramatist 4:348, Apr 1913
    Everybody's 28:520, Apr 1913
    Green Book 9:566-8+, Apr 1913
    Independent 74:265-6, Jan 30, 1913
    Life (NY) 61:200, Jan 23, 1913
    Munsey 48:1014-15, Mar 1913
           50:473, Dec 1913
    National Magazine 39:417-20, Dec 1913
    New York Dramatic News 57:19, Jan 11, 1913
                           57:22, Jan 18, 1913

Joseph and His Brethren (cont.)
New York Times II,p.13, Jan 26, 1913
VII,p.6, Jan 26, 1913
Red Book 20:1073-7, Apr 1913
Theatre Magazine 17:33-4+, Feb 1913
17:94-6+, Mar 1913

The Lady of Coventry
Productions:
Opened November 21, 1911 for 16 performances.
Reviews:
Dramatic Mirror 66:7-8, Nov 29, 1911
Green Book 7:286-7, Feb 1912
Theatre Magazine 15:xi-xii, Jan 1912

The Paper Chase
Productions:
Opened November 25, 1912 for 25 performances.
Reviews:
Blue Book 16:926-8, Mar 1913
Dramatic Mirror 68:7, Nov 27, 1912
Everybody's 28:259, Feb 1913
Green Book 9:367, Feb 1913
Theatre Magazine 17:1-3, Jan 1913

Pomander Walk
Productions:
Opened December 20, 1910 for 143 performances.
Reviews:
American Mercury 71:797-801, Apr 1911
Blue Book 13:16-18, May 1911
Book News 30:498-500, Mar 1912
Bookman 23:606, Feb 1911
Canadian Magazine 36:475-8, Mar 1911
Collier's 46:19, Jan 28, 1911
Dramatic Mirror 64:7+, Dec 28, 1910
Everybody's 24:559-60, Apr 1911
Green Book 5:455-7+, Mar 1911
6:860-4, Oct 1911
Harper's Weekly 55:18+, Jan 21, 1911
Independent 70:151-2, Jan 19, 1911
Leslie's Weekly 112:11, Jan 5, 1911
Life (NY) 57:124, Jan 12, 1911
Metropolitan Magazine 34:126-7, Apr 1911
Munsey 44:708-9, Feb 1911
Pearson 25:385-6, Mar 1911
Red Book 16:945-9, Mar 1911
Theatre Magazine 13:34-5+, Feb 1911

Rosemary (with Murray Carson)
    Productions:
        Opened January 12, 1915 for 15 performances.
    Reviews:
        Dramatic Mirror 73:8, Jan 20, 1915
        New York Times p. 9, Jan 13, 1915
                        VII, p. 6, Jan 17, 1915

Phillips, Stephen
    Herod
    Productions:
        Opened October 26, 1909 for 31 performances.
    Reviews:
        Collier's 44:9, Nov 13, 1909
                  44:21, Dec 4, 1909
        Dramatic Mirror 62:5, Nov 6, 1909
        Everybody's 22:127-8, Jan 1910
        Forum 42:578-9, Dec 1909
        Harper's Weekly 53:24, Nov 13, 1909
        Independent 67:1124, Nov 18, 1909
        Leslie's Weekly 109:462, Nov 11, 1909
        Life (NY) 54:672, Nov 11, 1909
        Metropolitan Magazine 31:528-9, Jan 1910
        Munsey 42:595-6, Jan 1910
        Theatre Magazine 10:169-70, Jan 1910
    Paolo and Francesca
    Productions:
        Opened December 2, 1924 for 8 performances.
        Opened April 1, 1929 for 16 performances.
    Reviews:
        Catholic World 129:200-1, May 19, 1929
        Commonweal 9:684, Apr 17, 1929
        New York Times p. 24, Dec 3, 1924
                        VIII, p. 5, Dec 7, 1924
                        p. 28, Apr 2, 1929
        Theatre Magazine 6:282, Nov 1906

Pinero, Arthur Wing
    The Amazons
    Productions:
        Opened April 28, 1913 for 48 performances.
    Reviews:
        Bookman 37:430, Jun 1913
        Dramatic Mirror 69:6, Apr 30, 1913
        Green Book 10:4-6+, Jul 1913
        New York Dramatic News 57:20, May 3, 1913

The Enchanted Cottage
  Productions:
    Opened March 31, 1923 for 65 performances.
  Reviews:
    Independent 110:302, Apr 28, 1923
    Life (NY) 81:18, Apr 19, 1923
    New York Times p. 22, Apr 2, 1923
                    VIII, p. 1, Apr 8, 1923
The Gay Lord Quex
  Productions:
    Opened November 12, 1917 for 40 performances.
  Reviews:
    Bookman 46:475-7, Dec 1917
    Book News 36: 219, Feb 1918
    Dramatic Mirror 77:5, Nov 24, 1917
    Dramatist 9:897, Apr 1918
    Life (NY) 70:836, Nov 22, 1917
    New York Times p. 11, Nov 13, 1917
The Magistrate
  Productions:
    (Off Broadway) Opened March 8, 1963 for 9
      performances.
  No Reviews.
Mid-Channel
  Productions:
    Opened January 31, 1910 for 96 performances.
  Reviews:
    Dramatic Mirror 63:8, Feb 12, 1910
    Dramatist 3:205-6, Oct 1911
    Everybody's 22:696-8, May 1910
    Green Book 3:764-5, Apr 1910
    Hampton 24:569, Apr 1910
    Harper's Weekly 54:24, Apr 2, 1910
    Life (NY) 55:244, Feb 10, 1910
    Literary Digest 40:350-1, Feb 19, 1910
    Metropolitan Magazine 32:394-5, Jun 1910
    Pearson 23:553-4, Apr 1910
    Theatre Magazine 11:68+, Mar 1910
The Mind-the-Paint Girl
  Productions:
    Opened September 9, 1912 for 13 performances.
  Reviews:
    Blue Book 16:252-6, Dec 1912
    Collier's 50:28, Oct 5, 1912
    Dramatic Mirror 68:6, Sep 11, 1912
    Dramatist 4:335-6, Jan 1913
    Everybody's 27:668-70, Nov 1912

Green Book 8:772, Nov 1912
        8:988, Dec 1912
Leslie's Weekly 115:497+, Nov 14, 1912
Life (NY) 60:1812-13, Sep 19, 1912
Literary Digest 44:534-5, Mar 16, 1912
McClure 40:63-4+, Mar 1913
Metropolitan Magazine 36:33-6, Oct 1912
Munsey 47:985, Sep 1912
        48:349-50, Nov 1912
Red Book 19:945+, Sep 1912

Preserving Mr. Panmure

Productions:
Opened February 27, 1912 for 31 performances.
Reviews:
American Playwright 1:108-10, Apr 1912
Blue Book 15:241+, Jun 1912
Bookman 35:173-4, Apr 1912
Collier's 48:34-5+, Mar 16, 1912
Dramatic Mirror 67:6, Mar 6, 1912
Dramatist 3:256-7, Jul 1912
Everybody's 26:686-8, May 1912
Green Book 7:900-2+, May 1912
        7:974-6, May 1912
Leslie's Weekly 114:293, Mar 14, 1912
Life (NY) 59:540, Mar 14, 1912
Munsey 47:130, Apr 1912
Red Book 19:181-7, May 1912
Theatre Magazine 15:xiv, Apr 1912

The Second Mrs. Tanqueray

Productions:
Opened February 3, 1913 for 16 performances.
Opened October 27, 1924 for 72 performances.
Reviews:
Dramatic Mirror 69:6, Feb 5, 1913
Dramatist 4:334, Jan 1913
Fortnightly Review 118:345-8, Aug 1922
Green Book 6:837-42, Oct 1911
Independent 113:551, Dec 20, 1924
Life (NY) 84:18, Nov 13, 1924
Nation 119:551-2, Nov 19, 1924
New York Times p. 11, Feb 5, 1913
        p. 27, Oct 28, 1924
        VIII,p. 1, Nov 2, 1924
        VIII,p. 1, Nov 9, 1924
Theatre Arts 17:xxix, Mar 1913
Theatre Magazine 40:20, Jan 1925
Yale Review 5:121-2, Oct 1915

The Thunderbolt
  Productions:
    Opened November 12, 1910 in repertory.
    Opened November 16, 1911 in repertory.
  Reviews:
    Blue Book 12:867-8, Feb 1911
    Bookman 23:164-7, Jan 1911
    Columbian Magazine 3:701+, Jan 1911
    Current Literature 50:184-91, Feb 1911
    Dramatic Mirror 66:8, Nov 29, 1911
    Dramatist 2:115-18, Jan 1911
    Everybody's 24:412+, Mar 1911
    Harper's Weekly 54:28-9, Dec 10, 1910
    Life (NY) 56:910, Nov 24, 1910
    Metropolitan Magazine 33:798, Mar 1911
    Munsey 44:562-3, Jan 1911
    Nation 91:479, Nov 17, 1910
    Pearson 25:117-21, Jan 1911
    Theatre 12:163-4+, Dec 1910
Trelawny of the Wells
  Productions:
    Opened January 1, 1911 for 48 performances.
    Opened June 1, 1925 for eight performances.
    Opened January 31, 1927 for 56 performances.
    (Off Broadway) Opened November 25, 1961 for nine
      performances.
  Reviews:
    Bookman 65:204, Apr 1927
    Dramatic Mirror 65:11, Jan 4, 1911
    Dramatist 18:1336-7, Apr 1927
    Life (NY) 57:125, Jan 12, 1911
              89:21, Feb 24, 1927
    Munsey 44:710, Feb 1911
    New Republic 49:275, Jan 26, 1926
    New York Times p. 16, Jun 2, 1925
                  p. 24, Feb 1, 1927
                  VII, p. 1, Feb 6, 1927
    Outlook 145:396-7, Mar 30, 1927
    Pearson 25:386-7, Mar 1911
    Theatre Magazine 13:42+, Feb 1911

Pinter, Harold
  The Caretaker
    Productions:
      Opened October 4, 1961 for 165 performances.
      (Off Broadway) Opened January 30, 1964 for 94
        performances.

Reviews:
    America 106:376, Dec 9, 1961
    Christian Century 78:1403-6, Nov 22, 1961
    Commonweal 75:122-3, Oct 27, 1961
                77:366, Dec 28, 1962
    Life 51:195-6, Nov 17, 1961
    Nation 193:276, Oct 21, 1961
    National Review 11:424, Dec 16, 1961
    New Republic 145:29-30, Oct 23, 1961
    New York Theatre Critics' Reviews 1961:247
    New York Times p. 42, Oct 5, 1961
                II, p. 1, Oct 15, 1961
                p. 16, Jan 31, 1964
    New Yorker 36:60-1, Jul 9, 1960
                37:162, Oct 14, 1961
    Newsweek 58:101, Oct 16, 1961
    Reporter 23:48, Oct 13, 1960
    Saturday Review 44:34, Oct 21, 1961
    Theatre Arts 45:12, Dec 1961
    Time 78:58, Oct 13, 1961
The Collection
  Productions:
    (Off Broadway) Opened November 26, 1962 for 578
      performances.
  Reviews:
    Commonweal 77:367, Dec 28, 1962
    Nation 195:430, Dec 15, 1962
    New York Times p. 44, Nov 27, 1962
                II, p. 5, Dec 9, 1962
    New Yorker 38:148-50, Dec 8, 1962
    Saturday Review 45:30, Dec 15, 1962
    Theatre Arts 47:10-11, Jan 1963
    Time 80:73, Dec 7, 1962
The Dumbwaiter
  Productions:
    (Off Broadway) Opened November 26, 1962 for 578
      performances.
  Reviews:
    Commonweal 77:367, Dec 28, 1962
    Nation 195:429-30, Dec 15, 1962
    New York Times p. 44, Nov 27, 1962
                II, p. 5, Dec 9, 1962
    New Yorker 38:148-50, Dec 8, 1962
    Saturday Review 45:30, Dec 15, 1962
    Theatre Arts 47:10-11, Jan 1963
    Time 80:72-3, Dec 7, 1962
The Lover

The Lover (cont.)
  Productions:
    (Off Broadway) Opened January 4, 1964 for 89
      performances.
  Reviews:
    Commonweal 79:484-5, Jan 24, 1964
    Nation 198:106, Jan 27, 1964
    New Republic 150:28+, Feb 1, 1964
    New York Times p. 35, Jan 6, 1964
    New Yorker 39:69-70, Jan 11, 1964
    Saturday Review 47:25, Jan 25, 1964
    Time 83:64, Jan 17, 1964
    Vogue 143:22, Feb 15, 1964
The Room
  Productions:
    (Off Broadway) Opened December 9, 1964 for 343
      performances.
  Reviews:
    Commonweal 82:193, Apr 30, 1965
    Nation 199:523, Dec 28, 1964
    New York Times p. 62, Dec 10, 1964
    New Yorker 40:68+, Dec 19, 1964
    Newsweek 64:75-6, Dec 21, 1964
    Saturday Review 47:33, Dec 26, 1964
    Time 84:86, Dec 18, 1964
    Vogue 145:98, Feb 1, 1965
A Slight Ache
  Productions:
    (Off Broadway) Opened Dec 16, 1962 for 16
      performances.
    (Off Broadway) Opened December 9, 1964 for 343
      performances.
  Reviews:
    Commonweal 82:194, Apr 30, 1965
    Nation 199:523, Dec 28, 1964
    New York Times p. 62, Dec 10, 1964
    New Yorker 40:68+, Dec 19, 1964
    Newsweek 64:75-6, Dec 21, 1964
    Saturday Review 47:33, Dec 26, 1964
    Time 84:86, Dec 18, 1964
    Vogue 145:98, Feb 1, 1965

Pirandello, Luigi
As You Desire Me
  Productions:
    Adapted by Dmitri Ostrow. Opened January 28, 1931
      for 142 performances.

190

Reviews:
  Arts and Decoration 34:84, Apr 1931
  Bookman 73:409-10, Jun 1931
  Catholic World 132:721, Mar 1931
  Commonweal 13:415, Feb 11, 1931
  Drama 21:9, Apr 1931
  Life (NY) 97:18, Feb 20, 1931
  Living Age 338:290-1, May 1, 1930
  Nation 132:198, Feb 18, 1931
  New Republic 66:19, Feb 18, 1931
              66:209, Apr 8, 1931
  New York Times p. 21, Jan 29, 1931
  Outlook 158:36, May 13, 1931
  Sketch Book 8:25, Apr 1931
  Theatre Arts 15:277, Apr 1931
  Theatre Magazine 53:28-9, Mar 1931
              53:26, Apr 1931

Call It Virtue
  Productions:
    (Off Broadway) Translated by Edward Eager. Opened
      March 27, 1963 for 24 performances.
  Reviews:
    New York Times p. 8, Mar 28, 1963
    Newsweek 61:85, Apr 8, 1963

Floriani's Wife
  Productions:
    Adapted by Ann Sprague MacDonald. Opened
      October 13, 1923 for 16 performances.
  Reviews:
    New Republic 36:207, Oct 17, 1923
    New York Times p. 10, Oct 1, 1923
              IX, p. 1, Oct 7, 1923

Henry IV (see The Living Mask)

Lazarus
  Productions:
    (Off Broadway) Opened April 2, 1963 for six
      performances.
  No Reviews.

The Living Mask (Henry IV)
  Productions:
    Opened January 21, 1924 for 28 performances.
  Reviews:
    American Mercury 1:371-2, Mar 1924
    Arts and Decoration 20:32, Mar 1924
    Freeman 8:544-5, Feb 13, 1924
    New Republic 37:287, Feb 6, 1924

The Living Mask (Henry IV) (cont.)
    New York Times p. 15, Jan 22, 1924
Naked
    Productions:
        Opened October 20, 1924 in repertory.
        Translated by Arthur Livingston. Opened November 8,
            1926 for 32 performances.
    Reviews:
        Nation 123:539-40, Nov 24, 1926
        New Republic 49:16-17, Nov 24, 1926
        New York Times p. 27, Oct 28, 1924
                        VII,p. 1, Nov 2, 1924
                        p. 31, Nov 9, 1926
Right You Are If You Think You Are
    Productions:
        Opened March 2, 1927 for 48 performances.
        (Off Broadway) English version by Eric Bentley.
        Opened March 4, 1964 for 53 performances.
    Reviews:
        American Mercury 11:116-7, May 1927
        Life (NY) 89:23, Mar 17, 1927
        Nation 124:295, Mar 16, 1927
        New Republic 50:141-2, Mar 23, 1927
        New York Times p. 27, Feb 24, 1927
                        VII,p. 1, Mar 6, 1927
                        p. 37, Mar 5, 1964
        New Yorker 40:109, Mar 14, 1964
        Vogue 69:86-7, Apr 15, 1927
Rules of the Game
    Productions:
        (Off Broadway) Season of 1960-1961.
    Reviews:
        New York Times p. 44, Dec 20, 1960
                        p. 22, Jan 24, 1961
        New Yorker 36:43-4, Dec 31, 1960
        Theatre Arts 45:68, Mar 1961
Say It With Flowers
    Productions:
        Translated by Alice Rohe. Opened December 3, 1926
            for two performances.
    Reviews:
        Dramatist 18:1332-3, Jan 1927
        New York Times p. 29, Dec 6, 1926
Six Characters in Search of an Author
    Productions:
        Opened October 30, 1922 for 136 performances.
        Opened February 6, 1924 for 17 performances.

Translated by Edward Storer. Opened April 15, 1931
for 13 performances.
Translated by Frank Fauritz. Adapted by Tyrone
Guthrie and Michael Wagner. Opened December 11,
1955 for 65 performances.
(Off Broadway) Translated by Paul Aliva Mayer.
Opened March 8, 1963 for 529 performances.
Reviews:
America 94:384, Dec 31, 1955
Arts and Decoration 35:46, Jun 1931
Catholic World 116:505-7, Jan 1923
182:385-6, Apr 19, 1956
Commonweal 63:483-4, Feb 10, 1956
78:105-6, Apr 19, 1963
Drama 13:130-1, Jan 1923
Dramatist 14:1177-8, Jul 1923
Life (NY) 80:18, Nov 23, 1922
Nation 115:556, Nov 22, 1922
181:582, Dec 31, 1955
191:334, Apr 20, 1963
New Republic 32:335-6, Nov 22, 1922
33:97, Dec 20, 1922
148:30, Mar 30, 1963
New York Clipper 70:20, Nov 8, 1922
New York Theatre Critics' Reviews 1955:189
New York Times VIII,p.1, Nov 5, 1922
p.11, Dec 31, 1922
p.29, Apr 16, 1931
p.38, Dec 12, 1955
II,p.3, Dec 25, 1955
p.7, Mar 11, 1963
New Yorker 31:46-7, Dec 24, 1955
39:74-5, Mar 23, 1963
Newsweek 46:53, Dec 26, 1955
Saturday Review 38:25, Dec 31, 1955
46:28, Mar 23, 1963
Theatre Arts 15:450-1, Jun 1931
40:75+, Feb 1956
47:13-14, May 1963
Theatre Magazine 37:23, Jan 1923
Time 66:30, Dec 26, 1955

Plunkett, E. J. M. D. (see Dunsany, Lord)

Priestley, J. B.
Dangerous Corner

Dangerous Corner (cont.)
  Productions:
    Opened October 27, 1932 for 206 performances.
    Opened July 17, 1933 for 90 performances.
  Reviews:
    Catholic World 136:334-5, Dec 1932
                   137:724, Sep 1933
    New Outlook 161:47, Dec 1932
    New York Times p. 20, Jul 18, 1933
    Stage 10:34, Dec 1932
    Theatre Arts 16:712-13, Sep 1932
                 17:22-3, Jan 1933
    Vanity Fair 39:20-21, Jan 1933
Eden End
  Productions:
    Opened October 21, 1935 for 24 performances.
  Reviews:
    Commonweal 23:48, Nov 8, 1935
    Nation 141:547-8, Nov 6, 1935
    New York Times p. 17, Oct 22, 1935
    Theatre Arts 19:894+, Dec 1935
The Good Companions (with Edward Knoblock)
  Productions:
    Opened October 1, 1931 for 68 performances.
  Reviews:
    Catholic World 134:208-9, Nov 1931
    Life (NY) 98:19, Oct 23, 1931
    New York Times p. 31, Oct 2, 1931
                   VIII,p. 1, Oct 11, 1931
                   p. 29, Nov 27, 1931
    Theatre Arts 15:982-3, Dec 1931
I Have Been Here Before
  Productions:
    Opened October 13, 1938 for 20 performances.
  Reviews:
    Commonweal 29:21, Oct 28, 1938
    New York Times p. 26, Oct 14, 1938
    Newsweek 12:34, Oct 24, 1938
    Theatre Arts 22:861, Dec 1938
    Time 32:56, Oct 24, 1938
An Inspector Calls
  Productions:
    Opened October 21, 1947 for 95 performances.
  Reviews:
    Catholic World 166:265, Dec 1947
    Commonweal 47:119, Nov 14, 1947
    Forum 109:25, Jan 1948

New Republic 117:35, Nov 10, 1947
New York Theatre Critics' Reviews 1947:291
New York Times p. 38, Oct 22, 1947
New Yorker 23:47-8, Nov 1, 1947
Newsweek 30:76+, Nov 3, 1947
School and Society 66:422-3, Nov 29, 1947
Theatre Arts 31:61, Dec 1947
                32:11, Jan 1948
Time 50:71, Nov 3, 1947

Laburnum Grove

Productions:
Opened January 14, 1935 for 131 performances.
Reviews:
Commonweal 21:403, Feb 1, 1935
Catholic World 140:722, Mar 1935
New Republic 81:336, Jan 1935
New York Times p. 23, Jan 15, 1935
                X,p. 1, Jan 20, 1935
Newsweek 5:32, Jan 12, 1935
Time 25:62, Jan 24, 1935

The Linden Tree

Productions:
Opened March 2, 1948 for seven performances.
Reviews:
Harper's Bazaar 82:133, Apr 1948
New Republic 118:28, Mar 15, 1948
New York Theatre Critics' Reviews 1948:317
New York Times p. 28, Mar 3, 1948
                II,p. 1, Mar 14, 1948
New Yorker 24:48+, Mar 13, 1948
Newsweek 31:78, Mar 15, 1948
Theatre Arts 31:44+, Nov 1947
Time 51:65, Mar 15, 1948
Vogue 111:192, Apr 1, 1948

A Severed Head (with Iris Murdoch)

Productions:
Opened October 28, 1964 for 29 performances.
Reviews:
Commonweal 81:354, Dec 4, 1964
New York Theatre Critics' Reviews 1964:177
New York Times p. 40, Oct 29, 1964
New Yorker 39:96+, Sep 7, 1963
Saturday Review 47:53, Nov 14, 1964
Time 84:52, Nov 6, 1964

Time and the Conways

Productions:
Opened January 3, 1938 for 32 performances.

Time and the Conways (cont.)
  Reviews:
    Catholic World 146:598, Feb 1938
    Commonweal 27:358, Jan 21, 1938
    Nation 146:81, Jan 15, 1938
    New Republic 93:310, Jan 19, 1938
    New York Times p. 19, Jan 4, 1938
    One Act Play Magazine 1:847-8, Jan 1938
    Stage 15:50, Feb 1938
    Theatre Arts 21:847, Nov 1937
                22:97-8, Feb 1938
    Time 31:61, Jan 17, 1938
When We Are Married
  Productions:
    Opened December 25, 1939 for 156 performances.
  Reviews:
    Commonweal 31:245, Jan 5, 1940
    New York Theatre Critics' Reviews 1940:433
    New York Times p. 22, Dec 26, 1939
                IX,p. 12, Feb 18, 1940
    Theatre Arts 24:168-9, Mar 1940

Quintero, Serafin and Joaquin Alvarez
  A Hundred Years Old
    Productions:
      English translation by Helen and Harley Granville-
      Barker. Opened October 1, 1929 for 39 per-
      formances.
    Reviews:
      American Mercury 18:503-4, Dec 1929
      Catholic World 130:329-30, Dec 1929
      Commonweal 10:616, Oct 16, 1929
      Life (NY) 94:22, Oct 25, 1929
      Nation 129:474, Oct 23, 1929
      New Republic 60:244-5, Oct 16, 1929
      New York Times p. 28, Dec 2, 1929
      Outlook 135:314, Oct 23, 1929
      Review of Reviews 80:158, Dec 1929
      Theatre Arts 13:877-8, Dec 1929
      Theatre Magazine 50:50, Dec 1929
  Malvaloca
    Productions:
      Translated by Jacob J. Fassett, Jr. Opened
      October 2, 1922 for 48 performances.
    Reviews:
      Forum 68:972-3, Nov 1922
      Nation 104:275, Mar 18, 1917

New Republic 32:223-4, Oct 25, 1922
                    33:284-6, Feb 7, 1923
    New York Clipper 70:20, Oct 11, 1922
    New York Times p. 22, Oct 3, 1922
    Theatre Magazine 36:373, 376, Dec 1922
A Sunny Morning
    Productions:
    Opened December 7, 1935 for 1 performance.
    No Reviews.
The Women Have Their Way
    Productions:
    Adapted by Harley and Helen Granville-Barker.
        Opened January 27, 1930 for 25 performances.
    Opened December 1, 1935 for 1 performance.
    Reviews:
    Commonweal 11:424, Feb 12, 1930
    Nation 130:226, Feb 19, 1930
    New York Times p. 28, Jan 28, 1930
    Vogue 75:108, Mar 15, 1930

Rappaport, Solomon (see Ansky, S.)

Rattigan, Terence
    The Browning Version
        Productions:
        Opened October 12, 1949 for 69 performances.
        Reviews:
        Catholic World 170:227, Dec 1949
        Life 27:93, Oct 31, 1949
        New Republic 121:21, Nov 7, 1949
        New York Theatre Critics' Reviews 1949:253
        New York Times p. 32, Oct 13, 1949
        New Yorker 25:60, Oct 22, 1949
        Newsweek 34:84, Oct 24, 1949
        Saturday Review 32:26-7, Nov 5, 1949
        School and Society 71:26, Jan 14, 1950
        Theatre Arts 33:12, Dec 1949
        Time 54:58, Oct 24, 1949
    College Sinners (see First Episode)

The Deep Blue Sea
    Productions:
    Opened November 5, 1952 for 132 performances.
    Reviews:
    Catholic World 176:306-7, Jan 1953
    Commonweal 57:197-8, Nov 28, 1952
    Nation 175:472-3, Nov 22, 1952

The Deep Blue Sea (cont.)
New York Theatre Critics' Reviews 1952:207
New York Times p.38, Nov 6, 1952
                II,p.3, Dec 14, 1952
New Yorker 28:69, Nov 15, 1952
Newsweek 40:74, Nov 17, 1952
Saturday Review 35:36-7, Nov 22, 1952
School and Society 76:402-3, Dec 20, 1952
Theatre Arts 37:21-2, Jan 1953
Time 60:102, Nov 17, 1952
First Episode (College Sinners) (with Philip Heinmann)
Productions:
Opened September 17, 1934 for 40 performances.
Reviews:
New York Times p.18, Sep 18, 1934
Flare Path
Productions:
Opened December 23, 1942 for 14 performances.
Reviews:
Commonweal 37:326, Jan 15, 1943
Current History ns 3:550, Feb 1943
New York Theatre Critics' Reviews 1942:138+
New York Times p.20, Dec 24, 1942
Theatre Arts 27:77-8, Feb 1943
French Without Tears
Productions:
Opened September 28, 1937 for 111 performances.
Reviews:
Catholic World 146:216, Nov 1937
Commonweal 26:580, Oct 15, 1937
New Republic 92:270, Oct 13, 1937
New York Times p.19, Sep 29, 1937
Scribner's Magazine 102:68, Sep 1937
Theatre Arts 21:828, Nov 1937
Time 30:55, Oct 11, 1937
Grey Farm (with Hector Bolitho)
Productions:
Opened May 3, 1940 for 35 performances.
Reviews:
New York Theatre Critics' Reviews 1940:317+
Harlequinade
Productions:
Opened October 12, 1949 for 69 performances.
Reviews:
Catholic World 170:227, Dec 1949
Life 27:94-5, Oct 31, 1949
New Republic 121:21, Nov 7, 1949

New York Theatre Critics' Reviews 1949: 253
New York Times p. 32, Oct 13, 1949
School and Society 71: 26, Jan 14, 1950
Theatre Arts 33: 12, Dec 1949
Time 54: 58, Oct 24, 1949
Love in Idleness (see O Mistress Mine)

Man and Boy
Productions:
Opened November 12, 1963 for 54 performances.
Reviews:
New York Theatre Critics' Reviews 1963: 199
New York Times p. 13, Jun 29, 1963
p. 17, Sep 27, 1963
p. 34, Nov 13, 1963
II, p. 1, Dec 1, 1963
New Yorker 39: 143, Nov 23, 1963
Newsweek 62: 71, Nov 25, 1963
Saturday Review 46: 24, Nov 30, 1963
Time 82: 71, Nov 22, 1963

O Mistress Mine (Love in Idleness)
Productions:
Opened January 23, 1946 for 452 performances.
Reviews:
Catholic World 162: 551, Mar 1946
Forum 105: 659-60, Mar 1946
Life 20: 49-50+, Feb 18, 1946
New Republic 114: 158, Feb 4, 1946
New York Theatre Critics' Reviews 1946: 474
New York Times II, p. 1, Sep 1, 1946
New Yorker 21: 34+, Feb 2, 1946
Newsweek 27: 80, Feb 4, 1946
Theatre Arts 30: 133, Mar 1946
Time 47: 61, Feb 4, 1946

Ross
Productions:
Opened December 26, 1961 for 159 performances.
Reviews:
Commonweal 75: 435-6, Jan 19, 1962
New Republic 146: 20+, Jan 22, 1962
New York Theatre Critics' Reviews 1961: 139
New York Times p. 20, Dec 27, 1961
II, p. 1, Jan 7, 1962
New Yorker 36: 59-60, Jul 9, 1960
37: 55, Jan 6, 1962
Newsweek 55: 78, May 30, 1960
59: 44, Jan 8, 1962
Saturday Review 45: 51, Jan 13, 1962

Ross (cont.)
          Theatre Arts 45: 58-60, Feb 1961
                          46: 57-8, Mar 1962
          Time 75: 56, May 23, 1960
                    79: 52, Jan 5, 1962
Separate Tables (Table by the Window and Table Number Seven)
     Productions:
          Opened October 25, 1956 for 332 performances.
     Reviews:
          America 96: 281+, Dec 1, 1956
          Catholic World 184: 303, Jan 1957
          Christian Century 73: 1328-9, Nov 14, 1956
          Commonweal 65: 234, Nov 30, 1956
          Life 41: 89-90, Dec 3, 1956
          Nation 183: 416, Nov 10, 1956
          New Republic 135: 23, Nov 12, 1956
          New York Theatre Critics' Reviews 1956: 246
          New York Times p. 33, Oct 26, 1956
                          II, p. 1, Nov 4, 1956
                          II, p. 1, Sep 15, 1957
          New Yorker 32: 68+, Nov 3, 1956
          Newsweek 48: 78, Nov 5, 1956
          Reporter 13: 43, Oct 20, 1955
          Saturday Review 38: 33, Sep 17, 1955
                          39: 29, Nov 3, 1956
          Theatre Arts 41: 19-20, Jan 1957
          Time 68: 75, Nov 5, 1956
          Vogue 128: 72, Oct 15, 1956
The Sleeping Prince
     Productions:
          Opened November 1, 1956 for 60 performances.
     Reviews:
          America 96: 359, Dec 22, 1956
          Catholic World 184: 307, Jan 1957
          Commonweal 65: 235, Nov 30, 1956
          Nation 183: 485, Dec 1, 1956
          New York Theatre Critics' Reviews 1956: 226
          New York Times p. 31, Nov 2, 1956
          New Yorker 29: 163, Dec 12, 1953
                          32: 112-14, Nov 10, 1956
          Newsweek 48: 54, Nov 12, 1956
          Saturday Review 39: 28, Nov 17, 1956
          Theatre Arts 41: 24, Jan 1957
          Time 68: 71, Nov 12, 1956
Table by the Window (see Separate Tables)

Table Number Seven (see Separate Tables)

While the Sun Shines
  Productions:
      Opened September 19, 1944 for 39 performances.
  Reviews:
      Catholic World 160: 169, Nov 1944
      Commonweal 40: 589, Oct 6, 1944
      Nation 159: 389, Sep 30, 1944
      New York Theatre Critics' Reviews 1944: 130
      New York Times p. 21, Sep 20, 1944
                    II, p. 1, Sep 24, 1944
      New Yorker 20: 38, Sep 30, 1944
      Newsweek 24: 99, Oct 2, 1944
      Theatre Arts 28: 641, Nov 1944
      Time 44: 59, Oct 2, 1944
The Winslow Boy
  Productions:
      Opened October 29, 1947 for 215 performances.
  Reviews:
      Catholic World 166: 264, Dec 1947
      Commonweal 47: 120, Nov 14, 1947
      Forum 109: 25, Jan 1948
      Life 23: 97-8+, Nov 24, 1947
      Nation 165: 537, Nov 15, 1947
      New Republic 117: 35, Nov 10, 1947
      New York Theatre Critics' Reviews 1947: 283
      New York Times p. 32, Oct 30, 1947
      New Yorker 23: 52, Nov 8, 1947
      Newsweek 30: 74, Nov 10, 1947
      Saturday Review 30: 24-9, Nov 29, 1947
      School and Society 67: 315-16, Apr 24, 1948
      Theatre Arts 30: 597, Oct 1946
                    31: 43, Jun 1947
                    32: 12, Jan 1948
      Time 50: 100, Nov 10, 1947

Robinson, Lennox
  Church Street
    Productions:
        Opened November 19, 1934 for one performance.
        (Off Broadway) Season of 1947-1948.
    Reviews:
        New Republic 118: 30, Feb 23, 1948
        School and Society 67: 166, Feb 28, 1948
  Crabbed Youth and Age
    Productions:
        Opened May 8, 1924 for one performance.
        Opened October 21, 1932 in repertory.

201

Crabbed Youth and Age (cont.)
 Reviews:
  New York Times p. 25, Nov 4, 1932
Drama at Inish (Is Life Worth Living?)
 Productions:
  Opened November 9, 1933 for 12 performances.
  Opened November 14, 1934 for 3 performances.
  Opened December 13, 1937 for 4 performances.
 Reviews:
  Commonweal 27: 272, Dec 31, 1927
  New York Times X, p. 1, Sep 17, 1933
             p. 24, Nov 15, 1934
             p. 33, Dec 14, 1937
  Theatre Arts 18: 13-14, Jan 1934
The Far Off Hills
 Productions:
  Opened October 18, 1932 for 13 performances.
  Opened November 14, 1934 for one performance.
  Opened October 11, 1937 for 47 performances.
 Reviews:
  Nation 145: 484, Oct 30, 1937
  New York Times p. 22, Oct 19, 1932
             p. 30, Oct 12, 1937
  Theatre Arts 21: 928, Dec 1937
Harvest
 Productions:
  Opened November 20, 1911 in repertory (The Irish Players).
 Reviews:
  Dramatic Mirror 66: 7, Dec 20, 1911
  New York Dramatic News 65: 6, Feb 16, 1918
Is Life Worth Living? (see Drama At Inish)

The Lost Leader
 Productions:
  Opened November 11, 1919 for 31 performances.
 Reviews:
  Current Opinion 67: 166-7, Sep 1919
              68: 47-53, Jan 1920
  Dramatic Mirror 80: 1825, Nov 27, 1919
  Living Age 302: 399-401, Aug 16, 1919
  New York Times p. 11, Nov 12, 1919
  Theatre Magazine 30: 368, Dec 1919
  Weekly Review 1: 238-9, Jul 26, 1919
Patriots
 Productions:
  Opened February 4, 1913 in repertory (The Irish Players).
 Reviews:

Collier's 50: 25, Mar 15, 1913
Dramatic Mirror 69: 6-7, Feb 19, 1913
New York Times p. 15, Feb 12, 1913

The White Headed Boy
  Productions:
    Opened September 15, 1921 for 60 performances.
    Opened October 21, 1932 in repertory.
  Reviews:
    Bookman 54: 231-2, Nov 1921
    Dramatic Mirror 84: 448, Sep 24, 1921
    Independent 107: 36, Oct 8, 1921
    Life (NY) 78: 18, Oct 6, 1921
    Nation 113: 428, Oct 12, 1921
    New Republic 28: 161, Oct 5, 1921
    New York Clipper 69: 17, Sep 21, 1921
    New York Times p. 20, Sep 16, 1921
    Theatre Magazine 34: 386, Dec 1921
                    53: 50, Jan 1931
    Weekly Review 3: 601-2, Dec 15, 1920

Rostand, Edmond
  L'Aiglon (The Eagle)
  Productions:
    Opened December 5, 1910 in repertory.
    Opened June 19, 1911 in repertory.
    Opened October 20, 1924 for 48 performances.
    Translated by Louis N. Parker. Opened December 26,
      1927 for eight performances.
    Adapted by Clemence Dane. Opened November 3, 1934
      for 58 performances.
  Reviews:
    Catholic World 140: 337-8, Dec 1934
    Commonweal 21: 96, Nov 16, 1934
    Dramatic Mirror 64: 6-7, Dec 7, 1910
    Dramatist 4: 382-3, Jul 1913
    Nation 119: 527-8, Nov 12, 1924
            139: 601, Nov 21, 1934
    New Republic 81: 78, Nov 28, 1934
    New York Times p. 21, Oct 21, 1924
                    p. 24, Dec 27, 1927
                    p. 22, Nov 5, 1934
    Stage 14: 87, Aug 1937
    Theatre Arts 19: 12, Jan 1935
    Theatre Magazine 47: 62, Mar 1928
    Vanity Fair 43: 31, Jan 1935
    Vogue 84: 72, Dec 15, 1934

Chantecler
  Productions:
    Adapted by Louis N. Parker. Opened January 23, 1911
      for 96 performances.
  Reviews:
    Blue Book 12: 1092-5, Apr 1911
    Bookman 31: 397-401, Jun 1910
              32: 154-6, Oct 1910
    Canadian Magazine 36: 482+, Mar 1911
    Collier's 46: 19+, Feb 4, 1911
    Colonnade 9: 205-15, Jun 1915
    Columbian 4: 347-8+, May 1911
    Current Literature 48: 319-21, Mar 1910
                        48: 544-9, May 1910
                        49: 304-16, Sep 1910
                        50: 513-15, Mar 1911
    Dramatic Mirror 65: 7, Jan 25, 1911
    Everybody's Magazine 24: 553-4, Apr 1911
    Fortnightly Review 93: 575-90, Mar 1910
    Independent 68: 680-5, Apr 27, 1910
                70: 406-7, Feb 23, 1911
    Leslie's Weekly 110: 260+, Mar 7, 1910
                    112: 153, Feb 9, 1911
    Life (NY) 57: 260, Feb 2, 1911
    Literary Digest 40: 103, Jan 15, 1910
                    40: 349-50, Feb 19, 1910
                    40: 441-2, Mar 5, 1910
                    40: 1265, Jun 25, 1910
                    42: 208-9, Feb 4, 1911
    Living Age 264: 696, Mar 12, 1910
               265: 37-43, Apr 2, 1910
    Munsey 44: 871-2, Mar 1911
    Nation 90: 491-2, May 12, 1910
           92: 264, Mar 16, 1911
    New England Magazine ns42: 227-31, Apr 1910
    Outlook 94: 373, Feb 9, 1910
            97: 251-2, Feb 4, 1911
    Red Book 16: 1137-43+, Apr 1911
    Theatre Magazine 13: 70-1+, Mar 1911
Cyrano de Bergerac
  Productions:
    Opened November 1, 1923 for 232 performances.
    English version by Brian Hooker. Opened February 18,
      1926 for 96 perfromances.
    English version by Brian Hooker. Opened December 25,
      1928.
    Adapted by Brian Hooker. Opened December 26, 1932

for 16 performances.
Translated by Brian Hooker. Opened April 27, 1946 for
40 performances.
English version by Brian Hooker. Opened October 8,
1946 for 193 performances.
Adapted by Brian Hooker. Opened November 11, 1953
for 15 performances.
(Off Broadway) Opened January 11, 1964 for eight per-
formances.
Reviews:
American Mercury 64: 53-5, Jan 1947
Bookman 48: 676-9, Feb 1919
Catholic World 164: 168-9, Nov 1946
            178: 308-9, Jan 1954
Classic 18: 48+, Feb 1924
Commonweal 24: 76, May 15, 1936
            45: 70, Nov 1, 1946
Golden Book 16: 250-8, Sep 1932
Life (NY) 82: 18, Nov 22, 1923
          83: 18, Feb 28, 1924
          87: 20, Mar 25, 1926
Literary Digest 79: 28, Nov 24, 1923
               109: 18, Jun 13, 1931
Modern Language Notes 37: 47-9, Jan 1922
National Magazine 52: 422, Mar 1924
New Republic 37: 18, Nov 28, 1923
            115: 518, Oct 21, 1946
New York Theatre Critics' Reviews 1946: 321
                                  1953: 214
New York Times p. 14, Nov 2, 1923
               VIII, p. 1, Nov 11, 1923
               p. 18, Feb 19, 1926
               p. 14, Dec 26, 1928
               p. 11, Dec 27, 1932
               p. 16, Dec 29, 1932
               p. 1, Apr 17, 1936
               p. 33, Oct 9, 1946
               II, p. 1, Nov 3, 1946
               p. 24, Nov 13, 1953
New Yorker 22: 57-8, Oct 19, 1946
           29: 88, Nov 21, 1953
Newsweek 7: 44, May 9, 1936
         28: 93, Oct 21, 1946
         42: 64, Nov 23, 1953
Outlook 151: 299, Feb 20, 1929
Saturday Review 29: 28-30, Nov 2, 1946
               48: 18, Sep 1, 1962

Cyrano de Bergerac (cont.)
    Theatre Arts 30: 690+, Dec 1946
                31: 50, Jan 1947
                38: 25, Jan 1954
                47: 69, Aug 1963
    Theatre Magazine 39: 23, Jan 1924
    Time 48: 78, Oct 1, 1946
         49: 48, Mar 3, 1947
The Eagle (see L'Aiglon)

The Lady of Dreams
    Productions:
        Adapted by Louis N. Parker from Rostand's La Princesse
        Lointaine.   Opened February 28, 1912 for 21 per-
        formances.
    Reviews:
        American Playwright 1: 114-16, Apr 1912
        Dramatic Mirror 67: 6-7, Mar 6, 1912
        Everybody's Magazine 26: 688-9, May 1912
        Green Book 7: 810-12+, May 1912
                    7: 973-4, May 1912
        Life (NY) 59: 540-1, May 14, 1912
        Munsey 47: 130, Apr 1912
        Theatre Magazine 15: 107-8+, Apr 1912
Last Night of Don Juan
    Productions:
        Translated by Sidney Howard.   Opened November 9, 1925
        for 16 performances.
    Reviews:
        Drama 16: 133, Jan 1926
        Life (NY) 86: 22, Nov 26, 1925
        Nation 121: 603-4, Nov 25, 1925
        New Republic 45: 86-7, Dec 9, 1925
        New York Times p. 23, Nov 10, 1925
        Theatre Arts 10: 5-7, Jan 1926
        Vanity Fair 25: 40, Jan 1926
La Samaritaine
    Productions:
        Opened December 5, 1910 in repertory.
    Reviews:
        Bookman 23: 602-4, Feb 1911
        Current Literature 50: 193-6, Feb 1911
        Literary Digest 41: 1203, Dec 24, 1910

Sartre, Jean-Paul
    The Condemned of Altona (Les Sequestres d' Altona)
        Productions:

Adapted by Justin O'Brien.   Opened February 3, 1966
     for 46 performances.
Reviews:
     America 114: 272-3, Feb 19, 1966
     Nation 189: 492-3, Dec 26, 1959
               202: 222-4, Feb 21, 1966
     New Republic 154: 42-3, Feb 26, 1966
     New York Theatre Critics' Reviews 1966: 372
     New York Times p. 21, Feb 4, 1966
     New York Times Magazine p. 84, Nov 29, 1959
     New Yorker 41: 206+, Oct 2, 1965
                41: 110+, Feb 12, 1966
     Newsweek 67: 88, Feb 14, 1966
     Saturday Review 49: 52, Feb 19, 1966
     Time 87: 67, Feb 18, 1966
     Vogue 147: 58, Mar 15, 1966
The Flies
  Productions:
     (Off Broadway) Opened April 17, 1947.
  Reviews:
     Commonweal 46: 93-4, May 9, 1947
     Forum 107: 541-5, Jun 1947
     New York Times p. 26, Apr 18, 1947
     New Yorker 23: 52, May 24, 1947
No Exit
  Productions:
     Adapted by Paul Bowles.   Opened November 26, 1946
        for 31 performances.
  Reviews:
     Catholic World 164: 358, Jan 1947
     Commonweal 45: 229, Dec 13, 1946
     Harper's Bazaar 80: 220, Dec 1946
     Nation 163: 708, Dec 14, 1946
     New Republic 115: 764, Dec 9, 1946
     New York Theatre Critics' Reviews 1946: 241
     New York Times p. 21, Nov 27, 1946
     New Yorker 22: 69, Dec 7, 1946
     Newsweek 28: 92, Dec 9, 1946
     Saturday Review 29: 26-8, Dec 28, 1946
     Theatre Arts 30: 641+, Nov 1946
                 31: 16+, Jan 1947
                 31: 70, Dec 1947
     Time 48: 83, Dec 9, 1946
     Vogue 108: 200, Dec 1, 1946
Red Gloves
  Productions:
     Adapted by Daniel Teradash.   Opened December 4, 1948

Red Gloves (cont.)
    for 113 performances.
Reviews:
    Catholic World 168: 322-3, Jan 1949
    Forum 111: 162, Mar 1949
    Harper's Bazaar 82: 92, Dec 1948
    Life 26: 49+, Jan 3, 1949
    Nation 167: 731-2, Dec 25, 1948
           168: 19, Jan 1, 1949
    New Republic 119: 28-9, Dec 20, 1948
    New York Theatre Critics' Reviews 1948: 132
    New York Times p. 28, Dec 6, 1948
               II, p. 3, Dec 12, 1948
    New York Times Magazine p. 20, Jul 1948
    New Yorker 24: 57-8, Dec 11, 1948
    Newsweek 32: 84, Dec 13, 1948
    Saturday Review 32: 24-7, Jan 1, 1949
    School and Society 69: 84-6, Jan 29, 1949
    Theatre Arts 33: 18+, Jan 1949
    Time 52: 69, Dec 13, 1948
The Respectful Prostitute
Productions:
    Adapted by Eva Wolas. Opened March 16, 1948 for 348
      performances.
Reviews:
    Catholic World 167: 71, Apr 1948
    Commonweal 47: 566, Mar 19, 1948
    Life 24: 83-4, Mar 29, 1948
    Nation 166: 257, Feb 28, 1948
    New Republic 118: 29, Feb 23, 1948
    New York Times p. 27, Feb 10, 1948
               II, p. 1, Feb 15, 1948
    New Yorker 24: 50+, Mar 27, 1948
    Saturday Review 31: 26-7, Mar 13, 1948
    School and Society 67: 166, Feb 28, 1948
    Theatre Arts 31: 45, Feb 1947
            32: 21, Oct 1948
            32: 31-2, Apr 1948
    Time 51: 46, Apr 5, 1948
    U. N. World 1: 60, Feb 1947
    Vogue 111: 150-51, Apr 1, 1948
Les Sequestres d' Altona (see The Condemned of Altona)

The Victors
Productions:
    (Off Broadway) Opened December 1948.
Reviews:

Commonweal 49: 352, Jan 14, 1949
Forum 111: 162-3, Mar 1949
New Republic 120: 19, Jan 10, 1949
New York Times p. 17, Dec 27, 1948
               II, p. 1, Jan 2, 1949
               II, p. 2, Jan 9, 1949
School and Society 69: 85, Jan 29, 1949
Theatre Arts 31: 44, Feb 1947
             33: 17, Mar 1949
Time 53: 49, Jan 3, 1949
U. N. World 1: 60-1, Feb 1947

Savior, Alfred
Banco
  Productions:
      Adapted by Clare Kummer. Opened September 20, 1922
        for 69 performances.
  Reviews:
      Life 80: 10, Oct 12, 1922
      New York Clipper 70: 39, Oct 4, 1922
      New York Times p. 18, Sep 21, 1922
      Theatre Magazine 36: 297, Nov 1922
Bluebeard's Eighth Wife
  Productions:
      Adapted by Charlton Andrews. Opened September 19,
        1921 for 155 performances.
  Reviews:
      Dramatic Mirror 84: 448, Sep 24, 1921
      Independent 107: 63, Oct 15, 1921
      Life (NY) 78: 18, Oct 6, 1921
      Nation 112: 427-8, Oct 12, 1921
      New York Clipper 69: 28, Sep 28, 1921
      New York Times p. 12, Sep 20, 1921
      Theatre Magazine 34: 386-7, Dec 1921
The Grand Duchess and the Waiter
  Productions:
      Opened October 13, 1925 for 31 performances.
  Reviews:
      Bookman 62: 479, Dec 1925
      Life (NY) 86:22, Nov 5, 1925
      New York Times p. 31, Oct 14, 1925
He
  Productions:
      Adapted by Chester Erskin. Opened September 21, 1931
        for 40 performances.
  Reviews:
      Bookman 74: 299, Nov 1931

He (cont.)
    Catholic World 134: 209, Nov 1931
    Commonweal 14: 555, Oct 7, 1931
    Nation 133: 373-4, Oct 7, 1931
    New Republic 68: 207-9, Oct 7, 1931
    New York Times p. 33, Sep 22, 1931
    Vanity Fair 37: 36, 80, Nov 1931
The Lion Tamer
    Productions:
    Translated by Winifred Katzin. Opened October 7, 1926
        for 29 performances.
    Reviews:
    Life (NY) 88: 19, Oct 28, 1926
    Nation 123: 408-9, Oct 20, 1926
    New Republic 48: 323-4, Nov 10, 1926
    New York Times p. 26, Oct 8, 1926
                        VIII, p. 1, Oct 17, 1926
    Theatre Arts 10: 812-13, Dec 1926

Schnitzler, Arthur
    The Affairs of Anatol (also see Anatol)
    Productions:
    Opened October 14, 1912 for 72 performances.
    Reviews:
    American Playwright 1: 367-8, Nov 1912
    Blue Book 16: 458-62, Jan 1913
    Collier's 50: 18+, Nov 2, 1912
    Dramatic Mirror 68: 6, Oct 16, 1912
    Everybody's 28: 111, Jan 1913
    Green Book 8: 818-24, Nov 1912
                    9: 64+, Jan 1913
    Life (NY) 60: 2050, Oct 24, 1913
    Munsey 48: 527, Dec 1912
    New York Dramatic News 56: 19, Oct 19, 1912
    Red Book 20: 497-500, Jan 1913
    Theatre Magazine 16: 106+, Oct 1912
                        16: 131, Nov 1912
    Anatol (also see The Affairs of Anatol)
    Productions:
    Adapted by Harley Granville-Barker. Opened January 16,
        1931 for 45 performances.
    Reviews:
    Bookman 73: 71, Mar 1931
    Catholic World 132: 720-1, Mar 1931
    Commonweal 13: 385, Feb 4, 1931
    Life (NY) 97: 18, Feb 6, 1931
    Nation 132: 134-5, Feb 4, 1931

New Republic 65: 323, Feb 4, 1931
New York Times p. 23, Jan 17, 1931
Outlook 157: 190, Feb 4, 1931
Theatre Magazine 53: 25-6, Mar 1931
The Big Scene
Productions:
 Translated by Charles Henry Meltzer. Opened April 15,
 1918 in repertory (The Greenwich Village Players).
Reviews:
 New York Times p. 13, Apr 19, 1918
The Call of Life
Productions:
 English version by Dorothy Donnelly. Opened October 9,
 1925 for 19 performances.
Reviews:
 Bookman 62: 478, Dec 1925
 Nation 121: 494-5, Oct 28, 1925
 New Republic 44: 255-6, Oct 28, 1925
 New York Times p. 10, Oct 10, 1925
The Green Cockatoo
Productions:
 Translated by Philip Littel and George Rublee. Opened
 April 11, 1910 for 16 performances.
 Opened October 6, 1930 in repertory.
Reviews:
 Bookman 31: 418, Jun 1910
 Dramatic Mirror 63: 7, Apr 23, 1910
 New York Times p. 20, Oct 10, 1910
 Theatre Magazine 11: xxix, Jun 1910
Literature
Productions:
 Opened October 4, 1915 in repertory (Washington Square
 Players).
 Translated by Andre Tridon. Opened August 30, 1916 in
 repertory (Washington Square Players).
Reviews:
 Bookman 42: 646+, Feb 1916
 Dramatic Mirror 74: 8, Nov 13, 1915
 New York Times p. 13, Nov 10, 1915

Shaffer, Peter
Five Finger Exercise
Productions:
 Opened December 2, 1959 for 337 performances.
Reviews:
 America 102: 428, Jan 9, 1960
 Christian Century 77: 16, Jan 6, 1960

Five Finger Exercise (cont.)
    Commonweal 71: 395, Jan 1, 1960
    Life 48: 93-4+, Mar 21, 1960
    New York Theatre Critics' Reviews 1959: 207
    New York Times p. 45, Dec 3, 1959
                II, p. 3, Dec 13, 1959
    New Yorker 35: 100-2, Dec 12, 1959
    Reporter 22: 36-7, Jan 7, 1960
    Saturday Review 42: 24, Dec 19, 1959
    Theatre Arts 44: 14, Feb 1960
    Time 74: 77, Dec 14, 1959
The Private Ear
  Productions:
    Opened October 9, 1963 for 163 performances.
  Reviews:
    America 109: 752, Dec 7, 1963
    Nation 197: 306, Nov 9, 1963
    New York Theatre Critics' Reviews 1963: 248
    New York Times p. 51, Oct 10, 1963
                II, p. 1, Oct 20, 1963
    Newsweek 62: 104, Oct 21, 1963
    Theatre Arts 48: 65, Jan 1964
    Time 82: 76+, Oct 18, 1963
The Public Eye
  Productions:
    Opened October 9, 1963 for 163 performances.
  Reviews:
    America 109: 752, Dec 7, 1963
    New York Theatre Critics' Reviews 1963: 248
    New York Times p. 51, Oct 10, 1963
                II, p. 1, Oct 20, 1963
    Newsweek 62: 104, Oct 21, 1963
    Saturday Review 46: 32, Oct 26, 1963
    Theatre Arts 48: 65, Jan 1964
    Time 82: 76+, Oct 18, 1963
Royal Hunt of the Sun
  Productions:
    Opened October 26, 1965 for 261 performances.
  Reviews:
    America 113: 648-9, Nov 20, 1965
    Commonweal 83: 215, Nov 19, 1965
    Dance Magazine 39: 138-9, Dec 1965
    Life 59: 134-5+, Dec 10, 1965
    Nation 201: 397, Nov 22, 1965
    National Review 18: 37, Jan 11, 1966
    New Republic 153: 45-6, Nov 27, 1965
    New York Theatre Critics' Reviews 1965: 293

New York Times p. 36, Oct 27, 1965
                   II, p. 1, Nov 14, 1965
New Yorker 41: 115, Nov 6, 1965
Newsweek 66: 96, Nov 8, 1965
Saturday Review 48: 31, May 29, 1965
                   48: 71, Nov 13, 1965
                   49: 72, Nov 19, 1966
Time 86: 77, Nov 5, 1965
Vogue 144: 112, Oct 1, 1964

Shairp, Mordaunt
  The Green Bay Tree
    Productions:
      Opened October 20, 1933 for 166 performances.
      Opened February 1, 1951 for 20 performances.
    Reviews:
      Catholic World 138: 339-40, Dec 1933
      Commonweal 53: 494, Feb 23, 1951
      Literary Digest 116: 19, Nov 4, 1933
      Nation 137: 548+, Nov 4, 1933
      New Outlook 162: 46, Dec 1933
      New Republic 77: 17-19, Nov 15, 1933
      New York Theatre Critics' Reviews 1951: 368
      New York Times IX, p. 3, Nov 12, 1933
                      p. 21, Mar 12, 1934
                      IV, p. 7, Aug 5, 1934
                      p. 18, Feb 2, 1951
      New Yorker 26: 60, Feb 10, 1951
      Newsweek 37: 72, Feb 12, 1951
      Player's Magazine 10: 13+, Nov-Dec 1933
      Review of Reviews 89: 39, Feb 1934
      Saturday Review 34: 24-6, Feb 24, 1951
      Stage 11: 20-21, Dec 1933
      Theatre Arts 17: 335+, May 1933
                  17: 912+, Dec 1933
      Time 22: 30, Oct 30, 1933
             57: 55, Feb 12, 1951
      Vanity Fair 41: 41, Jan 1934
  The Offense
    Productions:
      Opened November 16, 1925 for four performances.
    Reviews:
      New York Times p. 25, Nov 16, 1925

Shaw, George Bernard
  Admirable Bashville
    Productions:

Admirable Bashville (cont.)
    (Off Broadway) 1955-1956.
  Reviews:
      Catholic World 183: 150, May 1956
      New York Times p. 38, Feb 21, 1956
      Saturday Review 39: 26, Mar 17, 1956
Androcles and the Lion
  Productions:
      Opened January 27, 1915 in repertory.
      Opened November 23, 1925 for 68 performances.
      Opened December 16, 1938 for 104 performances.
      Opened December 19, 1946 for 40 performances.
      (Off Broadway) Opened November 21, 1961 for 48 per-
        formances.
  Reviews:
      American Playwright 4: 49-52, Feb 1915
      Book News 33: 353-4, Mar 1915
      Catholic World 100: 577-9, Feb 1915
                      148: 601, Feb 1939
                      164: 456, Feb 1947
      Collier's 52: 14, Oct 4, 1913
      Commonweal 45: 325, Jan 10, 1947
      Current Opinion 55: 330-1, Nov 1913
                      57: 244-8, Oct 1914
      Dramatic Mirror 73: 8, Feb 3, 1915
      Green Book 13: 767-8, Apr 1915
                  13: 695-6, Apr 1915
      Independent 116: 48, Jan 9, 1946
      Life (NY) 65: 240, Feb 11, 1915
      Life 21: 109, Dec 23, 1946
      Nation 100: 150, Feb 4, 1915
             121: 688-9, Dec 9, 1925
             164: 25, Jan 4, 1947
      New Republic 1: 25, Jan 30, 1915
                   116: 42, Jan 6, 1947
      New York Theatre Critics' Reviews 1946: 217
      New York Times p. 9, Jan 8, 1915
                      p. 28, Nov 24, 1925
                      II, p. 1, Nov 29, 1925
                      p. 10, Dec 17, 1938
                      p. 29, Dec 20, 1946
                      II, p. 1, Dec 29, 1946
                      p. 24, Nov 22, 1961
      New Yorker 22: 36+, Dec 28, 1946
                 37: 119, Dec 2, 1961
      Newsweek 28: 71, Dec 30, 1946
      North American Review 201: 439-42, Mar 1915

Saturday Review 30: 24-7, Jan 11, 1947
School and Society 65: 251, Apr 5, 1947
Theatre Arts 10: 8-10, Jan 1926
            31: 17-18, Feb 1947
Theatre Magazine 21: 110-111, Mar 1915
            43: 16-17, Feb 1926
Time 32: 25, Dec 26, 1938
      48: 34, Dec 30, 1946
Vogue 67: 130, Jan 15, 1926

The Apple Cart

Productions:
    Opened February 24, 1930 for 88 performances.
    Opened October 18, 1956 for 124 performances.
Reviews:
    America 96: 359, Dec 22, 1956
    Catholic World 131: 78-9, Apr 1930
            184: 225, Dec 1956
    Christian Century 73: 1328, Nov 14, 1956
    Commonweal 10: 497-8, Sep 18, 1929
            11: 535, Mar 12, 1930
    Drama 20: 6-8, Oct 1929
    Life (NY) 95: 18, Mar 14, 1930
    Literary Digest 101: 25, Jun 8, 1929
                102: 19-20, Jul 20, 1929
                104: 23-4, Mar 15, 1930
    Nation 130: 338, Mar 19, 1930
            183: 374, Nov 3, 1956
    New Republic 62: 99, Mar 12, 1930
                135: 21-2, Dec 3, 1956
    New York Theatre Critics' Reviews 1956: 258
    New York Times p. 30, Feb 25, 1930
                p. 23, Oct 19, 1956
                II, p. 1, Oct 20, 1956
    New Yorker 29: 66+, Jul 18, 1953
            32: 117-18, Oct 27, 1956
    Newsweek 48: 76, Oct 29, 1956
    Outlook 154: 429, Mar 12, 1930
    Review of Reviews 81: 144-5, Apr 1930
    Saturday Review 36: 24, Aug 1, 1953
                39: 24, Nov 10, 1956
    Theatre Arts 13: 729-33, Oct 1929
            14: 370, May 1930
    Time 68: 98+, Oct 29, 1956
    Vogue 75: 132, Apr 12, 1930
    Yale Review 20: 815-16, Summer 1931

Arms and the Man

Productions:

Arms and the Man (cont.)
Opened May 3, 1915 in repertory.
Opened September 14, 1925 for 180 performances.
Opened October 19, 1950 for 110 performances.
(Off Broadway) Opened April 27, 1964 for 23 performances.
(Off Broadway) Opened January 14, 1966 for 10
matinees (ANTA).
Reviews:
Bookman 62: 321, Nov 1925
Catholic World 172: 227, Dec 1950
Christian Science Monitor Magazine p. 8, Oct 28, 1950
Commonweal 53: 121, Nov 10, 1950
Dramatic Mirror 73: 8, May 5, 1915
Dramatist 17: 1291-2, Jan 1926
Nation 100: 545, May 13, 1915
121: 364, Sep 30, 1925
New Republic 3: 18, May 8, 1915
123: 20, Nov 13, 1950
New York Theatre Critics' Reviews 1950: 235
New York Times p. 15, May 4, 1915
IX, p. 1, Oct 4, 1925
p. 34, Oct 20, 1950
p. 41, Apr 28, 1964
Newsweek 36: 78, Oct 30, 1950
Theatre Magazine 21: 280-1, Jun 1915

Augustus Does His Bit
Productions:
Opened March 12, 1919 for five performances.
Reviews:
Current Opinion 62: 405, Jun 1917
Life (NY) 73: 504, Mar 27, 1919
New York Times p. 9, Nov 13, 1919
Back to Methuselah
Productions:
Opened February 27, 1922 for 25 performances.
Two act version by Arnold Moss. Opened March 26, 1958
for 29 performances.
Reviews:
Arts and Decoration 16: 426-7, Apr 1922
Bookman 53: 550, Aug 1921
55: 279, Aug 1922
Catholic World 187: 226-7, Jan 1958
Century 102: 631-5, Aug 1921
Dial 72: 444, Apr 1922
Everybody's 46: 141-8, Jun 1922
Fortune 120: 827-34, Nov 1923

Independent 108: 310, Mar 25, 1922
Life (NY) 79: 18, Mar 16, 1922
Nation 114: 323, Mar 15, 1922
      186: 349, Apr 19, 1958
New Republic 30: 80-1, Mar 15, 1922
      38: 21, Apr 1958
New York Clipper 70: 20, Mar 22, 1922
New York Theatre Critics' Reviews 1958: 322
New York Times p. 8, Jan 23, 1922
      IV, p. 1, Feb 5, 1922
      p. 11, Mar 7, 1922
      p. 11, Mar 14, 1922
      p. 41, Mar 27, 1958
      II, p. 1, Apr 6, 1958
Theatre Arts 38: 24-5, Jun 1954
Theatre Magazine 35: 290+, May 1922
Yale Review 11: 429, Jan 1922

Buoyant Billions
Productions:
(Off Broadway) Season of 1959-1960.
Reviews:
America 101: 438, Jun 13, 1959
New York Times p. 30, Jun 3, 1959
      II, p. 1, Jun 7, 1959
New Yorker 35: 120+, Jun 6, 1959

Caesar and Cleopatra
Productions:
Opened in the fall of 1913 in repertory (Forbes-Robertson).
Opened April 13, 1925 for 48 performances.
Opened December 21, 1949 for 149 performances.
Opened December 19, 1951 for 67 performances.
Reviews:
American Mercury 5: 244, Jan 1925
Catholic World 170: 384, Feb 1950
      174: 389-90, Feb 1952
Christian Science Monitor Magazine p. 5, Mar 4, 1950
Colliers 128: 21+, Dec 22, 1951
Commonweal 51: 390, Jan 13, 1950
      55: 349, Jan 11, 1952
Dial 78: 525, Jun 1925
Dramatic Mirror 70: 7, Oct 22, 1913
Life 28: 46-8, Jan 30, 1950
    31: 82-4, Dec 17, 1951
Life (NY) 62: 791, Nov 6, 1913
      85: 20, Apr 30, 1925

Caesar and Cleopatra (cont.)
    Nation 120: 500, Apr 29, 1925
            169: 650-1, Dec 31, 1949
            174: 17-18, Jan 5, 1952
    New Republic 42: 262-3, Apr 29, 1925
            122: 21, Jan 2, 1950
            126: 22, Jan 21, 1952
    New York Theatre Critics' Reviews 1949: 193
                                    1951: 132
    New York Times p. 27, Apr 14, 1925
            p. 28, Dec 22, 1949
            II, p. 1, Jan 8, 1950
            p. 32, May 11, 1951
            II, p. 1, Dec 30, 1951
            II, p. 1, Jan 6, 1952
    New York Times Magazine p. 16, Dec 18, 1949
    New Yorker 25: 38+, Dec 31, 1949
            27: 50, Dec 29, 1957
    Newsweek 35: 48, Jan 2, 1950
            38: 53, Dec 31, 1957
    Saturday Review 33: 26-8, Jan 14, 1950
            35: 24-7, Jan 12, 1952
    School and Society 71: 215-17, Apr 8, 1950
            75: 104-6, Feb 16, 1952
    Theatre Arts 34: 8, Mar 1950
            35: 10-11, Dec 1957
    Time 55: 52, Jan 2, 1950
            58: 44-7, Dec 31, 1951
Candida
    Productions:
        Opened May 18, 1915 in repertory.
        Opened March 22, 1922 for 43 performances.
        Opened December 12, 1924 for 143 performances.
        Opened November 9, 1925 for 24 performances.
        Opened March 10, 1937 for 50 performances.
        Opened April 27, 1942 for 27 performances.
        Opened April 3, 1946 for 24 performances.
        Opened April 22, 1952 for 31 performances.
        (Off Broadway) Season of 1955-56.
        (Off Broadway) Opened December 7, 1963 for eight per-
        formances.
    Reviews:
        American Mercury 4: 244, Feb 1925
        Bookman 55: 388, Jun 1922
        Canadian Magazine 64: 74-5, Apr 1925
        Catholic World 145: 211-13, May 1937
                155: 338-40, Jun 1942

163: 167, May 1946
Commonweal 25: 612, Mar 26, 1937
36: 135-6, May 29, 1942
56: 140, May 16, 1952
Delineator 111: 38, Oct 1927
Dramatic Mirror 73: 8, May 26, 1915
Dramatist 2: 164, Apr 1911
Fortnightly Review 177: 122-7, Feb 1952
Life 19: 65-6, Aug 20, 1945
Literary Digest 84: 28-9, Feb 7, 1925
123: 28, Mar 20, 1937
Living Age 274: 781, Sep 28, 1912
McCalls 90: 28, Mar 1963
Nation 144: 361-2, Mar 27, 1937
162: 487, Apr 20, 1945
New Republic 90: 322, Apr 21, 1937
New York Clipper 70: 20, Mar 29, 1922
New York Theatre Critics' Reviews 1942: 301
1946: 412
1952: 307
New York Times p. 13, May 21, 1915
p. 11, Nov 23, 1922
p. 12, Dec 13, 1924
VIII, p. 1, Dec 21, 1924
p. 9, Dec 31, 1924
p. 16, Jul 24, 1925
p. 23, Nov 10, 1925
p. 20, Nov 11, 1937
XI, p. 1, Nov 21, 1937
p. 24, Apr 28, 1942
p. 33, Apr 4, 1946
II, p. 1, Nov 3, 1946
p. 23, Apr 23, 1952
New Yorker 21: 36, Aug 18, 1945
28: 68, May 3, 1952
Newsweek 9: 22, Mar 20, 1937
19: 42+, May 25, 1942
26: 89, Aug 20, 1945
27: 84, Apr 15, 1946
39: 94, May 5, 1952
Saturday Review 29: 28-30, May 4, 1946
Stage 14: 78, Apr 1937
Theatre Arts 21: 344, May 1937
26: 421-2, Jul 1942
Theatre Magazine 35: 374, 379, Jun 1922
40: 64, Feb 1925
Time 39: 40, May 11, 1942

Candida (cont.)
        47: 91, Apr 15, 1946
        59: 54, May 5, 1952
Captain Brassbound's Conversion
    Productions:
        Opened March 29, 1916 in repertory.
        Opened December 27, 1950 for 15 performances.
    Reviews:
        Catholic World 172: 388, Feb 1951
        Christian Science Monitor Magazine p. 6, Jan 6, 1951
        Commonweal 53: 374, Jan 19, 1951
        Dramatic Mirror 75: 8, Apr 8, 1916
        Green Book 15: 978, 982, Jun 1916
        Harper's Weekly 62: 398, Apr 15, 1916
        Nation 102: 392, Apr 6, 1916
               172: 18, Jan 6, 1951
        New Republic 6: 269, Apr 8, 1916
                    118: 32, Jan 5, 1948
        New York Theatre Critics' Reviews 1950: 157
        New York Times p. 11, Mar 30, 1916
                       II, p. 1, Apr 2, 1916
                       p. 21, Dec 28, 1950
        Newsweek 31: 68, Jan 5, 1948
                 37: 67, Jan 8, 1951
        School and Society 73: 101-2, Feb 17, 1951
        Theatre Arts 35: 14, Mar 1951
        Theatre Magazine 23: 273, May 1916
                         51: 71, Jan 5, 1948
                         57: 30, Jan 8, 1951
The Devil's Disciple
    Productions:
        Opened April 23, 1923 for 64 performances.
        Opened January 25, 1950 for 127 performances.
        (Off Broadway) Opened January 4, 1963 for nine per-
          formances.
    Reviews:
        Catholic World 170: 468, Mar 1950
        Christian Science Monitor Magazine p. 5+, Mar 4, 1950
        Commonweal 51: 535-6, Feb 24, 1950
        Dial 75: 100, Jul 1923
        Life 28: 53-4+, Mar 6, 1950
        Literary Digest 106: 16, Sep 27, 1930
        Nation 170: 114, Feb 4, 1950
              116: 578, May 16, 1923
        New Republic 34: 299-300, May 9, 1923
                    122: 20, Feb 27, 1950
        New York Clipper 71: 14, Apr 25, 1923

New York Theatre Critics' Reviews 1950: 344
New York Times p. 24, Apr 24, 1923
              p. 23, Jan 26, 1950
              II, p. 1, Feb 5, 1950
School and Society 71: 215-17, Apr 8, 1950
Theatre Arts 34: 13, Apr 1950
Theatre Magazine 38: 17, 20, Jul 1923
Time 55: 66, Feb 6, 1950

The Doctor's Dilemma

Productions:
Opened March 26, 1915 in repertory.
Opened November 21, 1927 for 115 performances.
Opened March 11, 1941 for 121 performances.
Opened January 11, 1955 for 48 performances.
Reviews:
Bookman 41: 279, May 1915
Book News 33: 453, May 1915
Catholic World 153: 216, May 1941
              180: 468-9, Mar 1955
Commonweal 61: 524-5, Feb 18, 1955
Current Literature 50: 419, Apr 1911
Dramatic Mirror 73: 8, Mar 31, 1915
Green Book 13: 1045-8, Jun 1915
Harpers' Bazaar 75: 54, Mar 15, 1941
Life (NY) 65: 624, Apr 8, 1915
           90: 21, Dec 15, 1927
Life 10: 82-4, May 5, 1941
Nation 92: 325, Mar 30, 1911
      100: 364, Apr 1, 1915
      125: 690, Dec 14, 1927
      152: 331, Mar 22, 1941
      180: 107, Jan 29, 1957
      203: 427-8, Oct 24, 1957
New Republic 2: 264, Apr 10, 1915
          53: 96-7, Dec 14, 1927
          104: 404, Mar 24, 1941
          132: 22, Feb 7, 1955
New York Theatre Critics' Reviews 1941: 364
                              1955: 397
New York Times p. 11, Mar 27, 1915
              p. 33, Nov 22, 1927
              X, p. 1, Dec 4, 1927
              p. 18, Mar 12, 1941
              IX, p. 1, Mar 30, 1941
              p. 22, Jan 12, 1955
              II, p. 1, Jan 23, 1955
New Yorker 17: 36, Mar 22, 1941

The Doctor's Dilemma (cont.)
    Newsweek 17: 70, Mar 24, 1941
    Outlook 147: 532, Dec 28, 1927
    Saturday Review 4: 372, Dec 3, 1927
                 38: 24, Jan 29, 1955
    Theatre Arts 12: 94-6, Feb 1928
              25: 327-9, May 1941
              39: 92, Mar 1955
    Theatre Magazine 21: 228, May 1915
                  47: 38, 40, Feb 1928
    Time 37: 43, Mar 24, 1941
    Vogue 71: 120, Jan 15, 1928
Don Juan in Hell (Act III of Man and Superman)
    Productions:
    Opened April 6, 1952 for 105 performances.
    (Off Broadway) Season of 1960-1961.
    (Off Broadway) Opened June 19, 1962 for 17 performances.
    Reviews:
    New York Theatre Critics' Reviews 1952: 193
    New York Times II, p. 3, Jan 6, 1952
                  II, p. 1, Jun 1, 1952
                  p. 47, Oct 4, 1960
    New York Times Magazine p. 21, Nov 4, 1951
    Theatre Arts 36: 50-66, Apr 1952
    Time 58: 63-4+, Nov 5, 1951
Fanny's First Play
    Productions:
    Opened September 16, 1912 for 256 performances.
    Reviews:
    American Playwright 1: 321-4, Oct 1912
    Blue Book 16: 478-80, Jan 1913
    Book News 32: 178-9, Nov 1913
    Collier's 50: 24+, Oct 5, 1912
    Dramatic Mirror 68: 7, Sep 18, 1912
    Dramatist 4: 245-6, Apr 1913
    Everybody's 27: 808-12, Dec 1912
    Green Book 8: 932-4, 987, Dec 1912
    Independent 73: 1095-6, Nov 7, 1912
    Leslie's Weekly 115: 497, Nov 14, 1912
    Life (NY) 60: 1859, Sep 26, 1912
    McClure's 40: 64-6, Mar 1913
    Munsey 48: 352-3, Nov 1912
    National Magazine 40: 186-90, May 1914
    New York Dramatic News 56: 11-12, Sep 27, 1912
    North American Review 200: 147-52, Jul 1914
    Red Book 19: 958, Sep 1912

Theatre Magazine 16: 15, Oct 1912
Geneva
Productions:
Opened January 30, 1940 for 15 performances.
Reviews:
Canadian Forum 19: 288, Dec 1939
Catholic World 150: 729, Mar 1940
Commonweal 31: 367, Feb 16, 1940
New York Theatre Critics' Reviews 1940: 403
New York Times p. 14, Jan 30, 1940
             p. 15, Jan 31, 1940
Newsweek 15: 38, Feb 12, 1940
Nineteenth Century 125: 88-90, Feb 1939
              126: 449-57, Oct 1939
Theatre Arts 23: 100, Feb 1939
           24: 238, Apr 1940
Time 34: 59-60, Nov 13, 1939
Getting Married
Productions:
Opened November 6, 1916 for 112 performances.
Opened March 30, 1931 for 48 performances.
Opened May 7, 1951 for 16 performances.
Reviews:
Bookman 73: 411, Jun 1931
Book News 35: 206, Jan 1917
Catholic World 133: 207, May 1931
Commonweal 13: 666, Apr 15, 1931
Drama 21: 9, May 1931
Dramatic Mirror 76: 4, 7, Nov 18, 1916
Hearst 32: 38, 79, Jul 1917
Green Book 17: 5, Jan 1917
Life (NY) 68: 904-5, Nov 23, 1916
        97: 20, Apr 17, 1931
Nation 92: 325, Mar 30, 1911
      103: 470, Nov 16, 1916
      132: 430, Apr 15, 1931
New Republic 10: 77, Feb 17, 1917
           66: 236, Apr 15, 1931
New York Dramatic News 63: 11, Nov 11, 1916
New York Theatre Critics' Reviews 1951: 268
New York Times p. 9, Nov 7, 1916
            II, p. 6, Nov 12, 1916
            p. 25, Mar 31, 1931
            p. 28, May 14, 1951
New Yorker 35: 84, Jun 13, 1959
North American Review 203: 925, Dec 1916
                204: 925-7, Dec 1917

223

Getting Married (cont.)
    Outlook 157: 538, Apr 1915
    Theatre Magazine 24: 358, Jan 1916
                    25: 32, 56, Jan 1917
    Vogue 77: 100, 102, Jun 15, 1931
The Great Catherine
Productions:
    Opened December 18, 1916 in repertory (Gertrude
    Kingston).
    Opened May 13, 1936 for three performances.
Reviews:
    Collier's 58: 38, Jan 27, 1917
    Dramatic Mirror 76: 7, Nov 25, 1916
    Everybody's 32: 193-212, Feb 1915
    New York Times p. 9, Nov 15, 1916
                    p. 28, May 14, 1936
Heartbreak House
Productions:
    Opened November 10, 1920 for 125 performances.
    Opened April 29, 1938 for 48 performances.
    (Off Broadway) Season of 1955-56.
    Opened October 18, 1959 for 112 performances.
Reviews:
    America 102: 218, Nov 14, 1959
    Arts and Decoration 14: 213, Jan 1921
    Bookman 52: 565-6, Feb 1921
    Catholic World 147: 344-5, Jun 1938
                    171: 148, May 1950
    Christian Century 76: 1345, Nov 18, 1959
    Commonweal 28: 77, May 14, 1938
    Current Opinion 67: 228-32, Oct 1919
                    70: 207-9, Feb 1921
    Dramatic Mirror 181: 947, Nov 20, 1920
    Dramatist 12: 1041-2, Jan 1921
    Independent 104: 289, Nov 27, 1920
    Hearst 39: 41-3+, Feb 1921
    Life (NY) 76: 1100, Dec 9, 1920
    Living Age 334: 733-5, Apr 15, 1928
    Nation 111: 623, Dec 1920
            146: 556-7, May 14, 1938
            177: 152, Aug 22, 1953
            189: 338, Nov 2, 1959
    New Republic 95: 130, Jun 8, 1938
                    141: 20-1, Nov 2, 1959
    New York Clipper 68: 32, Nov 17, 1920
    New York Theatre Critics' Reviews 1959: 258
    New York Times p. 11, Nov 11, 1920

VI, p. 1, Nov 21, 1920
p. 18, Apr 30, 1938
X, p. 1, May 8, 1938
p. 37, Oct 19, 1959
II, p. 1, Oct 25, 1959
New Yorker 35: 131, Oct 31, 1959
Newsweek 54: 97-8, Nov 2, 1959
Outlook 127: 131, Jan 26, 1921
Reporter 21: 33-5, Nov 26, 1959
Saturday Review 42: 26, Oct 31, 1959
Theatre Arts 43: 85+, Dec 1959
Theatre Magazine 33: 31-2, Jan 1921
Time 74: 32, Nov 2, 1959
Weekly Review 3: 540-41, Dec 1, 1920

How He Lied to Her Husband
   Productions:
      Opened December 18, 1916 in repertory (Gertrude
      Kingston).
   No Reviews.
In Good King Charles' Golden Days
   Productions:
      (Off Broadway) Season of 1956-1957.
   Reviews:
      Catholic World 185: 387, Aug 1957
      Nation 185: 99, Aug 31, 1957
      New York Times p. 16, Jan 25, 1957
                        II, p. 1, Feb 3, 1957
      Newsweek 49: 78, Feb 4, 1957
      Saturday Review 40: 25, Feb 9, 1957
John Bull's Other Island
   Productions:
      Opened February 10, 1948 for eight performances.
   Reviews:
      Catholic World 167: 71, Apr 1948
      Commonweal 47: 494, Feb 27, 1948
      Nation 166: 219-21, Feb 21, 1948
      New Republic 118: 24, Mar 1, 1948
      New York Theatre Critics' Reviews 1948: 351
      New York Times p. 33, Feb 11, 1948
      New Yorker 23: 53, Feb 21, 1948
      Newsweek 31: 80, Feb 23, 1948
      Time 51: 56, Feb 23, 1948
Major Barbara
   Productions:
      Opened December 9, 1915 in repertory.
      Opened November 19, 1928 for 84 performances.

<u>Major Barbara</u> (cont.)
    Opened October 30, 1956 for 232 performances.
Reviews:
    America 96: 358, Dec 22, 1956
    Bookman 42: 648-50, Feb 1916
                63: 32-6, Mar 1916
    Catholic World 184: 305, Jan 1957
    Christian Century 74: 658, May 22, 1957
    Collier's 57: 23, May 13, 1916
    Commonweal 60: 558, Sep 10, 1954
                65: 228-9, Dec 14, 1956
    Current Opinion 60: 172-5, Mar 1916
    Dial 86: 169-70, Feb 1929
    Dramatic Mirror 74: 8, Dec 18, 1915
    Green Book 15: 311-13, Sep 1916
    Harper's Bazaar 75: 55, Mar 15, 1941
    Harper's Weekly 61: 611, Dec 25, 1915
    International 10: 28-9, Jan 1916
    Life (NY) 66: 1242-3, Dec 23, 1915
                92: 13, Dec 24, 1928
    Life 41: 123-4, Dec 10, 1956
    Literary Digest 52: 438-9, Feb 19, 1916
    Nation 101: 725-6, Dec 16, 1915
                127: 666-7, Dec 12, 1928
                183: 439, Nov 27, 1956
    New Republic 5: 175, Dec 18, 1915
                135: 22-3, Dec 3, 1956
                136: 23, May 20, 1957
    New York Dramatic News 62: 17, Dec 18, 1915
    New York Theatre Critics' Reviews 1956: 233
    New York Times p. 13, Jan 7, 1915
                VII, p. 6, Jan 10, 1915
                X, p. 1, Dec 2, 1928
                p. 27, Oct 31, 1956
    New Yorker 32: 114+, Nov 10, 1957
    Newsweek 48: 54-5, Nov 12, 1956
    North American Review 203: 136-8, Jan 1916
    Review of Reviews 79: 152-4, Jan 1929
    Saturday Review 39: 28, Nov 17, 1956
    Theatre Arts 41: 21-2, Jan 1957
    Theatre Magazine 23: 5+, Jan 1916
    Time 68: 72, Nov 12, 1956
    Vogue 128: 118, Sep 15, 1956
<u>Man and Superman</u>
  Productions:
    Opened September 30, 1912 for 32 performances.
    Opened October 8, 1947 for 295 performances.

Opened May 16, 1949 for 16 performances.
Opened April 6, 1952 (see Don Juan in Hell).
(Off Broadway) Opened December 6, 1964 for 100 perform-
ances.
Reviews:
Catholic World 166: 169, Nov 1947
Commonweal 47: 41, Oct 24, 1947
Everybody's 27: 812-13, Dec 1912
Life 23: 107-8+, Oct 27, 1947
     58: 10, Jan 15, 1965
Munsey 48: 528, Dec 1912
Nation 165: 454, Oct 25, 1947
     177: 158, Aug 22, 1953
     199: 522-3, Dec 28, 1964
New Republic 117: 38, Oct 20, 1947
     152: 33, Jan 30, 1965
New York Theatre Critics' Reviews 1947: 308
New York Times p. 31, Oct 19, 1947
     II, p. 1, Mar 9, 1947
     p. 28, May 17, 1949
     p. 45, Dec 7, 1964
New York Times Magazine pp. 36-7, Oct 5, 1947
New Yorker 23: 58-9, Oct 18, 1947
     40: 66+, Dec 19, 1964
Newsweek 30: 88+, Oct 20, 1947
Saturday Review 30: 28-32, Nov 1, 1947
     47: 33, Dec 26, 1964
School and Society 67: 314-15, Apr 24, 1948
Theatre Arts 31: 18, Nov 1947
     31: 12, Dec 1947
Time 50: 73, Oct 20, 1947
Vogue 110: 181, Sep 1, 1947
     110: 112, Nov 15, 1947
The Man of Destiny
Productions:
Opened November 23, 1925 for 68 performances.
(Off Broadway) Season of 1955-56.
Reviews:
New York Times p. 28, Nov 24, 1925
     p. 38, Apr 26, 1956
Vogue 67: 87+, Jan 15, 1926
The Millionairess
Productions:
Opened October 17, 1952 for 83 performances.
Reviews:
Catholic World 176: 227, Dec 1952
Commonweal 57: 198-9, Nov 28, 1952

The Millionairess (cont.)
    Life 33: 163-5, Oct 13, 1952
    Nation 175: 413, Nov 1, 1952
    New Republic 127: 22-3, Nov 3, 1952
    New York Theatre Critics' Reviews 1952: 228
    New York Times II, p. 1, Oct 26, 1952
    New York Times Magazine p. 17, Jul 13, 1952
    New Yorker 28: 65, Jul 19, 1953
               28: 74+, Oct 25, 1952
    Newsweek 40: 76, Oct 27, 1952
    Theatre Arts 36: 18-20, Nov 1952
    Time 60: 75, Oct 27, 1952

Misalliance
Productions:
    Opened September 27, 1917 for 52 performances.
    Opened February 18, 1953 for 146 performances.
    (Off Broadway) Opened September 25, 1961 for 156
      performances.
Reviews:
    America 88: 632, Mar 7, 1953
    Catholic World 177: 68-9, Apr 1953
    Commonweal 57: 648-9, Apr 3, 1953
               75: 38-9, Jan 5, 1962
    Current Opinion 63: 315-16, Nov 1917
    Dramatic Mirror 77: 5, Oct 6, 1917
    Green Book 18: 965-8, Dec 1917
    Life (NY) 70: 590, Oct 11, 1917
    Life 34: 155-6, Apr 8, 1953
    Nation 176: 212, Mar 7, 1953
    New Republic 12: 276, Oct 6, 1917
    New York Theatre Critics' Reviews 1953: 354
    New York Times p. 9, Sep 28, 1917
               p. 20, Feb 19, 1953
               II, p. 1, Mar 22, 1953
               p. 32, Sep 26, 1961
    New Yorker 29: 60, Mar 7, 1953
               37: 132-3, Oct 21, 1961
    Newsweek 41: 84, Mar 2, 1953
    Saturday Review 36: 34, Mar 7, 1953
    Theatre Arts 37: 16+, May 1953
               37: 63-4+, Jul 1953
               45: 71, Dec 1961
    Theatre Magazine 26: 280, 291, Nov 1917
    Time 61: 74+, Mar 2, 1953
        78: 88, Oct 6, 1961

Mrs. Warren's Profession
Productions:

Opened March 11, 1918 in repertory (The Washington
   Square Players).
Opened February 22, 1922 for 25 performances.
(Off Broadway) Opened November 1950.
(Off Broadway) Opened April 24, 1963 for 15 performances.
Reviews:
   Catholic World 172: 226-7, Dec 1950
   Christian Science Monitor Magazine p. 6, Nov 4, 1950
   Dramatic Mirror 78: 7, Mar 23, 1918
   Life (NY) 71: 518, Mar 28, 1918
   Nation 171: 418, Nov 4, 1950
   New Republic 123: 21, Nov 13, 1950
   New York Times p. 11, Mar 12, 1918
                 p. 39, Oct 26, 1950
                 p. 39, Apr 25, 1963
   New Yorker 39: 93, May 4, 1963
   Newsweek 36: 89, Nov 6, 1950
   Theatre Magazine 27: 218, Apr 1918
   Time 56: 58, Nov 6, 1950
O'Flaherty, V. C.
   Productions:
   Opened June 1920.
   Reviews:
   Current Opinion 61: 103, Aug 1916
                   63: 167-70, Sep 1917
   Dial 59: 551, Dec 9, 1915
   Dramatic Mirror 76: 3, Jul 22, 1916
   Hearst 32: 88-91, 158-9, Aug 1917
         38: 41-3, Sep 1920
   Literary Digest 53: 69-70, Jul 8, 1916
   New York Times p. 9, Jun 22, 1920
   Weekly Review 3: 114-16, Aug 4, 1920
On the Rocks
   Productions:
   Opened June 15, 1938 for 66 performances (Federal
      Theatre Project).
   Reviews:
   Commonweal 28: 273, Jul 1, 1938
   Literary Digest 118: 24, Aug 18, 1934
   New Republic 95: 251, Jul 6, 1938
   New York Times p. 20, Jun 16, 1938
   Theatre Arts 18: 98-9, Feb 1934
   Time 31: 33, Jun 27, 1938
Overruled
   Productions:
   Opened December 18, 1916 in repertory (Gertrude
      Kingston).

Overruled (cont.)
  Reviews:
    New York Times p. 11, Feb 3, 1917
The Philanderer
  Productions:
    Opened December 30, 1913 for 103 performances.
    (Off Broadway) Season of 1955-56.
  Reviews:
    American Mercury 77: 104, Jun 1914
    American Playwright 3: 42-7, Feb 1914
    Bookman 38: 610-11, Feb 1914
    Collier's 52: 24, Feb 21, 1914
    Dramatic Mirror 70: 6, Dec 31, 1913
    Green Book 11: 413-14, Mar 1914
    Harper's Weekly 58: 22, Jan 17, 1914
    Independent 77: 59, Jan 12, 1914
    International 8: 68, Feb 1914
    New York Times p. 7, Dec 29, 1913
    Outlook 106: 391, Feb 21, 1914
    Theatre Magazine 19: 58+, Feb 1914
Pygmalion
  Productions:
    Opened October 12, 1914 for 72 performances.
    Opened November 15, 1926 for 143 performances.
    Opened January 25, 1938 for two performances. (WPA
      New York State Federal Theatre Project)
    Opened December 26, 1945 for 179 performances.
  Reviews:
    American Mercury 79: 42, Feb 1915
    Bookman 40: 413-14, Dec 1914
            64: 731, Feb 1927
    Collier's 54: 9, Jan 2, 1915
    Commonweal 27: 496, Feb 25, 1938
    Current Opinion 56: 30-1, Jan 1914
                    56: 358-9, May 1914
    Forum 100: 921-32, May 1914
          105: 562-4, Feb 1946
    Dramatic Mirror 71: 12, Apr 1, 1914
                    72: 8-9, Oct 21, 1914
    Dramatist 6: 538-40, Jan 1915
              6: 602-4, Jul 1915
              17: 1319, Oct 1926
    Green Book 12: 1057-8, Dec 1914
              13: 118, Jan 1915
    Harper's Weekly 58: 14-15, Apr 11, 1914
                    59: 483, Nov 21, 1914
    International 8: 132, Apr 1914

Life 20: 67-8, Jan 14, 1946
Life (NY) 64: 120, Oct 22, 1914
Literary Digest 48: 1180-1, May 16, 1914
Mademoiselle 44: 104-6, Dec 1956
Munsey 53: 555-6, Dec 1914
Nation 99: 504-5, Oct 22, 1914
          100: 150, Dec 4, 1915
          123: 566-7, Dec 1, 1926
          162: 176, Feb 9, 1946
New Republic 1: 25, Nov 7, 1914
              49: 41-2, Dec 1, 1926
             114: 91, Jan 21, 1946
New York Dramatic News 60: 18-19, Oct 17, 1914
New York Theatre Critics' Reviews 1945: 57
New York Times p. 11, Mar 25, 1914
                 p. 11, Oct 13, 1914
                 p. 24, Nov 16, 1926
                 VIII, p. 1, Nov 21, 1926
                 p. 16, Jan 27, 1938
                 II, p. 1, Jan 6, 1946
New Yorker 21: 40, Jan 5, 1946
Newsweek 27: 82, Jan 7, 1946
North American Review 200: 933-4, Dec 1914
Saturday Review 29: 24-6, Jan 12, 1946
Stage 14: 76, Aug 1937
Theatre Arts 30: 69-71, Feb 1946
          30: 134+, Mar 1946
          40: 29-31, Dec 1956
Theatre Magazine 20: 262, Dec 1914
               45: 15+, Jan 1927
Time 47: 88, Jan 7, 1946
Vogue 69: 82-3, Jan 15, 1927
      144: 152-5+, Nov 1, 1964

Saint Joan
  Productions:
    Opened December 28, 1923 for 195 performances.
    Opened March 9, 1936 for 89 performances.
    Opened October 4, 1951 for 142 performances.
    Opened September 11, 1956 for 77 performances.
    Opened February 20, 1962 in repertory (Old Vic Company).
  Reviews:
    America 95: 630-2, Sep 29, 1956
    American Mercury 1: 241-3, Feb 1924
    Arts and Decoration 20: 17, Feb 1924
    Bookman 59: 60-1, Mar 1921
    Catholic World 119: 196-205, May 1924
              143: 85-6, Apr 1936

Saint Joan (cont.)
                174: 147-8, Nov 1951
                184: 146-7, Nov 1956
        Christian Century 73: 1138, Oct 3, 1956
        Commonweal 23: 609, Mar 27, 1936
                        55: 38, Oct 19, 1951
                        65: 46-7, Oct 12, 1956
                        75: 666-7, Mar 23, 1962
        Current Opinion 76: 316-29, Mar 1924
        Dial 76: 206, Feb 1924
        Drama 14: 178-9, Feb 1924
        Freeman 8: 447-9, Jan 16, 1924
        Independent 112: 55, Jan 19, 1924
        Independent World 25: 101-2, Apr 1946
        Life (NY) 83: 18, Jan 24, 1924
        Life 31: 141-2, Oct 22, 1951
            41: 59-60, Sep 10, 1956
            41: 90-7, Oct 15, 1956
        Literary Digest 80: 267, Jan 19, 1924
                        121: 19, Mar 21, 1936
        Living Age 322: 175-8, Jul 26, 1924
        Metropolitan Magazine 59: 42, May 1924
        Nation 118: 96-7, Jan 23, 1924
                142: 392, Mar 25, 1936
                173: 360-1, Oct 27, 1951
                183: 274-5, Sep 27, 1962
                194: 221, Mar 10, 1962
                199: 60, Aug 10, 1964
        New Republic 37: 205-6, Jan 16, 1924
                     40: 380-1, Aug 27, 1924
                     86: 198, Mar 25, 1936
                     88: 173, Sep 23, 1936
                     125: 29-30, Oct 29, 1951
                     146: 37-8, Mar 5, 1962
        New York Theatre Critics' Reviews 1952: 220
                                          1956: 233
                                          1962: 344
        New York Times p. 27, Mar 10, 1936
                        X, p. 1, Mar 15, 1936
                        p. 23, Oct 5, 1951
                        II, p. 1, Oct 14, 1951
                        p. 42, Sep 12, 1956
                        II, p. 1, Sep 16, 1956
                        p. 57, Feb 21, 1962
        New Yorker 27: 83, Oct 13, 1951
                   32: 96, Sep 22, 1956
                   38: 93, Mar 3, 1962

Newsweek 7: 22, Mar 21, 1936
        38: 84, Oct 15, 1951
        48: 102, Sep 24, 1956
Outlook 136: 338, Feb 27, 1924
Saturday Review 37: 32, Oct 23, 1954
        39: 70-1, Sep 1955
School and Society 74: 405-6, Dec 22, 1951
Stage 13: 30-33, Apr 1936
Survey 87: 525-6, Dec 1951
Theatre Arts 20: 329-38, May 1936
        20: 463-4, Jun 1936
        35: 3, Dec 1951
        36: 34-5, Jun 1952
        39: 70-1, Dec 1955
        40: 80-1, Nov 1956
        41: 30+, Mar 1957
Theatre Magazine 39: 14-16, Mar 1924
Time 27: 55, Mar 23, 1936
     58: 73, Oct 15, 1951
     68: 78+, Sep 24, 1956
     79: 64, Mar 2, 1962
Woman Citizen 8: 13, Feb 9, 1924

The Shewing-up of Blanco Posnet

Productions:

Opened November 20, 1911 in repertory.

Opened February 4, 1913 in repertory (The Irish Players).

Opened October 16, 1923 for 49 performances.

Reviews:

American Playwright 3: 79-84, Mar 1914

Collier's 50: 25, Mar 13, 1915

Dramatic Mirror 66: 8-9, Nov 29, 1911

Everybody's 28: 680, May 1913

Munsey 46: 589-90, Jan 1912

Nation 92: 325-6, Mar 30, 1911

New Republic 36: 257, Oct 31, 1923

New York Times p. 14, Oct 17, 1923

The Simpleton of Unexpected Isles

Productions:

Opened February 18, 1935 for 40 performances.

Reviews:

Catholic World 141: 87-8, Apr 1935

Commonweal 21: 542, Mar 8, 1935

Literary Digest 119: 23, Mar 2, 1935

Nation 140: 286-7, Mar 6, 1935

New Republic 82: 105, Mar 6, 1935

New York Times p. 27, Feb 19, 1935

The Simpleton of Unexpected Isles (cont.)
         VIII, p. 1, Feb 24, 1935
         p. 7, Jul 30, 1935
         X, p. 1, Aug 25, 1935
    Saturday Review 14: 10, Jun 13, 1936
    Stage 12: 12-13, Aug 1935
    Theatre Arts 19: 244, 247, 283-4, Apr 1935
    Time 25: 39, Mar 4, 1935
Too True To Be Good
  Productions:
    Opened April 4, 1932 for 57 performances.
    Opened March 12, 1963 for 94 performances.
  Reviews:
    America 108: 591, Apr 20, 1963
    Bookman 75: 75-6, Apr 1932
    Catholic World 135: 206-7, May 1932
    Commonweal 15: 691, Apr 20, 1932
    Literary Digest 113: 14, Apr 30, 1932
                  114: 15, Nov 12, 1932
    Nation 134: 477-8, Apr 20, 1932
           177: 157, Aug 22, 1953
           196: 275, Mar 30, 1963
    New Republic 70: 271-3, Apr 20, 1932
                  148: 29, Mar 30, 1963
    New York Theatre Critics' Reviews 1963: 315
    New York Times p. 1, Mar 6, 1932
                   p. 8, Mar 14, 1963
                   p. 5, Mar 23, 1963
    New Yorker 39: 73, Mar 23, 1963
    Newsweek 61: 97, Mar 25, 1963
    Stage 9: 5-7, May 1932
    Theatre Arts 16: 437-9, Jun 1932
                 16: 877-8, Nov 1932
                 47: 69, May 1963
    Theatre Guild Magazine 9: 14-17, Apr 1932
    Time 81: 74, Mar 22, 1963
    Vogue 79: 76, Jun 1, 1932
Village Wooing
  Productions:
    (Off Broadway) May 1943.
  Reviews:
    Catholic World 181: 63, Oct 1955
    Newsweek 3: 39, Apr 28, 1934
    Saturday Review 38: 37, Nov 19, 1955
    Time 23: 26, Apr 30, 1934
Widower's Houses
  Productions:

(Off Broadway) Opened February 1939 for one per-
formance (Irish Repertory Players).
Reviews:
New York Times p. 39, Mar 3, 1959
New Yorker 35:102-3, Mar 21, 1959
You Never Can Tell
Productions:
Opened April 5, 1915 in repertory.
Opened May 16, 1948 for 39 performances.
Reviews:
Canadian Magazine 42: 634-7, Apr 1914
Catholic World 167:169, May 1948
Commonweal 48:635, Apr 16, 1948
Dramatic Mirror 73:9, Apr 14, 1915
Nation 100:424-5, Apr 15, 1915
         166:361, Mar 27, 1948
New Republic 118:30, Mar 29, 1948
New York Theatre Critics' Reviews 1948:307
New York Times VII, p. 6, Apr 11, 1915
                 p. 31, Nov 17, 1948
New Yorker 24:49, Mar 27, 1948
Newsweek 31:82, Mar 29, 1948
Saturday Review 31:32-4, Apr 24, 1948
Theatre Arts 32:47, Jan 1948
Time 51:56, Mar 29, 1948

Sherriff, R. C.
Journey's End
Productions:
Opened March 22, 1929 for 485 performances.
Opened September 18, 1939 for 16 performances.
Reviews:
American Mercury 17: 245-7, Jun 1929
                 17: 376-7, Jul 1929
Bookman 69:173-6, Apr 1929
Catholic World 129:201-2, May 1929
               130:326-7, Dec 1929
               150:214-15, Nov 1939
Christian Century 46:1332, Oct 30, 1929
Collier's 83:7, Jun 8, 1929
Commonweal 9:656-7, Apr 10, 1929
           30:519, Sep 29, 1939
Life (NY) 93:28, Apr 19, 1929
          95:20, May 2, 1930
Literary Digest 100: 22-3, Mar 30, 1939
                105:18-19, May 3, 1930
Nation 128:434, Apr 10, 1929

Journey's End (cont.)
>130: 141, Feb 5, 1930
>130: 524-5, Apr 30, 1930
>149: 355-7, Sep 30, 1939
>New Republic 58: 225-6, Apr 10, 1929
>New York Times p. 23, Mar 23, 1929
>>VIII, p. 1, Mar 31, 1929
>>IX, p. 2, May 5, 1929
>>p. 20, Jan 17, 1930
>>p. 29, Sep 19, 1939
>>IX, p. 1, Sep 24, 1939
>Newsweek 14: 35, Oct 2, 1939
>>14: 44, Oct 16, 1939
>Nineteenth Century 105: 844-8, Jun 1929
>Outlook 151: 590, Apr 10, 1929
>>154: 670, Apr 23, 1930
>Saturday Review 5: 1021, May 18, 1929
>Theatre Arts 13: 325-30, May 1929
>>13: 493-7, Jul 1929
>>14: 738, Sep 1930
>>23: 777-9, Nov 1939
>Theatre Magazine 49: 43-5, Jun 1929
>>50: 25-6+, Sep 1929
>>52: 44, Jul 1930
>Time 34: 38, Oct 2, 1939
>Vanity Fair 32: 52-3+, Jun 1929
>Vogue 73: 186, May 11, 1929
>>73: 74-5, Jun 8, 1929

Saint Helena (with Jeanne de Casalis)
Productions:
Opened October 6, 1936 for 63 performances.
Reviews:
>Catholic World 144: 212-13, Nov 1936
>Commonweal 24: 617, Oct 23, 1936
>Nation 143: 457, Oct 17, 1936
>New Republic 88: 314, Oct 21, 1936
>New York Times p. 32, Oct 7, 1936
>>X, p. 1, Oct 11, 1936
>Newsweek 8: 28-9, Oct 17, 1938
>Saturday Review 15: 17, Oct 31, 1936
>Theatre Arts 20: 840+, Nov 1936
>Time 28: 44, Oct 19, 1936

Shiels, George
The New Gosson
Productions:
Opened October 21, 1932 for 14 performances.

Opened November 13, 1934 for 2 performances.
Opened November 29, 1937 for 8 performances (Abbey
Theatre Players).
Reviews:
Literary Digest 114: 17, Nov 19, 1932
Nation 139: 629, Nov 28, 1934
New York Times p. 18, Oct 22, 1932
                p. 26, Nov 30, 1937

Sierra, Gregorio Martinez (see Martinez-Sierra, Gregorio)

Sigurjonsson, Johann
  Eyvind of the Hills
    Productions:
      Opened February 1921 for 24 performances.
    Reviews:
      Dramatic Mirror 83: 288, Feb 12, 1921
      New York Clipper 69: 19, Feb 9, 1921
      New York Times p. 14, Feb 2, 1921
      Theatre Magazine 33: 261, Apr 1921
      Weekly Review 4: 255, Mar 16, 1921

Simonov, Konstantin
  The Russian People (The Russians)
    Productions:
      American acting version by Clifford Odets. Opened
        December 29, 1942 for 39 performances.
    Reviews:
      Catholic World 156: 599, Feb 1943
      Commonweal 37: 349, Jan 22, 1943
      Current History ns3: 549, Feb 1943
      Nation 156: 103, Jan 16, 1943
      New York Theatre Critics' Reviews 1942: 127+
      New York Times p. 17, Dec 30, 1942
      Newsweek 21: 66, Jan 11, 1943
      Theatre Arts 27: 70-1, Feb 1943
                   27: 141-2+, Mar 1943
  The Whole World Over
    Productions:
      Adapted by Thelma Schnee. Opened March 27, 1947
        for 100 performances.
    Reviews:
      Catholic World 165: 168-9, May 1947
      Commonweal 46: 15, Apr 18, 1947
      Nation 164: 459, Apr 19, 1947
      New York Theatre Critics' Reviews 1947: 411
      New York Times p. 28, Mar 28, 1947

The Whole World Over (cont.)
New Yorker 23: 50+, Apr 5, 1947
Newsweek 29: 80, Apr 7, 1947
School and Society 65: 403-4, May 31, 1947
Time 49: 78, Apr 7, 1947

Simpson, N. F.
Hole
Productions:
(Off Broadway) Season of 1960-1961.
Reviews:
New York Times p. 42, Apr 4, 1961
New Yorker 37: 76+, Apr 15, 1961
One Way Pendulum
Productions:
(Off Broadway) Opened September 18, 1961 for 40 performances.
Reviews:
America 106: 29, Oct 7, 1961
Commonweal 75: 94, Oct 20, 1961
New York Times p. 38, Sep 19, 1961
New Yorker 36: 104, May 28, 1960
         37: 118-20, Sep 30, 1961
Saturday Review 44: 38, Oct 7, 1961
Theatre Arts 45: 58-9, Nov 1961
Resounding Tinkle
Productions:
(Off Broadway) Season of 1960-1961.
Reviews:
New York Times p. 42, Apr 4, 1961
New Yorker 37: 76+, Apr 15, 1961

Smith, Dodie
Autumn Crocus (written under the pseud. C. L. Anthony)
Productions:
Opened November 19, 1932 for 210 performances.
Reviews:
Catholic World 136: 465-6, Jan 1933
Commonweal 17: 469, Feb 22, 1933
         17: 525, Mar 8, 1933
Nation 135: 577, Dec 7, 1932
New Republic 73: 99-100, Dec 7, 1932
New York Times p. 20, Nov 21, 1932
Stage 10: 9-10, Jan 1933
Theatre Arts 15: 461-2, Jun 1931
         17: 109-10, Feb 1933
Town and County 87: 38, Dec 15, 1932

Vogue 81: 39+, Jan 15, 1933

Call It a Day
Productions:
Opened January 28, 1936 for 194 performances.
Reviews:
Catholic World 142: 724, Mar 1936
Commonweal 23: 440, Feb 14, 1936
Literary Digest 121: 20, Feb 8, 1936
Nation 142: 201-2, Feb 12, 1936
New Republic 86: 78, Feb 26, 1936
New York Times p. 26, Jan 21, 1936
                 p. 15, Jan 29, 1936
              X, p. 1, Feb 9, 1936
Newsweek 7: 25-6, Feb 8, 1936
Theatre Arts 20: 183, Mar 1936
Time 27: 47-8, Feb 10, 1936

Dear Octopus
Productions:
Opened January 11, 1939 for 53 performances.
Reviews:
Catholic World 148: 731, Mar 1939
Commonweal 29: 413, Feb 3, 1939
Nation 148: 128, Jan 28, 1939
New Republic 97: 343, Jan 25, 1939
New York Times p. 22, Jan 12, 1939
Theatre Arts 23: 171-2, Mar 1939
Time 33: 21, Jan 23, 1939

Lovers and Friends
Productions:
Opened November 29, 1943 for 168 performances.
Reviews:
Catholic World 158: 393, Jan 1944
Commonweal 39: 231, Dec 17, 1943
Nation 157: 740, Dec 18, 1943
New York Theatre Critics' Reviews 1943: 210
New York Times p. 23, Nov 30, 1943
                 II, p. 5, Dec 5, 1943
New York Times Magazine p. 16, Nov 21, 1943
Newsweek 22: 90, Dec 13, 1943
Theatre Arts 28: 74+, Feb 1944
Time 42: 44, Dec 13, 1943

Strindberg, August
The Bridal Crown
Productions:
Opened February 5, 1938 for one performance.
Reviews:

The Bridal Crown (cont.)
>New York Times p. 11, Feb 7, 1938
>Newsweek 11: 28, Feb 21, 1938
>Time 31: 36, Feb 14, 1938

Countess Julia (see Miss Julie)
>Productions:
>Opened May 2, 1913 for three performances.
>Reviews:
>New York Times p. 9, Apr 29, 1913

The Creditors
>Productions:
>Season of 1921-1922.
>(Off Broadway) Adapted by Paul Shyer.   Opened January
>25, 1962 for 46 performances.
>Reviews:
>Commonweal 51: 267-8, Dec 9, 1949
>   75: 543, Feb 16, 1962
>Forum 113: 26-7, Jan 1950
>Nation 194: 126, Feb 10, 1962
>New Republic 122: 22, Jan 2, 1950
>   146: 20-1, Feb 19, 1962
>New York Clipper 70: 20, May 10, 1922
>New York Times p. 27, May 3, 1922
>   p. 19, Jan 26, 1962
>New Yorker 37: 72, Feb 3, 1962
>Theatre Arts 46: 63+, Apr 1962

Crime and Crime
>Productions:
>(Off Broadway) Translated by Elizabeth Sprigge.   Opened
>December 16, 1963 for one performance.
>Reviews:
>New York Times p. 51, Dec 17, 1963

The Dance of Death (see also The Last Dance)
>Productions:
>Season of 1919-1920.
>(Off Broadway) Adapted by John Bowman.   Opened
>September 13, 1960 for 32 performances.
>Reviews:
>Dramatic Mirror 86: 1146, May 22, 1920
>Independent 102: 273, May 29, 1920
>Nation 110: 774-5, Jan 5, 1920
>   118: 16-17, Jan 1924
>New York Times p. 51, Sep 14, 1960
>New York Clipper 68: 19, May 19, 1920
>Theatre Arts 44: 9, Nov 1960
>Theatre Magazine 15: xv, Jun 1912
>   32: 30, Jul-Aug 1920

The Dream Play
  Productions:
      Translated by Edwin Bjorkman. Opened January 30,
          1926 for 27 performances.
  Reviews:
      Nation 122: 122-3, Feb 3, 1926
      New York Times p. 18, Jan 21, 1926
      New Yorker 36: 103, Dec 3, 1960
      Theatre Magazine 15: xv, Jun 1912
Easter One Day More (Easter)
  Productions:
      Opened March 18, 1926 for 28 performances.
  Reviews:
      America 96: 511, Feb 2, 1957
      Dramatic Mirror 78: 29, Apr 6, 1918
      Life (NY) 87: 27, Apr 8, 1926
      New York Times p. 24, Mar 19, 1926
The Father
  Productions:
      Opened April 9, 1912 for 31 performances.
      English version by Robert Whittier. Opened May 11,
          1928 for eight performances.
      Opened October 8, 1931 for 20 performances.
      English version by Robert L. Joseph. Opened Novem-
          ber 16, 1949 for 69 performances.
      Opened May 14, 1962 for three performances.
      (Off Broadway) Opened November 10, 1965 for 11 per-
          formances.
  Reviews:
      American Playwright 1: 146, May 1912
      Arts and Decoration 36: 55, Dec 1931
      Blue Book 15: 694-6, Aug 1912
      Catholic World 170: 307-8, Jan 1950
      Commonweal 51: 267-8, Dec 9, 1949
      Dramatic Mirror 67: 6, Apr 17, 1912
      Forum 113: 26, Jan 1950
      Green Book 7: 1204, Jun 1912
                  8: 9-11+, Jul 1912
      Life (NY) 59: 869-72, Apr 25, 1912
      Munsey 47: 467, Jun 1912
      Nation 95: 153, Aug 15, 1912
             169: 525, Nov 26, 1949
      New Republic 68: 301, Oct 28, 1931
                   121: 22, Sep 19, 1949
                   121: 21, Dec 19, 1949
      New York Dramatic News 55: 17, Apr 13, 1912
                              55: 18, Apr 20, 1912

The Father (cont.)
New York Theatre Critics' Reviews 1949: 223
New York Times p. 9, May 12, 1928
                p. 21, Oct 9, 1931
                II, p. 1, Nov 27, 1949
                p. 49, May 15, 1962
New Yorker 25: 52, Nov 26, 1949
Newsweek 34: 67, Nov 28, 1949
Outlook 159: 280, Oct 28, 1931
Red Book 19: 564, Jul 1912
Theatre Arts 15: 981, Dec 1931
                34: 15, Jan 1950
Theatre Magazine 15: 176, Jun 1912
Time 54: 61, Nov 28, 1949
The Last Dance (see also Dance of Death)
Productions:
Adapted by Peter Goldbaum and Robin Short. Opened
    January 27, 1948 for seven performances.
Reviews:
Forum 109: 158, Mar 1948
New Republic 118: 34, Feb 9, 1948
New York Times p. 27, Jan 28, 1948
New Yorker 23: 42, Feb 7, 1948
Newsweek 31: 70, Feb 9, 1948
Miss Julie (Miss Julia) (see also Countess Julia)
Productions:
Adapted by George Tabori. Opened February 21, 1956
    for 33 performances.
Opened May 16, 1962 in repertory (Royal Dramatic The-
    atre of Sweden).
(Off Broadway) Opened November 10, 1965 for 11 per-
    formances.
Reviews:
Book News 32: 72-3, Sep 1913
Catholic World 183: 66, Apr 1956
Dramatic Mirror 69: 6, Apr 30, 1913
Life (NY) 61: 930, May 8, 1913
Nation 182: 205, Mar 10, 1956
New York Theatre Critics' Reviews 1956: 353
New York Times p. 23, Feb 22, 1956
                II, p. 1, Mar 4, 1956
                p. 31, May 17, 1962
                p. 42, Jun 9, 1965
Newsweek 32: 62+, Mar 3, 1956
Saturday Review 39: 25, Mar 10, 1956
Time 67: 47, Mar 5, 1956
Pariah

Productions:
  Translated by Edwin Bjorkman. Opened March 18, 1913
    for one performance.
  Opened 1917 in repertory (Washington Square Players).
Reviews:
  Dramatic Mirror 69: 6, Apr 2, 1913
              77: 7, Jun 9, 1917
  New York Times p. 13, May 29, 1917
  Theatre Magazine 26: 15+, Jul 1917
The Spook Sonata
Productions:
  Opened January 5, 1924 for 24 performances.
Reviews:
  Dial 76: 205, Feb 1924
  Freeman 8: 472, Jan 23, 1924
  Life (NY) 83: 18, Jan 24, 1924
  Nation 118: 147-8, Feb 6, 1924
  New Republic 37: 231-2, Jan 23, 1924
  New York Times p. 23, Jan 7, 1924
              VII, p. 1, Jan 13, 1924
The Stronger
Productions:
  Translated by Edith and Warner Oland. Opened March
    18, 1913 for one performance.
  Adapted by George Tabori. Opened February 21, 1956
    for 33 performances.
Reviews:
  Dramatic Mirror 69: 6, Apr 2, 1913
  New York Theatre Critics' Reviews 1956: 353
  New York Times p. 23, Feb 22, 1956
  Saturday Review 39: 25, Mar 10, 1956

Sudermann, Hermann
Magda
Productions:
  Translated by Charles Edward Amory Winslow. Opened
    January 26, 1926 for 24 performances.
Reviews:
  American Playwright 1: 192-7, Jun 1913
  New York Times p. 16, Jan 27, 1926
Song of Songs
Productions:
  Opened December 22, 1914 for 191 performances.
Reviews:
  Bookman 40: 637-8, Feb 1915
  Current Opinion 58: 97-8, Feb 1915
  Dramatic Mirror 72: 8, Dec 30, 1914

Song of Songs (cont.)
        Green Book 13: 478-9, Mar 1915
                13: 570-1, Mar 1915
        Hearst 27: 299-301; 316-17, Mar 1915
        Nation 100: 87, Jan 21, 1915
        New Republic 1: 25, Jan 2, 1915
        New York Times p. 13, Dec 5, 1914
                      VIII, p. 8, Dec 13, 1914
        Smart Set 45: 453-4, Jan 1915
        Theatre Magazine 21: 58, Feb 1915

Synge, John Millington
 Deirdre of the Sorrows
   Productions:
     Season of 1920-1921.
   Reviews:
     America 102: 217, Nov 14, 1959
     Forum 113: 27, Jan 1950
     New York Clipper 68: 19, Sep 29, 1920
     New York Times VI, p. 1, Sep 26, 1920
     New Yorker 35: 95, Oct 24, 1959
     Weekly Review 3: 297, Oct 1920
 In the Shadow of the Glen
   Productions:
     Opened November 20, 1911 in repertory (The Irish
       Players).
     Opened October 21, 1932 in repertory (Irish Repertory
       Company).
     Opened November 17, 1934 for one performance.
   Reviews:
     Catholic World 185: 148, May 1957
     Dramatic Mirror 66: 6-7, Dec 20, 1911
     New York Times p. 25, Nov 4, 1932
 Playboy of the Western World
   Productions:
     Opened November 20, 1911 in repertory (Irish Repertory
       Company).
     Opened February 4, 1913 in repertory (Irish Repertory
       Company).
     Opened April 16, 1921 in repertory (Irish Repertory
       Company).
     Opened June 2, 1930 in repertory (Irish Repertory
       Company).
     Opened October 21, 1932 in repertory (Irish Repertory
       Company).
     Opened November 17, 1934 for 7 performances.
     Opened November 20, 1937 for 9 performances.
     Opened October 26, 1946 for 81 performances.

(Off Broadway) Opened June 23, 1947.
(Off Broadway) Season of 1957-1958.
Reviews:
American Playwright 1: 24-5, Jan 1912
Bookman 32: 145-6, Oct 1910
Catholic World 164: 262-3, Dec 1946
                187: 312-13, Jul 1958
Collier's 48: 33-4, Feb 10, 1912
Commonweal 45: 95, Nov 8, 1946
             68: 303-4, Jan 20, 1958
Dramatic Mirror 66: 7+, Nov 29, 1911
              66: 6, Dec 6, 1911
Dramatist 3: 224-5, Jan 1912
Everybody's Magazine 26: 233+, Feb 1912
Forum 47: 380-1, Mar 1912
Green Book 7: 237-8+, Feb 1912
Harper's Bazaar 80: 220, Dec 1946
Life (NY) 58: 1090, Dec 14, 1911
Life 24: 85-6+, May 24, 1948
Munsey 46: 588-9, Jan 1912
Nation 93: 529, Nov 30, 1911
      163: 536, Nov 9, 1946
      166: 557, May 15, 1948
New Republic 27: 117, Jun 22, 1921
            115: 628, Nov 11, 1946
            118: 34, May 19, 1948
New York Clipper 69: 23, Apr 20, 1921
New York Theatre Critics' Reviews 1946: 287
New York Times p. 20, Jan 30, 1930
             p. 25, Oct 21, 1932
             p. 14, Nov 22, 1937
             p. 18, Oct 28, 1946
New Yorker 22: 57, Nov 2, 1946
Newsweek 28: 85, Nov 4, 1946
         31: 77, May 10, 1948
Red Book 18: 753-62, Feb 1912
Saturday Review 31: 20-1, May 29, 1948
Theatre Arts 16: 228-36, Mar 1932
          31: 21-2, Jan 1947
          32: 13+, Summer 1948
Theatre Magazine 15: ii+, Jan 1912
            34: 14+, Jul 1921
Time 48: 55, Nov 4, 1946
     51: 81, May 10, 1948
Weekly Review 4: 496-7, May 21, 1921
Riders to the Sea
Productions:

Riders to the Sea (cont.)
    Opened November 20, 1911 in repertory.
    Opened February 4, 1913 in repertory (The Irish Players).
    Opened in the Fall of 1934 in repertory for two per-
        formances (Abbey Theatre Players).
    (Off Broadway) Season of 1956-1957.
  Reviews:
    Catholic World 185: 148, May 1947
    Drama 15: 106, Feb 1925
    Dramatic Mirror 66: 7, Dec 13, 1911
    Green Book 7: 239+, Feb 1912
    New York Times p. 24, Mar 7, 1957
                    II, p. 1, Mar 17, 1957
    Weekly Review 3: 155-6, Aug 18, 1920
Tinker's Wedding
  Productions:
    (Off Broadway) Season of 1956-1957.
  Reviews:
    Catholic World 185: 148, May 1957
    New York Times p. 24, Mar 7, 1957
                    II, p. 1, Mar 17, 1957
The Well of the Saints
  Productions:
    Opened November 20, 1911 in repertory (The Irish
        Players).
    Opened January 21, 1932 for five performances.
    Opened November 21, 1934 for one performance.
  Reviews:
    Arts and Decoration 36: 42+, Mar 1932
    Catholic World 189: 243, Jun 1959
    Dramatic Mirror 66: 9, Nov 29, 1911
    New York Times p. 15, Jan 22, 1932
                    p. 26, Nov 22, 1934
    New Yorker 35: 82-3, Apr 18, 1959

Tabori, George
  Brecht on Brecht (stage reading)
    Productions:
    (Off Broadway) Arranged and translated by George
        Tabori. Opened January 3, 1962 for 424 performances.
    (Off Broadway) Arranged and translated by George
        Tabori. Opened July 9, 1963 for 47 performances.
  Reviews:
    New Republic 146: 23, Jan 22, 1962
    New York Times p. 26, Jan 4, 1962
                    II, p. 1, Jan 14, 1962
    Theatre Arts 46: 60-1, Mar 1962

The Emperor's Clothes
  Productions:
    Opened February 9, 1953 for 16 performances.
  Reviews:
    Commonweal 57: 551, Mar 6, 1953
    Nation 176: 174, Feb 21, 1953
    New Republic 128: 22-3, Feb 23, 1953
    New York Theatre Critics' Reviews 1953: 368
    New York Times p. 24, Feb 20, 1953
                II, p. 3, Feb 22, 1953
                II, p. 3, Mar 1, 1953
    New Yorker 29: 62, Feb 21, 1953
    Saturday Review 36: 37, Feb 28, 1953
                36: 33, Nov 7, 1953
    Theatre Arts 37: 28, Apr 1953
    Time 61: 86, Feb 23, 1953
Flight Into Egypt
  Productions:
    Opened March 18, 1952 for 46 performances.
  Reviews:
    Catholic World 175: 147, May 1952
    Commonweal 55: 638, Apr 4, 1952
    Nation 174: 306, Mar 29, 1952
              174: 328, Apr 5, 1952
    New York Theatre Critics' Reviews 1952: 341
    New York Times p. 33, Mar 19, 1952
                II, p. 1, Mar 30, 1952
                II, p. 3, Mar 30, 1952
    New Yorker 28: 60+, Mar 29, 1952
    Newsweek 39: 84, Mar 31, 1952
    Saturday Review 35: 28-9, Mar 22, 1952
                35: 27, May 3, 1952
    Theatre Arts 36: 90, May 1952
    Time 59: 68, Mar 31, 1952

Tagger, Theodor (see Bruckner, Ferdinand)

Thomas, Brandon
  Charley's Aunt
    Productions:
      Opened June 1, 1925 for 8 performances.
      Opened October 17, 1940 for 233 performances.
      Opened December 22, 1933 for 15 performances.
      (Off Broadway) Opened April 7, 1962 for 9 performances.
    Reviews:
      Catholic World 152: 334, Dec 1940
                  178: 387, Feb 1954

Charley's Aunt (cont.)
    Commonweal 33: 80, Nov 8, 1940
    Life 6: 72-3, May 29, 1939
        9: 47-50, Nov 18, 1940
    Nation 151: 431, Nov 2, 1940
    New Republic 103: 629, Nov 4, 1940
    New York Theatre Critics' Reviews 1940: 24
                                        1953: 179
    New York Times p. 16, Jun 2, 1925
                    p. 24, Oct 18, 1940
                    p. 22, Dec 23, 1953
    Theatre Arts 24: 848, Dec 1940
               38: 18, Mar 1954
    Time 36: 51, Nov 4, 1940
    Vogue 97: 34, Jan 1, 1941
Under Orders
  Productions:
    Opened August 20, 1918 for 167 performances.
  Reviews:
    Current Opinion 65: 299-302, Nov 1918
    Dramatic Mirror 79: 301, Aug 31, 1918
    Dramatist 11: 1016-17, Jul 1920
    Green Book 20: 772+, Nov 1918
    Life (NY) 72: 344, Sep 5, 1918
    New York Times p. 7, Aug 21, 1918
                 III, p. 4, Aug 25, 1918
    Theatre Magazine 28: 218-20, Oct 1918

Thomas, Dylan
  Under Milk Wood
    Productions:
    Opened October 15, 1957 for 39 performances.
    (Off Broadway) Opened March 29, 1961 for 202 perform-
    ances.
    (Off Broadway) Opened November 16, 1962 for 54 per-
    formances.
  Reviews:
    Christian Century 74: 1324, Nov 6, 1957
                     78: 535-7, Apr 26, 1961
    Commonweal 58: 297, Jun 26, 1953
              67: 151, Nov 8, 1967
    Nation 185: 309, Nov 2, 1957
    New York Theatre Critics' Reviews 1957: 223
    New York Times p. 42, Oct 16, 1957
                 II, p. 1, Nov 10, 1957
                 p. 25, Mar 30, 1961
                 II, p. 1, Apr 9, 1961

248

p. 13, Oct 6, 1962
New Yorker 33: 95, Oct 26, 1957
37: 132+, Apr 8, 1961
38: 132, Dec 15, 1962
Reporter 17: 39, Nov 14, 1962
Saturday Review 36: 24-5, Jun 6, 1953
39: 39, Oct 6, 1956
43: 30, Jun 4, 1960
Theatre Arts 41: 92-3, May 1957
41: 22-3, Dec 1957
Time 70: 93, Oct 28, 1957
Vogue 130: 212-13, Sep 1, 1957

Toller, Ernst
Bloody Laughter
Productions:
Adapted by Forrest Wilson and William Schack.
Opened December 4, 1931 for 35 performances.
Reviews:
Commonweal 15: 214, Dec 23, 1931
New York Times p. 20, Dec 5, 1931
Theatre Arts 16: 95-6, Feb 1932
Man and the Masses
Productions:
Translated by Louis H. Untermeyer. Opened April 14,
1924 for 32 performances.
Reviews:
American Mercury 2: 244, Jun 1924
Life (NY) 83: 20, May 8, 1924
Living Age 322: 175-8, Jul 26, 1924
Nation 118: 512-13, Apr 10, 1924
New Republic 38: 262, Apr 30, 1924
New York Times p. 25, Apr 15, 1924
Theatre Magazine 39: 54, Jun 1924
No More Peace
Productions:
Translated by Edward Crankshaw. Opened January 25,
1938 for 4 performances (Federal Theatre Project).
Reviews:
New York Times p. 13, Jan 29, 1938
One Act Play Magazine 1: 950, Feb 1938

Tolstoy, Leo
The Living Corpse (see Redemption)

The Power of Darkness
Productions:

249

The Power of Darkness (cont.)
     Opened January 15, 1920 for 40 performances.
  Reviews:
     Nation 110: 178, Feb 7, 1920
     New Republic 21: 296, Feb 4, 1920
     New York Times p. 22, Jan 22, 1920
                         VIII, p. 2, Jan 25, 1920
     New Yorker 35: 129-30, Oct 10, 1959
     Review 2: 137-8, Feb 7, 1920
Redemption (Living Corpse)
  Productions:
     Opened October 3, 1918 for 204 performances.
     Opened November 19, 1928 for 20 performances.   Adapted
     by August Scholz.
     Opened December 6, 1929.
  Reviews:
     Arts and Decoration 32: 96, Feb 1930
     Commonweal 11: 299, Dec 25, 1929
     Current Opinion 65: 305, Nov 1918
     Dramatic Mirror 79: 580, Oct 19, 1918
     Forum 60: 621-2, Nov 1918
     Green Book 20: 958-9, Dec 1918
     Nation 107: 459, Oct 19, 1918
            127: 640-1, Dec 5, 1928
            129: 785-6, Dec 25, 1929
     New Republic 17: 46, Nov 9, 1918
                  16: 349, Oct 19, 1918
     Theatre Arts 14: 107-8, Feb 1930
     Theatre Magazine 28: 277, Nov 1918
                      28: 358-9, Dec 1918
Tsar Fyodor Ivanovitch
  Productions:
     Opened January 1923 in repertory.
     Opened November 1923 in repertory.
  Reviews:
     Hearst 43: 93-5, Feb 1923
     Independent 110: 98, Feb 3, 1923
     New York Clipper 70: 14, Jan 17, 1923
     New York Times p. 14, May 22, 1923

Turgenev, Ivan
  Lady from the Provinces
     Productions:
        Opened February 1923 for 8 performances in repertory.
     No Reviews.
  A Month in the Country
     Productions:

Opened March 17, 1930 for 71 performances.
Reviews:
    Arts and Decoration 33: 62, May 1930
    Commonweal 11: 622, Apr 2, 1930
    Life (NY) 95: 16, Apr 4, 1930
    Nation 130: 430+, Apr 9, 1930
    New Republic 62: 246-7, Apr 16, 1930
    New York Times p. 30, Mar 18, 1930
    Outlook 154: 550, Apr 2, 1930
    Theatre Arts 14: 368+, May 1930
    Theatre Magazine 51: 42+, May 1930

Ustinov, Peter
  The Love of Four Colonels
    Productions:
    Opened January 15, 1953 for 141 performances.
    Reviews:
      Catholic World 176: 466-7, Mar 1953
      Commonweal 57: 450, Feb 6, 1953
      Harper 203: 110, Nov 1951
      Life 34: 95-6+, Feb 2, 1953
      Look 17: 17, Feb 24, 1953
      Nation 176: 132, Feb 7, 1953
      New Republic 128: 22-3, Feb 2, 1953
      New York Theatre Critics' Reviews 1953: 394
      New York Times p. 17, Jan 16, 1953
      New Yorker 28: 54+, Jan 24, 1953
      Newsweek 41: 95, Jan 26, 1953
      Saturday Review 36: 26, Jan 31, 1953
      Theatre Arts 37: 66-8, Mar 1953
      Time 61: 52, Jan 26, 1953
  Photo Finish
    Productions:
    Opened February 12, 1963 for 159 performances.
    Reviews:
      Nation 196: 214, Nov 9, 1963
      New York Theatre Critics' Reviews 1963: 377
      New York Times p. 5, Feb 14, 1963
      New Yorker 39: 112, Feb 23, 1963
      Newsweek 61: 60, Feb 25, 1963
      Saturday Review 46: 30, Mar 2, 1963
      Theatre Arts 47: 10-11, Apr 1963
      Time 81: 75, Feb 22, 1963
  Romanoff and Juliet
    Productions:
    Opened October 10, 1957 for 389 performances.
    Reviews:

Romanoff and Juliet (cont.)
   America 98: 355, Dec 14, 1957
   Catholic World 186: 225, Dec 1957
   Christian Century 74: 1424, Nov 27, 1957
   Commonweal 67: 175, Nov 15, 1957
   Life 43: 111-12, Nov 25, 1957
   Nation 185: 291, Oct 26, 1957
   New Republic 137: 20, Oct 28, 1957
   New York Theatre Critics' Reviews 1957: 228
   New York Times p. 24, Oct 11, 1957
   New Yorker 33: 81, Oct 19, 1957
   Newsweek 50: 99, Oct 21, 1957
   Reporter 15: 38, Nov 1, 1956
           17: 39, Nov 14, 1957
   Saturday Review, 39: 30, Oct 13, 1956
               40: 27, Oct 26, 1957
   Theatre Arts 41: 92, May 1957
                41: 19-20, Dec 1957
   Time 70: 57, Oct 21, 1957

Vajda, Ernst
  The Crown Prince
   Productions:
       Adapted by Zoe Akins.   Opened March 23, 1927 for 45
         performances.
   Reviews:
       Bookman 65: 448, Jun 1927
       Life (NY) 89: 18, Apr 14, 1927
       New York Times p. 23, Mar 24, 1927
  Fata Morgana (Mirage)
   Productions:
       Translated by James T. A. Burrell and Philip Moeller.
       Opened March 3, 1924 for 120 performances.
       Opened December 25, 1931 for 27 performances.
   Reviews:
       American Mercury 2: 116, May 1924
       Bookman 59: 331, May 1924
       Independent 112: 231-2, Apr 26, 1924
       Life (NY) 83: 18, Mar 27, 1924
       Nation 118: 321, Mar 19, 1924
       New Republic 38: 128, Mar 26, 1924
       New York Times p. 16, Mar 4, 1924
                     VIII, p. 1, Mar 9, 1924
                     p. 15, Dec 26, 1931
       Theatre Magazine 39: 15, May 1924
  Grounds for Divorce
   Productions:

252

Adapted by Guy Bolton. Opened September 23, 1924 for
127 performances.
Reviews:
Nation 119: 394-5, Oct 8, 1924
New York Times p. 20, Sep 24, 1924
The Harem
Productions:
Adapted by Avery Hopwood. Opened December 2, 1924
for 183 performances.
Reviews:
American Mercury 4: 245-6, Feb 1925
Bookman 60: 742, Feb 1925
Dramatist 16: 1255, Jan 1925
Life (NY) 84: 18, Dec 25, 1924
New York Times p. 24, Dec 3, 1924
Theatre Magazine 40: 16, Feb 1925
The Little Angel
Productions:
Adapted by J. Jacobus. Opened September 27, 1924 for
49 performances.
Reviews:
American Mercury 3: 374-5, Nov 1924
Life (NY) 84: 18, Oct 16, 1924
New York Times p. 10, Sep 29, 1924
                    VIII, p. 1, Oct 5, 1924
Mirage (see Fata Morgana)

Vane, Sutton
Outward Bound
Productions:
Opened January 7, 1924 for 144 performances.
Opened December 22, 1938 for 255 performances.
Reviews:
American Mercury 1: 372-3, Mar 1924
Classic 19: 46+, May 1924
Current Opinion 76: 443-50, Apr 1924
Dial 76: 293-4, Mar 1924
Freeman 8: 473, Jan 23, 1924
Independent 112: 231-2, Apr 26, 1924
Life (NY) 83: 18, Jan 31, 1924
Nation 148: 44, Jan 7, 1939
New York Times p. 26, Jan 8, 1924
              p. 16, Dec 23, 1938
              XI, p. 1, Jan 1, 1939
Stage 16: 12-13, Feb 1939
Theatre Arts 23:97+, Feb 1939
Theatre Magazine 39: 26+, May 1924
Time 33: 25, Jan 2, 1939

Outward Bound (cont.)
    Woman Citizen ns8: 23,   Mar 8, 1924

Vernueil, Louis
 Affairs of State
    Productions:
        Opened September 25, 1950 for 610 performances.
    Reviews:
        Catholic World 172: 149, Nov 1950
        Christian Science Monitor Magazine p. 6, Sep 30,   1950
        Commonweal 53: 15, Oct 13, 1950
        Nation 171: 321, Oct 7, 1950
        New Republic 123: 21, Oct 16, 1950
        New York Theatre Critics' Reviews 1950: 267
        New York Times p. 37, Sep 26, 1950
                            II, p. 1, Oct 1, 1950
                            II, p. 3, Feb 4, 1951
        New Yorker 26: 52, Oct 7, 1950
        Newsweek 36: 84, Oct 9, 1950
        Saturday Review 33: 24, Nov 4, 1950
        Theatre Arts 34: 12, Nov 1950
        Time 56: 85, Oct 9, 1950
 Cousin Sonia
    Productions:
        Translated by Herbert Williams.   Opened December 7,
            1925 for 30 performances.
    No Reviews.
 First Love
    Productions:
        Adapted by Zoe Akins from Pile ou Face.   Opened Novem-
            ber 8, 1926 for 50 performances.
    Reviews:
        Life (NY) 88: 23, Nov 25, 1926
        New York Times p. 31, Nov 9, 1926
        Theatre Magazine 45: 16+, Feb 1927
 Jealousy
    Productions:
        Adapted by Eugene Walter.   Opened October 22, 1928 for
            136 performances.
    Reviews:
        New York Times p. 32, Oct 23, 1928
        Theatre Magazine 49: 45-6, Jan 1929
                            49: 30-1+, Feb 1929
 Love and Let Love
    Productions:
        Opened October 19, 1951 for 51 performances.
    Reviews:

Catholic World 174: 229, Dec 1951
Commonweal 55: 117, Nov 9, 1951
New York Theatre Critics' Reviews 1951: 198
New York Times p. 11, Oct 20, 1951
New Yorker 27: 68, Oct 27, 1951
Newsweek 38: 84, Oct 29, 1951
Theatre Arts 35: 21+, Nov 1951
         35: 3, Dec 1951
Time 58: 38, Oct 29, 1951

The Love Habit

Productions:
Adapted by Gladys Unger. Opened March 14, 1923 for 69 performances.

Reviews:
New York Clipper 71: 14, Mar 21, 1923
New York Times p. 17, Mar 15, 1923
Theatre Magazine 37: 15, May 1923

Matrimony PFD.

Productions:
Adapted by Grace George and James Forbes. Opened November 12, 1936 for 61 performances.

Reviews:
Catholic World 144: 473, Jan 1937
Nation 143: 642, Nov 28, 1936
New York Times p. 28, Nov 6, 1936
         p. 26, Nov 13, 1936
Theatre Arts 21: 20+, Jan 1937
Time 28: 36, Nov 23, 1936

Oh Mama

Productions:
Adapted by Wilton Lackaye and Harry Wagstaff Gribble. Opened August 19, 1925 for 70 performances.

Reviews:
Dramatist 16: 1287-8, Oct 1925
New York Times p. 22, Aug 20, 1925
Theatre Magazine 42: 14-15, Oct 1925

Pile ou Face (see First Love)

Vildrac, Charles

Michel Auclair

Productions:
Opened March 4, 1925 for 19 performances.

Reviews:
Nation 120: 334-5, Mar 25, 1925
New York Times p. 23, Mar 5, 1925
Theatre Arts 8: 13-18, Jan 1942

S. S. Tenacity

S. S. Tenacity (cont.)
    Productions:
    Opened January 2, 1922 for 67 performances.
    Reviews:
        Bookman 55: 61, Mar 1922
        Dramatic Mirror 95: 17, Jan 7, 1922
        Independent 108: 92, Jan 28, 1922
        Nation 114: 103, Jan 25, 1922
        New Republic 29: 251, Jan 25, 1922
        New York Clipper 69: 20, Jan 18, 1922
        New York Times p. 20, Jan 3, 1922
                        VI, p. 1, Jan 15, 1922
                        VI, p. 1, Feb 5, 1922
        Theatre Magazine 35: 166-7, Mar 1922

Wedekind, Frank
    The Awakening of Spring (see also Birabeau's Dame Nature)
    Productions:
        (Off Broadway) Translated by Mascha Beyo. Adapted
        by Arthur A. Seidelman and Donald Levin. Opened
        May 12, 1964 for eight performances.
    Reviews:
        New York Times p. 50, May 13, 1964
    The Loves of Lulu
    Productions:
        Translated by Samuel A. Eliot, Jr. Opened May 11, 1925
        for 15 performances.
    Reviews:
        New Republic 43: 20-21, May 27, 1925
        New York Times p. 26, May 12, 1925
        New Yorker 34: 89-90, Oct 11, 1958
    The Tenor
    Productions:
        Adapted by Andre Tridon. Opened October 4, 1915 in
        repertory (Washington Square Players).
    Reviews:
        Dramatic Mirror 75: 8, Jan 22, 1916
        New York Times p. 11, Jan 11, 1916

Weiss, Peter
    Marat/Sade (The Persecution and Assassination of Marat as
                Performed by the Inmates of the Asylum of
                Charenton Under the Direction of the Marquis
                de Sade)
    Productions:
        Opened December 27, 1965 for 144 performances.
    Reviews:

256

America 114: 181-2, Jan 29, 1966
Catholic World 203: 63-4, Apr 1966
Commentary 41: 75-6, Mar 1966
Commonweal 83: 476-7, Jan 21, 1966
      83: 636-8, Mar 4, 1966
Harper's 232: 124, Apr 1966
Life 60: 26-27, Mar 11, 1966
Look 30: 106-10, Feb 22, 1966
Nation 202: 82-4, Jan 17, 1966
New Republic 154: 23-4+, Jan 22, 1966
New York Theatre Critics' Reviews 1965: 212
New York Times p. 35, Dec 28, 1965
      II, p. 1, Jan 9, 1966
Newsweek 67: 63, Jan 10, 1966
      69: 93, Jan 16, 1966
Reporter 34: 48-9, Jan 27, 1966
Saturday Review 49: 45+, Jan 15, 1966
Time 87: 51, Jan 7, 1966
Vogue 147: 102-5, Jan 1, 1966
      147: 56, Feb 15, 1966

Werfel, Franz
 The Eternal Road
  Productions:
   Adapted by William A. Drake. Translated by Ludwig
   Lewisohn. Opened January 7, 1937 for 153 perform-
   ances.
  Reviews:
   Nation 144: 109, Jan 23, 1937
   New Republic 90: 19-20, Feb 10, 1937
   New York Times p. 29, Dec 14, 1936
        X, p. 7, Dec 27, 1936
        X, p. 1, Jan 3, 1937
        X, p. 8, Jan 17, 1937
        p. 30, May 13, 1937
        p. 23, May 15, 1937
   Saturday Review 15: 17+, Feb 27, 1937
   Stage 13: 62-4, Dec 1935
   Theatre Arts 21: 180+, Mar 1937
   Time 29: 47-8, Jan 18, 1937
 The Goat Song
  Productions:
   Translated by Ruth Langner. Opened January 25, 1926
   for 58 performances.
  Reviews:
   Bookman 63: 213, Apr 1926
   Dramatist 17: 1289, Jan 1926

The Goat Song (cont.)
 Independent 116: 275, Mar 6, 1926
 Literary Digest 88: 25, Feb 13, 1926
 Nation 122: 187, Feb 17, 1926
 New Republic 46: 17, Feb 24, 1926
 New York Times p. 18, Jan 26, 1926
                        VII, p. 1, Feb 7, 1926
 Theatre Magazine 43: 16, Apr 1926
 Vogue 67: 134, Mar 15, 1926
Jacobowsky and the Colonel
 Productions:
 Adapted by S. N. Behrman. Opened March 14, 1944
  for 417 performances.
 Reviews:
 Catholic World 159: 169-70, May 1944
                159: 457-8, Aug 1944
 Commonweal 39: 589-90, Mar 31, 1944
 Life 16: 49-50+, Apr 10, 1944
 Nation 158: 373, Mar 25, 1944
          158: 429-30, Apr 8, 1944
 New Republic 110: 307, Mar 27, 1944
 New York Theatre Critics' Reviews 1944: 243
 New York Times VI, p. 24, Mar 5, 1944
                 II, p. 1, Mar 12, 1944
                 p. 17, Mar 15, 1944
                 II, p. 1, Mar 19, 1944
 New York Times Magazine pp. 24-5, Mar 5, 1944
                        p. 16+, Apr 9, 1944
 New Yorker 20: 52, Mar 25, 1944
 Newsweek 23: 105-6, Mar 27, 1944
 Theatre Arts 28: 143-5, Mar 1944
              28: 204, Apr 1944
              28: 261-2+, May 1944
 Time 43: 60+, Mar 27, 1944
Juarez and Maximillian
 Productions:
 Opened October 11, 1926 for 48 performances.
 Reviews:
 Dial 81: 522, Dec 1926
 Independent 117: 621, Nov 1927
 Life (NY) 88: 21, Nov 4, 1926
 Literary Digest 91: 26-7, Oct 30, 1926
 Nation 122: 587, May 26, 1926
        123: 435, Oct 27, 1926
 New Republic 48: 271-2, Oct 27, 1926
 New York Times p. 31, Oct 12, 1926
                VIII, p. 1, Oct 17, 1926

Theatre Arts 10: 813-14+, Dec 1926
Theatre Magazine 44: 15, Dec 1926
               44: 26-8+, Dec 1926
Vanity Fair 27: 63+, Nov 1926
Vogue 68: 83, Dec 1, 1926
Schweiger
  Productions:
    Translated by Jack Charash and William A. Drake.
    Opened March 23, 1926 for 30 performances.
  Reviews:
    Bookman 63: 467-8, Jun 1926
    Life (NY) 87: 23, Apr 15, 1926
    New York Times p. 20, Mar 24, 1926
    Theatre Magazine 43: 16, Jun 1926

Wesker, Arnold
  Chips with Everything
    Productions:
    Opened October 1, 1963 for 149 performances.
    Reviews:
      America 109: 496, Oct 26, 1963
      Commonweal 79: 139-41, Oct 25, 1963
                  79: 570-1, Feb 7, 1964
                  84: 473, Jul 22, 1966
      Nation 197: 267-8, Oct 19, 1963
      New Republic 149: 30-1, Oct 19, 1963
      New York Theatre Critics' Reviews 1963: 236
      New York Times p. 49, Oct 2, 1963
      New Yorker 38: 160, May 12, 1962
      Newsweek 62: 72, Oct 14, 1963
      Reporter 27: 48+, Sep 13, 1962
      Saturday Review 46: 30, Oct 19, 1963
      Theatre Arts 48: 10-11, Jan 1964
      Time 82: 72+, Oct 11, 1963
      Vogue 143: 62, Feb 1, 1964
  The Kitchen
    Productions:
    (Off Broadway) Opened May 9, 1966 for three performances
    (New Theatre Workshop).
    Reviews:
      Life 61: 17, Aug 12, 1966
      Newsweek 67: 89, Jun 27, 1966
      Saturday Review 49: 36, Jul 2, 1966
  Roots
    Productions:
    (Off Broadway) Opened March 6, 1961 for 72 perform-
    ances.

Roots (cont.)
   (Off Broadway) Opened January 8, 1965 for nine performances.
   Reviews:
      Horizon 3: 117-18, Jul 1961
      Nation 192: 272, Mar 25, 1961
      New Republic 144: 30, Mar 27, 1961
      New York Times p. 40, Mar 7, 1961
                    II, p. 1, Mar 19, 1961
      New Yorker 37: 126+, Mar 18, 1961
      Theatre Arts 45: 56, May 1961
      Time 77: 42+, Mar 17, 1961

Wheeler, Hugh
   Big Fish, Little Fish
   Productions:
      Opened March 15, 1961 for 101 performances.
   Reviews:
      Commonweal 74: 255-6, Jun 2, 1961
      Nation 192: 292, Apr 1, 1961
      New Republic 144: 22, Apr 1, 1961
      New York Theatre Critics' Review 1961: 323.
      New York Times p. 42, Mar 16, 1961
                    II, p. 1, Mar 26, 1961
      New Yorker 37: 113, Mar 25, 1961
      Newsweek 57: 82, Mar 27, 1961
      Reporter 24: 46, Apr 13, 1961
      Saturday Review 44: 32, Apr 1, 1961
      Theatre Arts 45: 56-7, May 1961
      Time 77: 52, Mar 24, 1961
   Look: We've Come Through
   Productions:
      Opened October 25, 1961 for five performances.
   Reviews:
      Commonweal 72: 210-11, Nov 17, 1961
      New York Theatre Critics' Reviews 1961: 198
      New York Times p. 40, Oct 26, 1961
      New Yorker 37: 128, Nov 4, 1961
      Newsweek 58: 69, Nov 6, 1961
      Reporter 25: 46, Nov 23, 1961
      Saturday Review 44: 39, Nov 18, 1961
      Theatre Arts 46: 14-15, Jan 1962

Wilde, Oscar
   An Ideal Husband
   Productions:
      Opened September 16, 1918 for 80 performances.

Reviews:
>   Dramatic Mirror 75: 8, Mar 18, 1916
>   79: 471, Sep 28, 1918
>   Independent 96: 37, Oct 12, 1918
>   Green Book 20: 952-4, Dec 1918
>   Life (NY) 77: 572-3, Apr 21, 1921
>   New York Clipper 69: 19, Apr 6, 1921
>   New York Times p. 11, Sep 17, 1918
>   IV, p. 2, Sep 22, 1918
>   Theatre Magazine 28: 278+, Nov 1918
>   Weekly Review 4: 378-80, Apr 20, 1921

The Importance of Being Earnest

Productions:
>   Opened November 14, 1910 for 48 performances.
>   Opened January 20, 1921 for 44 performances.
>   Opened May 3, 1926 for 50 performances.
>   Opened January 12, 1939 for 61 performances.
>   Opened March 3, 1947 for 81 performances.
>   (Off Broadway) Opened February 25, 1963 for 164 performances.

Reviews:
>   Blue Book 12: 892-3, Mar 1911
>   Catholic World 148: 730, Mar 1939
>   165: 70-1, Apr 1947
>   Commonweal 29: 413, Feb 3, 1939
>   45: 565-6, Mar 21, 1947
>   Life 22: 123-4+, Mar 31, 1947
>   Life (NY) 56: 911, Nov 24, 1910
>   Munsey 44: 564, Jan 1911
>   Nation 148: 128, Jan 28, 1939
>   164: 338-9, Mar 22, 1947
>   New Republic 116: 41, Mar 17, 1947
>   New York Theatre Critics' Reviews 1947: 439
>   New York Times p. 30, May 4, 1926
>   p. 16, Jan 13, 1939
>   p. 30, Mar 4, 1947
>   II, p. 1, Mar 9, 1947
>   p. 5, Feb 27, 1963
>   New Yorker 23: 53, Mar 15, 1947
>   39: 132+, Mar 9, 1963
>   Newsweek 29: 97, Mar 17, 1947
>   61: 86, Mar 11, 1963
>   Pearson 25: 121, Jan 1911
>   Saturday Review 108: 125, Dec 4, 1909
>   150: 79, Jul 19, 1930
>   30: 22-4, Mar 29, 1947
>   Theatre Arts 23: 174, Mar 1939

The Importance of Being Earnest (cont.)
            23: 253, Apr 1939
            31: 16-17+, Apr 1947
    Theatre Magazine 44: 14-15, Jul 1926
    Time 33: 21, Jan 23, 1939
         49: 39, Mar 17, 1947
    Weekly Review 4: 184- 5, Feb 23, 1921
Lady Windermere's Fan
  Productions:
    Opened March 14, 1914 for 72 performances.
    Opened January 26, 1932 for four performances.
    Opened October 14,   1946 for 228 performances.
  Reviews:
    Catholic World 164: 262, Dec 1946
    Commonweal 44: 551- 2, Sep 20, 1946
    Dramatic Mirror 71: 13, Apr 1, 1914
    Green Book 11: 1913-14, Jun 1914
    Life 20: 119-20+, Apr 15, 1946
    Nation 98: 372, Apr 2, 1914
           163: 510, Nov 2, 1946
    New Republic 115: 556, Oct 28, 1946
    New York Theatre Critics' Reviews 1946: 307
    New York Times p. 11, Mar 31, 1914
                   p. 19, Jan 27, 1932
                   II, p. 1, Oct 13, 1946
                   p. 29,   Oct 15, 1946
    New Yorker 22: 51, Oct 26, 1946
    Newsweek 28: 86, Oct 28, 1946
    Saturday Review 29: 34-6, Nov 9, 1946
    School and Society 65: 182-3, Mar 8, 1947
    Theatre Arts 30: 691+, Dec 1946
    Theatre Magazine 19: 259-60, May 1914
    Time 38: 63, Oct 28, 1946
Mr. and Mrs. Daventry
  Productions:
    Opened February 23, 1910 for four performances.
  Reviews:
    Dramatic Mirror 63: 6, Mar 5, 1910
Salome
  Productions:
    Opened October 31, 1917 in repertory (Washington
      Square Players).
    Opened May 22, 1922 for eight performances.
    Opened May 7, 1923 for eight performances.
  Reviews:
    Drama 12: 335-7, Sep 1922
    Dramatic Mirror 78: 620, May 4, 1918

Green Book 20: 4-5+, Jul 1918
Life (NY) 71: 722, May 2, 1918
Life 21: 87, Aug 5, 1946
New York Clipper 70: 20, May 31, 1922
New York Times p. 12, May 23, 1922
                p. 22, May 8, 1923
                VII, p. 1, May 20, 1923
Poet Lore 30: 433-5, Autumn 1919
Theatre Magazine 27: 355+, Jun 1918

A Woman of No Importance
  Productions:
  Opened April 14, 1916 for 56 performances.
  Reviews:
    Book News 34: 431-2, Jun 1916
    Dramatic Mirror 75: 8, Apr 29, 1916
    Green Book 16: 71, 80-1, Jul 1916
    Nation 102: 525, May 11, 1916
    New York Times p. 9, Apr 25, 1916
                   VII, p. 7, Apr 30, 1916
                   II, p. 6, May 14, 1916
    Saturday Review 36: 24, Aug 1, 1953
    Theatre Magazine 23: 334, Jun 1916

Williams, Emlyn
  The Corn Is Green
  Productions:
    Opened November 26, 1940 for 477 performances.
    Opened May 3, 1943 for 56 performances.
    Opened January 11, 1950 for 16 performances.
    (Off Broadway) Opened September 30, 1961 for 10
      performances.
  Reviews:
    Catholic World 152: 469-70, Jan 1941
                   155: 299, Jun 1943
    Commonweal 33: 209 Dec 13, 1940
    Independent Woman 20: 24, Jan 1941
    Life 9: 25-8, Dec 23, 1940
    Nation 151: 585, Dec 7, 1940
    New Republic 103: 789, Dec 9, 1940
    New York Theatre Critics' Reviews 1940: 209+
                                      1941: 454+
    New York Times p. 27, Nov 27, 1940
                   IV, p. 2, Apr 27, 1941
                   p. 18, May 4, 1943
                   II, p. 1, May 9, 1943
                   p. 33, Jan 12, 1950
                   II, p. 1, Jan 22, 1950

The Corn Is Green (cont.)
    Stage 1: 31, Dec 1940
        1: 19+, Jan 1941
    Theatre Arts 25: 91-3, Feb 1941
                34: 15, Mar 1950
    Time 36: 69, Dec 9, 1940
The Light of Heart (see Yesterday's Magic)

The Morning Star
  Productions:
    Opened September 14, 1942 for 24 performances.
  Reviews:
    Commonweal 36: 565, Oct 2, 1942
    Nation 155: 278, Sep 26, 1942
    New Republic 107: 381-2, Sep 28, 1942
    New Yorker 18: 34, Sep 26, 1942
    New York Theatre Critics' Reviews 1942: 239
    New York Times p. 18, Sep 15, 1942
                    VIII, p. 1, Sep 20, 1942
    Newsweek 20: 62, Sep 20, 1942
    Theatre Arts 26: 677-9, Nov 1942
    Time 40: 47, Sep 28, 1942
Night Must Fall
  Productions:
    Opened September 28, 1936 for 64 performances.
  Reviews:
    Catholic World 144: 213, Nov 1936
    Commonweal 24: 532, Oct 2, 1936
    Literary Digest 122: 28, Oct 10, 1936
    Nation 143: 426-7, Oct 10, 1936
    New Republic 88: 284, Oct 14, 1936
    New York Times p. 34, Sep 29, 1936
    Newsweek 8: 29, Oct 10, 1936
    Stage 14: 44-5, Oct 1936
    Theatre Arts 20: 847-8, Nov 1936
    Time 28: 52, Oct 12, 1936
Someone Waiting
  Productions:
    Opened February 14, 1956 for 15 performances.
  Reviews:
    America 94: 646, Mar 10, 1956
    New York Theatre Critics' Reviews 1956: 365
    New York Times p. 26, Feb 15, 1956
    New Yorker 32: 93-4, Feb 25, 1956
    Theatre Arts 40: 21, Apr 1956
    Time 67: 61, Feb 27, 1956
Yesterday's Magic (The Light of Heart)

Productions:
Opened April 14, 1942 for 55 performances.
Reviews:
Catholic World 155: 340, Jun 1942
Commonweal 36: 38, May 1, 1942
New York Theatre Critics' Reviews 1942: 312+
New York Times p. 27, Apr 15, 1942
New Yorker 8: 30, Apr 25, 1942
Theatre Arts 26: 357, 360, Jun 1942
Time 39: 61, Apr 27, 1942

Winter, Keith
  The Rats of Norway
    Productions:
      Opened April 15, 1948 for 4 performances.
    Reviews:
      New York Theatre Critics' Reviews 1948: 292
      New York Times p. 27, Apr 16, 1948
      New Yorker 24: 50, Apr 24, 1948
  The Shining Hour
    Productions:
      Opened February 13, 1934 for 121 performances.
    Reviews:
      Catholic World 139: 88-9, Apr 1934
      Nation 138: 258, Feb 28, 1934
      New Outlook 163: 32-3, Mar 1934
      New Republic 78: 78, Feb 28, 1934
      New York Times p. 22, Feb 14, 1934
      Newsweek 3: 34, Feb 24, 1934
      Review of Reviews 89: 57, Apr 1934
      Stage 11: 18-19, Mar 1934
            11: 18-21, Apr 1934
      Theatre Arts 18: 245+, Apr 1934

Wolf, Friedrich
  Professor Mamlock
    Productions:
      Translated by Anne Bromberger. Opened April 13, 1937
        for 74 performances (Federal Theatre Project).
    Reviews:
      New York Times p. 30, Apr 14, 1937
                      X, p. 1, Apr 25, 1937
  Sailors of Cattaro
    Productions:
      Translated by Keene Wallis. Adapted by Michael Blank-
        fort. Opened December 10, 1934 for 96 performances.
    Reviews:

Sailors of Cattaro (cont.)
    Catholic World 140: 600, Feb 1935
    Commonweal 21: 236, Dec 21, 1934
    Golden Book 21: 30a, Feb 1935
    Nation 139: 749, Dec 26, 1934
    New Republic 81: 223, Jan 2, 1935
    New York Times p. 28, Dec 11, 1934
    Theatre Arts 19: 100+, Feb 1935
    Time 24: 13, Dec 24, 1934

Yeats, William Butler
The Countess Cathleen
  Productions:
    Opened February 4, 1913 in repertory (The Irish Players).
  Reviews:
    Christian Science Monitor Magazine p. 5, Mar 18, 1950
    Dramatic Mirror 69: 7, Feb 26, 1913
    Everybody's Magazine 28: 680, May 1913
Kathleen ni Houlihan
  Productions:
    Opened November 20, 1911 in repertory.
    Opened February 4, 1913 in repertory (The Irish Players).
    Opened in the Fall of 1934 in repertory for one perform-
    ance (Abbey Theatre Players).
  Reviews:
    Dramatic Mirror 66: 6, Dec 6, 1911
    Weekly Review 3: 76, Jul 21, 1960
The Player Queen
  Productions:
    Opened October 16, 1923 for 49 performances.
  Reviews:
    Nation 117: 496, Oct 31, 1923
    New Republic 36: 257, Oct 3, 1923
    New York Times p. 14, Oct 17, 1923
The Resurrection
  Productions:
    Opened November 19, 1934 for one performance.
  Reviews:
    New York Times p. 24, Nov 20, 1934

Zweig, Stefan
Jeremiah
  Productions:
    Translated by Eden Paul and Cedar Paul. English
    Version by John Gassner and Washington Miner.
    Opened February 3, 1939 for 35 performances.
  Reviews:

Catholic World 148: 731, Mar 1939
Commonweal 29: 469, Feb 17, 1939
Nation 148: 212, Feb 18, 1939
New York Times p. 11, Feb 4, 1939
One Act Play Magazine 2: 747-8, Feb 1939
Theatre Magazine 23: 248, Apr 1939
Time 33: 24, Feb 13, 1939

Volpone
  Productions:
    Translated by Ruth Langner. Based on Ben Jonson's
      play. Opened April 9, 1928 for 46 performances.
    Opened March 10, 1930 for 8 performances.
  Reviews:
    Catholic World 127: 340-3, Jun 1928
    Dial 84: 528-30, Jun 1928
    Dramatist 19: 1365-6, Apr 1928
    Life 92: 12, Jul 12, 1928
    Nation 126: 495, Apr 25, 1928
    New Republic 54: 295-6, Apr 25, 1928
    New York Times p. 32, Apr 10, 1928
                   IX, p. 1, Apr 22, 1928
                   p. 24, Mar 11, 1938
    Outlook 148: 665, Apr 25, 1928
    Theatre Arts 12: 387-90, Jun 1928
    Theatre Magazine 47: 37-9, Jun 1928
    Vogue 71: 78, Jun 1, 1928

About the Dramatists

Dramatist	Nationality	Dates
Andreyev, Leonid Nikolayevitch	Russian	1871-1919
Anouilh, Jean	French	born 1910
Ansky, S.	Russian (Jewish)	1863-1920
Archer, William	English	1856-1924
Auden, W. H.	English	born 1907
Bagnold, Enid	English	born 1889
Bahr, Hermann	Austrian	1863-1934
Barrie, James M.	English	1860-1937
Baum, Vicki	German	1888-1960
Beckett, Samuel	Irish (writes in French)	born 1906
Becque, Henry	French	1837-1899
Behan, Brendan	Irish	1925-1964
Benavente, Jacinto	Spanish	1866-1954
Benelli, Sem	Italian	1877-1949
Bernard, Jean-Jacques	French	born 1888
Besier, Rudolph	English	1878-1942
Betti, Ugo	Italian	1892-1953
Birabeau, Andrè	French	born 1890
Bolitho, William	English	1890-1930
Bolt, Robert	English	born 1924
Bolton, Guy	English	born 1884
Bourdet, Edouard	French	1887-1945
Brecht, Bertolt	German	1898-1956
Bridie, James	Scottish	1888-1951
Brieux, Eugene	French	1858-1932
Bruckner, Ferdinand	Austrian	1891-1958
Camus, Albert	French	1913-1960
Capek, Karel	Czech	1890-1938
Carroll, Paul Vincent	Irish	born 1900
Casella, Alberto	Italian	born 1891
Chambers, C. Haddon	English	1861-1921
Chekhov, Anton	Russian	1860-1904
Chiarelli, Luigi	Italian	1886-1947
Christie, Agatha	English	born 1890
Claudel, Paul	French	1868-1955
Cocteau, Jean	French	1889-1963
Colton, John	English	1886-1946

Dramatist	Nationality	Dates
Copeau, Jacques	French	1878-1949
Coward, Noel	English	born 1899
Dane, Clemence	English	1888-1965
Delaney, Shelagh	English	born 1940
Deval, Jacques	French	born 1893
Drinkwater, John	English	1882-1937
Durrenmatt, Friedrich	Swiss	born 1921
Dunsany, Lord	English-Irish	1878-1957
Dyer, Charles	English	born 1928
Eliot, T. S.	American-English	1888-1965
Ervine, St. John	Irish	born 1883
Feydeau, Georges	French	1862-1921
Frank, Bruno	German	1887-1945
Friel, Brian	Irish	born 1930
Frisch, Max	Swiss	born 1911
Fry, Christopher	English	born 1907
Galsworthy, John	English	1867-1933
García-Lorca, Federico	Spanish	1899-1936
Genêt, Jean	French	born 1910
Geraldy, Paul	French	born 1885
Gide, Andre	French	1869-1951
Giraudoux, Jean	French	1882-1944
Gorki, Maxim	Russian	1868-1936
Greene, Graham	English	born 1904
Gregory, Lady	English-Irish	1859-1932
Guitry, Sacha	French	1885-1957
Hamilton, Patrick	English	born 1904
deHartog, Jan	Dutch	born 1914
Harwood, H. M.	English	1874-1959
Hauptmann, Gerhart	German	1862-1946
Heijermans, Herman	Dutch	1864-1924
Hochhuth, Rolf	German	born 1931
Houghton, Stanley	English	1881-1913
Housman, Laurence	English	1865-1959
Huxley, Aldous	English	1894-1963
Ibsen, Henrik	Norwegian	1828-1906
Ionesco, Eugene	French	born 1912
Jerome, Helen	Australian	born 1883
Job, Thomas	Welsh	1900-1947
Johnston, Denis	Irish	born 1901
Jones, Henry Arthur	English	1851-1929
Joyce, James	Irish	1882-1941
Kaiser, Georg	German	1878-1945
Katayev, Valentin	Russian	born 1897
Knott, Frederick	English	born 1919

Dramatist	Nationality	Dates
Lawler, Ray	Australian	born 1922
Lenormand, Henri René	French	1882-1951
Levy, Benn W.	English	born 1900
Lonsdale, Frederick	English	1881-1954
Maeterlinck, Maurice	Belgian	1862-1949
Marceau, Felicien	Belgian	born 1913
Martinez-Sierra, Gregorio	Spanish	1881-1947
Masefield, John	English	born 1878
Maugham, W. Somerset	English	1874-1965
Milne, A. A.	English	1882-1956
Molnar, Ferenc	Hungarian	1878-1952
Morley, Robert	English	born 1908
Munro, C. K.	English	born 1889
Murray, T. C.	Irish	1873-1959
Nichols, Robert	English	1893-1944
O'Casey, Sean	Irish	1884-1964
Osborne, John	English	born 1929
Pagnol, Marcel	French	born 1895
Parker, Louis N.	English	1852-1944
Phillips, Stephan	English	1868-1915
Pinero, Arthur Wing	English	1855-1934
Pinter, Harold	English	born 1932
Pirandello, Luigi	Italian	1867-1936
Priestley, J. B.	English	born 1894
Quintero, Joaquin Alvarez	Spanish	1873-1944
Quintero, Serafin	Spanish	1871-1938
Rattigan, Terence	English	born 1911
Robinson, Lennox	Irish	1886-1958
Rostand, Edmond	French	1869-1918
Sartre, Jean-Paul	French	born 1905
Savoir, Alfred	French	1883-1934
Schnitzler, Arthur	Austrian	1862-1931
Shaffer, Peter	English	born 1926
Shairp, Mordaunt	English	1887-1939
Shaw, George Bernard	English-Irish	1856-1950
Sherriff, R. C.	English	born 1896
Shiels, George	Irish	born 1886
Sigurjonsson, Johann	Icelandic	1880-1919
Simonov, Konstantin	Russian	born 1915
Simpson, N. F.	English	born 1919
Smith, Dodie	English	born 1896
Strindberg, August	Swedish	1849-1912
Sudermann, Hermann	German	1857-1928
Synge, John Millington	Irish	1871-1909
Tabori, George	Hungarian-English	born 1914

Dramatist	Nationality	Dates
Thomas, Brandon	English	1857-1914
Thomas, Dylan	Welsh	1914-1953
Toller, Ernst	German	1893-1939
Tolstoy, Leo Nikolayevitch	Russian	1828-1910
Turgenev, Ivan	Russian	1818-1883
Ustinov, Peter	English	born 1921
Vajda, Ernst	Hungarian-American	1887-1954
Vane, Sutton	English	1891-1963
Verneuil, Louis	French	1893-1952
Vildrac, Charles	French	born 1882
Wedekind, Frank	German	1864-1918
Weiss, Peter	German	born 1916
Werfel, Franz	Austrian	1890-1945
Wesker, Arnold	English	born 1932
Wheeler, Hugh	English	born 1916
Wilde, Oscar	English-Irish	1854-1900
Williams, Emlyn	English	born 1905
Winter, Keith	English	born 1906
Wolf, Frederich	German	1888-1953
Yeats, William Butler	Irish	1865-1939
Zweig, Stefan	Austrian	1881-1942

Successful Modern British and Continental Productions
(*Off Broadway Productions)

Performances	Play and Year of Production	Author
*1,408	The Blacks (1961)	Genet
1,295	Angel Street (1941)	Hamilton
*672	The Balcony (1960)	Genet
657	Blithe Spirit (1942)	Coward
648 (see 104)	Rain (1922)	Colton
645	Witness for the Prosecution (1954)	Christie
637	A Man for All Seasons (1961)	Bolt
632	The Fourposter (1951)	deHartog
610	Affairs of State (1950)	Verneuil
*582	Krapp's Last Tape (1960)	Beckett
*578	The Collection (1962)	Pinter
*578	The Dumbwaiter (1962)	Pinter
*545 (see 127)	The Hostage (1961)	Behan
*529 (see 136)	Six Characters in Search of An Author (1963)	Pirandello
522	Dial "M" for Murder (1952)	Knott
517	Victoria Regina (1935)	Housman
500	Bird In Hand (1929)	Drinkwater
485	Journey's End (1929)	Sherriff
477	The Corn Is Green (1940)	Williams
459	Grand Hotel (1930)	Baum
452	O Mistress Mine (1946)	Rattigan
430	Uncle Harry (1942)	Job
426	Ten Little Indians (1944)	Christie
*424	Brecht On Brecht (1962)	Tabori
417	Jacobowsky and the Colonel (1944)	Werfel
409	The Cocktail Party (1950)	Eliot
407	Look Back In Anger (1957)	Osborne
389	Romanoff and Juliet (1957)	Ustinov
385	The Last of Mrs. Cheyney (1925)	Lonsdale
376	A Taste of Honey (1960)	Delaney
373	Wait Until Dark (1966)	Knott
370	The Barretts of Wimpole Street (1931)	Besier

Performances	Play and Year of Production	Author
368	The Madwoman of Chaillot(1948)	Giraudoux
356	Tovarich (1936)	Deval
352	The First Mrs. Fraser (1929)	Ervine
348	The Respectful Prostitute (1948)	Sartre
*343	The Room (1964)	Pinter
*343	A Slight Ache (1964)	Pinter
*340	Hedda Gabler (1960)	Ibsen
337	Five Finger Exercise (1959)	Shaffer
332	Separate Tables (1956)	Rattigan
321	Mrs. Moonlight (1930)	Levy
321	Peter Pan (1950)	Barrie
316	The Deputy (1964)	Hochhuth
315	Polly with A Past (1917)	Bolton
312	Adam and Eva (1919)	Bolton
310	The Ivory Door (1927)	Milne
295 (see 100)	Man and Superman (1947)	Shaw
280	Disraeli (1911)	Parker
274	Shadow and Substance (1936)	Carroll
272	Anastasia (1954)	Bolton
264	The Concert (1910)	Bahr
261	Royal Hunt of the Sun (1965)	Shaffer
260	Edward, My Son (1948)	Morley
260 (see 244)	The Play's the Thing (1926)	Molnar
256	Fanny's First Play (1912)	Shaw
256(see 248)	Private Lives (1931)	Coward
255	Outward Bound (1938)	Vane
255	The Perfect Alibi (1928)	Milne
255	The Swan (1923)	Molnar
251	Spring Cleaning (1923)	Lonsdale
248	The Guardsman (1924)	Molnar
248 (see 256)	Private Lives (1948)	Coward
248	Time Remembered (1957)	Anouilh
246	Michael and Mary (1929)	Milne
244 (see 260)	The Play's the Thing (1948)	Molnar
240	Rhinoceros (1961)	Ionesco
239	Fallen Angels (1956)	Coward
233	Charley's Aunt (1940)	B. Thomas
233 (see 138)	The Constant Wife (1926)	Maugham
232 (see 193)	Cyrano de Bergerac (1923)	Rostand
232	Major Barbara (1956)	Shaw
229	The Lark (1955)	Anouilh
228	Lady Windermere's Fan (1946)	Wilde
220	Loyalties (1922)	Galsworthy
219	Pride and Prejudice (1935)	Jerome
218	Clutterbuck (1949)	Levy

Performances	Play and Year of Production	Author
217	Tiger At the Gates (1955)	Giraudoux
*216	Ghosts (1961)	Ibsen
215	The Winslow Boy (1947)	Rattigan
211	Luther (1963)	Osborne
210	Autumn Crocus (1932)	Smith
210	Cynara (1931)	Harwood
206	Dangerous Corner (1932)	Priestley
206	Shanghai Gesture (1926)	Colton
204	The Dover Road (1921)	Milne
204	Redemption (1918)	Tolstoy
*203	A Country Scandal (1960)	Chekhov
*202	Under Milk Wood (1961)	D. Thomas
199	Springtime for Henry (1931)	Levy
196	Write Me A Murder (1961)	Knott
195 (see 142)	Saint Joan (1923)	Shaw
194	Call It A Day (1936)	Smith
193	Abraham Lincoln (1919)	Drinkwater
193	Becket (1960)	Anouilh
193 (see 232)	Cyrano de Bergerac (1946)	Rostand
191	Song of Songs (1914)	Sudermann
189	Deburau (1920)	Guitry
189	The Visit (1958)	Duerrenmatt
184	Dear Brutus (1918)	Barrie
184	Polly Preferred (1923)	Bolton
184	R. U. R. (1923)	Capek
183	The Harem (1924)	Vajda
183	Old English (1924)	Galsworthy
182	The Chalk Garden (1955)	Bagnold
182	He Who Gets Slapped (1922)	Andreyev
180 (see 110)	Arms and the Man (1925)	Shaw
180	Death Takes A Holiday (1929)	Casella
180	Mima (1928)	Molnar
179	The Jest (1919)	Benelli
179 (see 143)	Pygmalion (1945)	Shaw
177	John Ferguson (1919)	Ervine
*176	Red Roses for Me (1961)	O'Casey
176	The Skin Game (1920)	Galsworthy
175	The Circle (1921)	Maugham
175	The Green Goddess (1921)	Archer
*175	Man Is Man (1962)	Brecht
*175	A Man's Man (1962)	Brecht
173	A Bill of Divorcement (1921)	Dane
173	Escape (1927)	Galsworthy
172	The Lie (1914)	Jones
168	Lovers and Friends (1943)	Smith

Performances	Play and Year of Production	Author
168	Secrets (1922)	Besier
167	Under Orders (1918)	B. Thomas
166	The Green Bay Tree (1933)	Shairp
166	Inadmissible Evidence (1965)	Osborne
165	The Caretaker (1961)	Pinter
*164	The Importance of Being Earnest (1963)	Wilde
163	The Private Ear (1963)	Shaffer
163	The Public Eye (1963)	Shaffer
161	The Nest (1922)	Geraldy
161	Sleeping Partners (1918)	Guitry
160	The Captive (1926)	Bourdet
159	Bitter Sweet (1929)	Coward
159	Photo Finish (1963)	Ustinov
159	Ross (1961)	Rattigan
159	Topaze (1930)	Pagnol
158	Present Laughter (1946)	Coward
157	Ondine (1954)	Giraudoux
157	This Year of Grace (1928)	Coward
157	The Vortex (1925)	Coward
*156 (see 146)	Misalliance (1961)	Shaw
156	When We Are Married (1939)	Priestley
155	Bluebeard's Eighth Wife (1921)	Savoir
153	Amphitryon 38 (1937)	Giraudoux
153	The Eternal Road (1937)	Werfel
152	A Kiss for Cinderella (1916)	Barrie
151	The Good Fairy (1931)	Molnar
151	The Lady's Not for Burning (1950)	Fry
150	Quadrille (1954)	Coward
149	Caesar and Cleopatra (1949)	Shaw
149	Chips With Everything (1963)	Wesker
147	Easy Virtue (1925)	Coward
146 (see 156)	Misalliance (1953)	Shaw
144	Chicken Feed (1923)	Bolton
144	A Doll's House (1937)	Ibsen
144	The High Road (1928)	Lonsdale
144	Marat/Sade (1965)	Weiss
144	Outward Bound (1924)	Vane
144	The Passion Flower (1920)	Benavente
143	Candida (1924)	Shaw
143	Pomander Walk (1910)	Parker
143	The Potting Shed (1957)	Greene
143 (see 179)	Pygmalion (1926)	Shaw
142	As You Desire Me (1931)	Pirandello

Performances	Play and Year of Production	Author
142 (see 195)	Saint Joan (1951)	Shaw
*141	The Exception and the Rule (1965)	Brecht
141	The Love of Four Colonels (1953)	Ustinov
141	Within the Gates (1934)	O'Casey
138 (see 233)	The Constant Wife (1951)	Maugham
136	Jealousy (1928)	Verneuil
136	The Legend of Leonora (1914)	Barrie
136	The Mind-the-Paint Girl (1912)	Pinero
136 (see 529)	Six Characters in Search of an Author (1922)	Pirandello
136	The White Steed (1939)	Carroll
135	Design for Living (1933)	Coward
135	Nobody Home (1915)	Bolton
132	The Deep Blue Sea (1952)	Rattigan
132	The Rubicon (1922)	Bourdet
132	The Waltz of the Toreadors (1957)	Anouilh
131	The Grand Duke (1921)	Guitry
131	Laburnum Grove (1935)	Priestley
128 (see 112)	Our Betters (1928)	Maugham
127	The Devil's Disciple (1950)	Shaw
127	An Enemy of the People (1927)	Ibsen
127	Grounds for Divorce (1924)	Vajda
127 (see 545)	The Hostage (1960)	Behan
127	Mary Rose (1920)	Barrie
127	The Phantom Rival (1914)	Molnar
125 (see 112)	Heartbreak House (1920)	Shaw
124	The Apple Cart (1956)	Shaw
124	Mr. Pim Passes By (1921)	Milne
124	Mixed Marriage (1920)	Ervine
124	Passers-by (1911)	Chambers
123 (see 119)	The Three Sisters (1942)	Chekhov
121 (see 115)	The Doctor's Dilemma (1941)	Shaw
121	Joseph and His Brethren (1913)	Parker
*121	Play (1964)	Beckett
121	The Shining Hour (1934)	Winter
120	The Betrothal (1918)	Maeterlinck
120 (see 111)	The Dybbuk (1925)	Ansky
120	Fata Morgana (1924)	Vajda
120	Peer Gynt (1923)	Ibsen
119	Philadelphia, Here I Come! (1966)	Friel
*119	Rosmersholm (1962)	Ibsen
119 (see 123)	The Three Sisters (1964)	Chekhov

Performances	Play and Year of Production	Author
118	Tonight At Eight-Thirty (1936)	Coward
117	The Confidential Clerk (1954)	Eliot
115 (see 121)	The Doctor's Dilemma (1927)	Shaw
113	Red Gloves (1948)	Sartre
112	Getting Married (1919)	Shaw
112 (see 125)	Heartbreak House (1959)	Shaw
112	Jane Clegg (1920)	Ervine
112 (see 128)	Our Betters (1917)	Maugham
112	Smith (1910)	Maugham
111 (see 120)	The Dybbuk (1926)	Ansky
111	French Without Tears (1937)	Rattigan
111	The World We Live In (1922)	Capek
110 (see 180)	Arms and the Man (1950)	Shaw
110	The Rehearsal (1963)	Anouilh
108	The Chinese Prime Minister (1964)	Bagnold
108	Hotel Paradiso (1957)	Feydeau
108	Squaring the Circle (1935)	Katayev
108	The Truth About Blayds (1922)	Milne
105	Don Juan in Hell (1952)	Shaw
105	Juno and the Paycock (1940)	O'Casey
105	Once Is Enough (1938)	Lonsdale
104	Androcles and the Lion (1938)	Shaw
104	Another Love Story (1943)	Lonsdale
104	Justice (1916)	Galsworthy
104	The Letter (1927)	Maugham
104	Prunella (1913)	Housman
104 (see 648)	Rain (1924)	Colton
*103	Corruption in the Palace of Justice (1963)	Betti
103	Mademoiselle (1932)	Deval
103	The Philanderer (1913)	Shaw
103	The Wild Duck (1925)	Ibsen
102	Too Many Husbands (1919)	Maugham
101	Big Fish, Little Fish (1961)	Wheeler
101	The Complaisant Lover (1961)	Greene
100	East of Suez (1922)	Maugham
100	Her Cardboard Lover (1927)	Deval
*100 (see 295)	Man and Superman (1964)	Shaw
100	Rope's End (1929)	Hamilton
100	The Whole World Over (1947)	Simonov

Popular Modern British and Continental Dramatists
(*Off Broadway Productions Included)

Dramatist	Productions (over 100 performances)	Plays (over 100 performances)
Shaw	24	16
Coward	12	11
Maugham	9	7
Ibsen	*7	*7
Molnar	7	6
Bolton	6	6
Milne	6	6
Rattigan	6	6
Anouilh	5	5
Barrie	5	5
Galsworthy	5	5
Lonsdale	5	5
Pinter	*5	*5
Ervine	4	4
Giraudoux	4	4
Shaffer	4	4
Brecht	*3	*2
Chekhov	*3	*2
Colton	3	2
Deval	3	3
Guitry	3	3
Knott	3	3
Levy	3	3
O'Casey	3	3
Osborne	3	3
Parker	3	3
Pirandello	*3	*2
Priestley	3	3
Smith	3	3
Ustinov	3	3
Vajda	3	3
Ansky	2	1
Bagnold	2	2
Beckett	*2	*2
Behan	*2	*1
Besier	2	2
Bourdet	2	2

Dramatist	Productions (over 100 performances)	Plays (over 100 performances)
Capek	2	2
Carroll	2	2
Christie	2	2
Drinkwater	2	2
Eliot	2	2
Genêt	*2	*2
Greene	2	2
Hamilton	2	2
Housman	2	2
Rostand	2	1
Sartre	2	2
B. Thomas	2	2
Vane	2	1
Verneuil	2	2
Werfel	2	2
Wilde	*2	*2

New York Drama Critics' Circle Awards (Best Foreign Play)

1937-1938 Shadow and Substance (Carroll)
1938-1939 The White Steed (Carroll)
1939-1940 no award
1940-1941 The Corn Is Green (Williams)
1941-1942 Blithe Spirit (Coward)
1942-1943 no award
1943-1944 Jacobowsky and the Colonel (Werfel)
1944-1945 no award
1945-1946 no award
1946-1947 No Exit (Sartre)
1947-1948 The Winslow Boy (Rattigan)
1948-1949 The Madwoman of Chaillot (Giraudoux)
1949-1950 The Cocktail Party (Eliot)
1950-1951 The Lady's Not for Burning (Fry)
1951-1952 Venus Observed (Fry)
1952-1953 The Love of Four Colonels (Ustinov)
1953-1954 Ondine (Giraudoux)
1954-1955 Witness for the Prosecution (Christie)
1955-1956 Tiger at the Gates (Giraudoux)
1956-1957 Waltz of the Toreadors (Anouilh)
1957-1958 Look Back in Anger (Osborne)
1958-1959 The Visit (Duerrenmatt)
1959-1960 Five Finger Exercise (Shaffer)
1960-1961 A Taste of Honey (Delaney)
1961-1962 A Man for All Seasons (Bolt)
1962-1963 no award
1963-1964 Luther (Osborne) Best play of the year regard-
           less of category.
1964-1965 no award
1965-1966 Marat/Sade (The Persecution and Assassination
           of Marat as Performed by the Inmates of the
           Asylum of Charenton Under the Direction of
           the Marquis de Sade) (Weiss) Best play of the
           year regardless of category.

Index of Authors, Adaptors, and Translators

Betti, Ugo 39-41
Beyo, Mascha 256
Bialik, H. N. 20
Birabeau, Andre 41
Bjorkman, Edwin 241, 243
Black, Kitty 15, 17
Blanchard, Benjamin F. 54
Blankfort, Michael 265
Bolitho, Hector 198
Bolitho, William 41
Bolt, Robert 42
Bolton, Guy 42-46, 162, 253
Booth, Howard 95
Borden, Ethel 131
Bourdet, Edouard 46-48
Bowles, Paul 207
Bowman, John 240
Boyd, Ernest 37, 85
Brecht, Bertolt 48, 51
Bridie, James 51-53, 96
Brieux, Eugene 53-55
Bromberger, Anne 265
Bromfield, Louis 47
Browne, Maurice 174
Bruckner, Ferdinand 55
Burell, Randal C. 56
Burrell, James T. A. 252

Calderon, George 62
Camus, Albert 56
Canfield, Mary Cass 131
Cannon, Denis 16
Capek, Joseph 57
Capek, Karel 56-58
Carlton, Tom 44
Carr, Philip 111
Carroll, Paul Vincent 58-60
Carson, Murray 185
de Casalis, Jeanne 236
Casella, Alberto 60
Caylor, Rose 67
Chambers, C. Haddon 60-62
Charash, Jack 259
Chekhov, Anton 62-68
Chiarelli, Luigi 68-69
Christie, Agatha 69
Claudel, Paul 69-70

282

284

Heijermans-Houwink, Caroline   124
Heimann, Philip 198
Helburn, Theresa 41
Hellman, Lillian 15
Herbert, Henry 53
Hill, Lucienne 13, 14, 16, 19
Hinton, Jane 47, 167
Hochhuth, Rolf 124-125
Hooker, Brian 118, 204, 205
Hopwood, Avery 253
Hornblow, Arthur, Jr. 46, 54, 118, 121
Houghton, Stanley 125-126
House, Ray Temple 62
Housman, Laurence 126-127
Howard, Sidney 170, 181, 206
Huxley, Aldous 127-128

Ibsen, Henrik 128-137
Ionesco, Eugene 137-139
Irving, Laurence 53, 55
Isherwood, Christopher 21
Ivan, Rosalind 73

Jacobs, W. W. 182
Jacobus, J. 253
James, Henry 43
Jay, William 44
Jerome, Helen 139
Jerrell, Randall 66
Jesse, F. Tennyson 120, 121, 122
Job, Thomas 140-141
John, Miriam 18
Johnson, Pamela Hansford 17
Johnston, Denis 141
Jones, Henry Arthur 141-144
Jonson, Ben 267
Joseph, Robert L. 241
Joyce, James 144

Kafka, Franz 108
Kaiser, Georg 144
Kanin, Garson 155
Kapek, Karel (see Capek, Karel)
Katayev, Valentin 144-145
Katzin, Winifred 146, 210
Kirkup, James 87
Knoblock, Edward 194

285

Knott, Frederick   145-146
Kronenberger, Louis   16
Kummer, Clare   209

Lackaye, Wilton   255
Langley, Noel   172
Langner, Ruth   257, 267
Laughton, Charles   49
Laurence, William L.   11
Lawler, Ray   146
Lawrence, William L.   112
LeGallienne, Eva   65, 130, 131, 132, 133, 135
LeGallienne, Julie   131
Lenormand, Henri Rene   146-147
Lessing, Gotthold Ephriam   55
Levin, Donald   256
Levy, Benn W.   97, 147-149, 181
Lewisohn, Ludwig   257
Leyssac, Paul   131
Littell, Philip   172, 211
Livingston, Arthur   192
Lonsdale, Frederick   149-152
Lorca, Federico García (see García-Lorca, Federico)
Lujan, James Graham   106
Lyons, Eugene   144

McCarthy, Kevin   65
MacDonald, Ann Sprague   191
Mack, Willard   95
Maeterlinck, Maurice   152-155
Malamuth, Charles   144
Mallen, Miles   56
Mandel, Frank   44, 45
Marceau, Felicien   155
Marcin, Max   45
Marquina, Eduardo   156
Martinez-Sierra, Gregorio   155-157
Mazefield, John   157
de Mattos, Alexander Teixeira   152
Maugham, W. Somerset   68, 157-163
Maurette, Marcelle   43
Mayer, Paul Aliva   193
Mayor, Osborne H. (see Bridie, James)
Meader, Clarence L.   12
Meinhard   183
Meltzer, Charles Henry   211
Meriwether, William   41

286

Priestley, J. B. 193-196
Prouse, Derth 138

Quintero, Serafin and Joaquin Alvarez 196-197

Rappaport, Solomon (see Ansky, S.)
Randolph, Clemence 72
Rattigan, Terence 197-201
Reed, Henry 39-40
Reznich, E. H. Von 183
Rice, Elmer 23
Richepin, Jean 36
Rizzo, Gino 41
Robinson, Lennox 201-203
Robson, Cecil 14
Roeder, Ralph 154, 181
Rohe, Alice 192
Rosen, Sam 66
Ross, Carmel 128, 130, 135
Rostand, Edmond 203-206
Rostova, Mina 65
Rothenberg, Jerome 124
Rubens, Paul 45
Rublee, George 211

Sartre, Jean-Paul 206-209
Saunders, Lilian 124
Savacool, John K. 110
Savior, Alfred 209-210
Schack, William 249
Schlitt, Robert 155
Schnee, Thelma 237
Schnitzler, Arthur 210-211
Scholz, August 250
Scott, Fred Newton 12
Seidelman, Arthur A. 256
Selver, Paul 56, 57
Semple, Lorenzo, Jr. 84
Shaffer, Peter 211-213
Shairp, Mordaunt 213
Sharpe, R. Farquharson 128, 130
Shaw, George Bernard 213-235
Sherriff, R. C. 235-236
Sherwood, Robert E. 85
Shiels, George 236-237
Short, Robin 242
Shyer, Paul 240

Sierra, Gregorio Martinez (see Martinez-Sierra, Gregorio)
Sigurjonsson, Johann 237
Sill, L. M. 70
Simonov, Konstantin 237-238
Simpson, N. F. 238
Skariatina, Irina 62
Smith, Dodie 238-239
Spottiswood, Sybil 38
Sprigge, Elizabeth 240
Storer, Edward 193
Stringberg, August 239-243
Sudermann, Hermann 243-244
Synge, John Millington 244-246
Szogyi, Alex 63, 65, 113

Tabori, George 48, 98, 242, 243, 246-247
Tagger, Theodor (see Bruckner, Ferdinand)
Teradash, Daniel 207
Thomas, Brandon 247-248
Thomas, Dylan 248-249
Toller, Ernst 249
Tolstoy, Leo Nikolayevitch 249-250
Tridon, Andre 211, 256
Turgenev, Ivan 250-251

Underhill, John Garrett 35, 155
Unger, Gladys 255
Untermeyer, Louis H. 249
Ustinov, Peter 251-252

Vajda, Ernst 252-253
Valency, Maurice 88, 110, 111
Vane, Sutton 253, 254
Verneuil, Louis 254, 255
Vidal, Gore 88
Vildrac, Charles 255-256

Wagner, Michael 193
Wallis, Keene 265
Walpole, Hugh 148
Walter, Eugene 254
Watson, Donald T. 137, 138, 139
Wedekind, Frank 41, 256
Weiss, Peter 256-257
Weissman, José A. 106
Wells, H. G. 95
Wendel, Beth 127

Index of Titles

291

292

293